SALVATION FOR ALL

Salvation for All

God's Other Peoples

GERALD O'COLLINS, SJ

OXFORD
UNIVERSITY PRESS

OXFORD
UNIVERSITY PRESS

Great Clarendon Street, Oxford OX2 6DP

Oxford University Press is a department of the University of Oxford.
It furthers the University's objective of excellence in research, scholarship,
and education by publishing worldwide in

Oxford New York

Auckland Cape Town Dar es Salaam Hong Kong Karachi
Kuala Lumpur Madrid Melbourne Mexico City Nairobi
New Delhi Shanghai Taipei Toronto

With offices in

Argentina Austria Brazil Chile Czech Republic France Greece
Guatemala Hungary Italy Japan Poland Portugal Singapore
South Korea Switzerland Thailand Turkey Ukraine Vietnam

Oxford is a registered trade mark of Oxford University Press
in the UK and in certain other countries

Published in the United States
by Oxford University Press Inc., New York

© Gerald O'Collins, SJ, 2008

British Library Cataloguing in Publication Data

Data available

Library of Congress Cataloging in Publication Data

Data available

Typeset by SPI Publisher Services, Pondicherry, India
Printed in Great Britain
on acid-free paper by
Biddles Ltd., King's Lynn, Norfolk

ISBN 978–0–19–923890–3 (Hbk)   978–0–19–923889–7 (Pbk)

1 3 5 7 9 10 8 6 4 2

Preface

This book takes me into a field that is weighed down with a century or more of debate. One might replay that modern discussion about those of other religious traditions by assembling a range of notable writers. Such a spectrum of views would move from Karl Barth (1886–1968), through Karl Rahner (1904–84) and Jacques Dupuis (1923–2004), and on to John Hick (b. 1922). Many further names cluster around these four figures and would enjoy a walk-on part in a study of what twentieth-century authors, official teachers, and significant assemblies—in particular, the Second Vatican Council (1962–5)—contributed to thinking about the salvation of those who do not belong to Judaism and Christianity. Much and all as I appreciate the importance of what has come from those modern sources, I do not wish to organize, distinguish, and appraise their contributions. In various articles and chapters of books (some of them listed in the bibliography), I have already taken part, albeit in a minor way, in that debate. But doing justice to the full story would require at least one large volume, and I wonder how much I might achieve by going over all that ground once again.

The purpose of this book is rather to assemble and assess the biblical testimony about the salvation of God's 'other peoples' or the 'others', before presenting some systematic conclusions and positions about the role of Jesus for the salvation of the world. In going through the Bible I will take up and explore testimony that illuminates the *universal* scope of God's love and offer of salvation. I want to show that this is a strong and lasting theme. Unquestionably, there are many biblical passages that catch the eye and that seem at odds with the universality of divine love (for example the OT oracles against the nations pronounced by various prophets). Here and there I will pay attention to this feature in the scriptural witness (as in examining teaching from the prophet Amos in Chapter 3). But my purpose is not to survey equally and appraise *both* the 'negative' *and* the 'positive' witness; to do that would call for a book twice the length of this one. My aim is to set out in detail all the major biblical testimony to the universal scope of God's offer of salvation—something that, as far as I know, has never been done before. The witness of the whole Bible to God's universal love is very impressive and should be appropriated much more in contemporary discussions of the 'other' religions and 'God's other peoples'. Before plunging into the intricate, contemporary debates, all parties—or at least all Christian parties—should listen attentively to the full scriptural witness to the universal divine benevolence.

Two central presuppositions undergird this project. First, I believe in the crucified and risen Jesus as the Saviour of all people—that is to say, of all men and women who have ever shared or will share in our common humanity. Along with this role, as we shall see, goes that of his being the universal Revealer or Light of the world. Salvation and revelation can and should be distinguished, but should never be separated.

Second, I accept the canonical scriptures (including the deutero-canonical books of the OT) as written under the inspiration of the Holy Spirit and therefore as normative and religiously authoritative. Some of the deutero-canonical books, such as the Wisdom of Solomon and Sirach (or the Wisdom of Ben Sira), yield important teaching on the divine relationship with all people. Respect for the inspired status of the whole Bible does not mean, however, putting every book on the same level or closing my eyes to developments (for example from the earlier to the later books of the OT).

From my fairly extensive reading in the area of interreligious studies, I do not think that Christian authors, not to mention others, have explored and appreciated the full range of scriptural testimony that is relevant to the role of Jesus for the redemption of the human race. At times they seem to adopt a position and then rustle up some biblical evidence in its support. The issues should be approached in the opposite direction, by hearing first the full range of scriptural voices and then attempting some systematic conclusions.

The novelty of this book comes from its shifting into focus, right from the outset, the biblical witness. That includes avoiding as far as possible the leaden jargon which has often come to dominate when Catholics and other Christians write and teach about world religions. Eventually I will have to move beyond the biblical testimony to evaluations which use such terms as 'presence'. But I want to delay that shift as long as possible, and certainly not begin by analysing various '-isms' like 'Christo-centrism', 'exclusivism', 'inclusivism', 'pluralism', and 'theo-centrism'. Introduced originally to sort matters out, these abstract nouns now groan under the weight of their many meanings and at times finish up confusing rather than clarifying discussion. The one unavoidable but relatively uncontroversial '-ism' that will turn up in the early chapters is 'universalism', used in the sense of God's benevolence towards everyone.

One terminological issue remains a nagging problem. With many others, I dislike such negative labels as 'non-Christian' and 'non-evangelized'. But how are we to name en bloc those of other religious traditions? In this book I decided to adopt the terms 'God's other peoples', 'others', and 'outsiders', understanding these general terms in a positive sense.

Beyond question, I want to arrive at some closing judgements, and not lay myself open to the criticism of being long on biblical detail but short on systematic conclusions. But, before moving to any such conclusions, a series of chapters will explore and retrieve what the Bible has to say about the human condition and about the religious life of 'others'. First, how do the scriptures account for the origin, nature, and destiny of human beings? Second, what did the chosen people of God (according to the OT) and Christians (according to the NT) think about the religious situation of 'others', those who did not (or did not yet) belong to their community of faith?

As a Christian I use the terminology of Old Testament (OT) and New Testament (NT). Here 'old' is understood as good and does not imply any 'supersessionism', or the view that the NT has rendered obsolete, replaced, and so 'superseded' the OT.

In dealing with the OT scriptures, I intend to follow more or less the sequence of the Hebrew Bible: the Law, the Prophets, and the Writings. I am well aware that this threefold ordering of the books—(1) the Pentateuch and the historical books, then (2) the prophets, and, finally, (3) the wisdom books—does *not* mean that the works found under (1) were all written before (2), or that the prophetic books were all written before (3). Further, the particular sequence of books within each of these three groupings does not represent—or at least does not necessarily represent—the order of their composition. As regards the final text of individual books, these can include a variety of traditions which should be dated to various periods. Such books as Genesis, Proverbs, and Isaiah classically exemplify this variety. In the case of the NT canon, the four Gospels precede the letters of St Paul. But the canonical texts of the Gospels were almost certainly put into their present shape *after* the Apostle wrote his letters. Once again the canonical order does not necessarily represent the chronological order in the composition of NT books (and of traditions that can enter into the final text). Occasionally this difference can prove significant to some arguments being developed in this book and will be included in the discussion.

One needs to examine carefully the testimony from both parts of the scriptural canon, in which the OT enjoys a certain advantage over the NT for thinking about the relations of 'others' to God. The OT scriptures emerged from oral traditions and writings that went on for over a thousand years, centuries in which the Israelites experienced many other peoples, cultures, and religions. The OT yields a rich variety of positive and negative reflections on the religious situation of the 'others'. Palestine itself served as a kind of 'sacred bridge' between Egypt and Mesopotamia, while years of exile outside Palestine also provided the Israelites with extensive first-hand contacts with the religious beliefs and practices of the 'others'. By way of contrast, the NT resulted from only seventy or so years of Christian experiences, even if those decades involved contacts around the Mediterranean, in North Africa, out to the Middle East, and even beyond. As regards the cradle of Christianity itself, Palestine admittedly was multi-lingual and, to some extent, multi-ethnic and multi-religious. But the experience of 'others' reflected in the 27 books of the NT cannot match the great variety of experiences, hopes, and wishes derived from Israel's long history and incorporated in the 45 books of the OT.

Israel's history had been shaped, to a large extent, by contacts with other peoples, and, since much of that history was one of suffering, what predominates in the sayings about the nations (e.g. Jer. 46–51; Ezek. 25–32, 35; Zeph. 2: 4–15) were words of judgement. But that, as we shall see, is not the whole story. Instead of proposing merely negative things about 'outsiders', the OT also acknowledges the gracious goodness of God towards the nations and foreigners. Traditional Judaism, which draws not only on the scriptures but also on rabbinic literature, also offers a generous view not only of the salvation of non-Jews, but also of their co-operation in God's plan, as we will see below.

This book begins then with the biblical witness. Some data will be treated several times. But I make no apology for that repetition. It seems important and even necessary to drive home the relevant teaching from the OT and the NT and the implications of such teaching.

I might have chosen another starting point: for instance, the conditions for inter-religious dialogue, its nature, and its aims. Engaging in such dialogue is obviously of immense importance as the human race moves further into the third millennium. The world has become increasingly interdependent—economically, politically, and religiously. It is not simply the mass media that has crossed national and continental frontiers. Our global situation has turned more and more multi-ethnic, multi-cultural, and multi-religious. Inter-religious dialogue at every level is a pressing necessity. In this book I hope to help in laying a foundation for such dialogue by exploring thoroughly what the scriptural witnesses would say to Christian (and also to non-Christian) partners in these exchanges.

I am most grateful to many people for their help and encouragement in writing this book: Michael Barnes, Abigail Brown, Brendan Byrne, Richard Clifford, Charles Conroy, Robert Doran, Gerald Goetz, Anne Hunt, Robert Joda, Nicholas King, Joseph Mueller, Maev O'Collins, Kevin O'Reilly, John Schmitt, Thomas Stegman, Jane Steingraeber, Roland Teske, David Twetten, the graduate students at Marquette University who took Theology 316 in the fall semester of 2006, and two anonymous readers for Oxford University Press. I also wish to express my warm thanks to three Jesuit communities for their support when I was composing this work: Jesuit Theological College (Parkville, Australia), Marquette University Jesuit Residence (Milwaukee, USA), and John Sinnott House (Wimbledon, England). With gratitude and affection I dedicate this book to the memory of Jacques Dupuis, a theologian of immense learning who always held that followers of other religions are persons to be encountered and are not 'cases' to be reduced to mere statements about them.

Gerald O'Collins, SJ

St Mary's University College, Twickenham
Easter, 2007

Contents

Abbreviations

ABD	D. N. Freedman (ed.), *Anchor Bible Dictionary*, 6 vols. (New York: Doubleday, 1992)
DzH	H. Denzinger and P. Hünermann (eds.), *Enchiridion symbolorum, definitionum et declarationum* (Freiburg im Breisgau: Herder, 17th edn., 1991)
LXX	Septuagint (the most important Greek version of the OT)
ND	J. Neuner and J. Dupuis (eds.), *The Christian Faith* (Bangalore/New York: Theological Publications in India/Alba House, 7th edn., 2001)
NT	New Testament
par. parr.	parallel passage(s) in the Synoptic Gospels
OT	Old Testament

1

From Adam and Eve to Abraham and Sarah

The Book of Genesis deploys a range of traditional figures and stories that symbolize the unity of humankind and God's loving concern for all human beings. This chapter picks out Adam and Eve, Noah and his family, and then the patriarch Abraham and his wife Sarah. Their stories show how God cares for everyone and shows a universal benevolence. Let us see the details of these ancient legends, along with their views of the human condition and its religious practices. Jewish history looks back not merely to Abraham and Sarah but also 'beyond' them to the 'parents' of the human race and the mythical 'time' when humanity was one.

ADAM AND EVE

The Hebrew word *'adam*, a common noun that signifies 'human being (man)' or 'humanity (mankind)', *also* functions in the Bible, albeit rarely, as the proper name for a male person, the first human being. The Book of Genesis uses the word as the name for the first human individual only after Adam and Eve have been expelled from Eden. Prior to that, the so-called Priestly tradition speaks of the creation of *'adam* in a collective sense (as 'humanity' or 'humankind') (Gen. 1: 26–8). The Yahwist tradition then depicts the creation and sin of *ha 'adam* ('the man') and makes it clear that is referring to the first male individual (Gen. 2: 4–3: 24). But the proper name

'Adam' occurs in the Hebrew text at Genesis 4: 25, when Adam is identified as the father of Seth.[1]

Thus at the start of Genesis, the story of the creation and of the subsequent sin of 'the man' and 'the woman' (e.g. Gen. 3: 2, 6, 12, 13, 15–16) works to depict symbolically the origin and present sinful state of humankind, or of everyman and everywoman. The figures of 'Adam' and 'Eve' may be individual, but are used to portray the whole human race and not merely the story of two human beings. The opening chapters of Genesis apply to the entire human community: first, their creation through the goodness of God and then their fall into sin that has affected all subsequent generations. What we read in those chapters refers universally to human beings, their origin, and their life in the presence of God.[2] What is at stake is the relationship between God, the lord of history and creator of the world, and human beings, the climax of the creative work of God. These are the headlines; let us now see the small print.

Human existence, according to Genesis, consists in relationships—between human beings and nature, among human beings, and between human beings and God. Human creation can respond to and collaborate with the creator—something clearly implied when God says: 'Let us make humankind in our image, according to our likeness' (Gen. 1: 26). This is to define human beings in terms of their relationship with God and their dialogue with God. The creation story, which attaches God-like attributes to human beings as such (and not specifically to Israelites, who have not yet appeared in the story) inspires a psalm to express wonder at the divine favour shown towards human beings: 'you have made them a little lower

[1] The Priestly tradition has normally been dated to the time of the Babylonian captivity in the sixth century BC. The Yahwist tradition used to be dated to the time of David and Solomon, but many scholars now lower the date by a century or more. Some even doubt the distinct existence of the Priestly and the Yahwist traditions. See E. Zenger *et al.*, *Einleitung in das Alte Testament* (Stuttgart: Kohlhammer, 5th edn., 2004), 90–123.

[2] F. Maass, "*Adham*', in G. J. Botterweck and H. Ringgren (eds.), *Theological Dictionary of the Old Testament*, i (Grand Rapids, Mich.: Eerdmans, 1974), 75–87, at 83–4: 'the use of the word *adham* in the OT presents one of the strongest evidences for ancient Israelite universalism. In most passages using *adham*, including the earliest texts, it is clear that this word is not intended to refer particularly to Israelites but to all men.'

than God [or 'the angels']; and crowned them with glory and honour' (Ps. 8: 5).

This sense of the unconditional dignity of all human beings and the sanctity of their life comes through a later, classical Jewish homily on the creation story. 'For this reason was one single man created: to teach you that anyone who destroys a single life is as though he destroyed the whole of mankind, and anyone who preserves a single life is as though he preserved the whole of mankind... [Since each of us is an Adam] everyone must say: "For my sake the world was created"' (*Sanhedrin*, 4. 5).[3]

In the older, Yahwist account of creation (Gen. 2), God places 'man' in the garden and then provides for all his needs. The later Priestly tradition (Gen. 1) shows God preparing the earth as a 'house' or 'tent' and then bringing in the human tenants: 'male and female' (Gen. 1: 27).[4] The 'house' belongs to the divine proprietor; humanity can only be God's steward and mouthpiece. Communication is both vertical (between God and humanity) and horizontal (among human beings themselves). The Yahwist account dwells on the fact that 'the man' needs a partner, while the Priestly version shows God creating humankind as a community. It is to humanity as a whole that God delivers the injunction: 'be fruitful and multiply; fill the earth and subdue it' (Gen. 1: 28). Here *'adam* is understood not as a single couple, still less as 'the man', but collectively as the 'composite whole as male and female' or a human dyad created in the divine image (Gen. 1: 26–7).[5]

Genesis expresses not only humanity's inherent dignity (as created by God and endowed with God-like qualities) but also the mission that issues from this dignity. Human images of God manifest the divine rule on earth and have the privileged task of being God's stewards, continuing and completing God's creative work by presiding in the divine name over the rest of creation. In particular, three

---

[3] See M. Greenberg, 'Mankind, Israel and the Nations in the Hebraic Heritage', in J. R. Nelson (ed.), *No Man Is Alien* (Leiden: Brill, 1971), 15–39, at 38.

[4] Some scholars argue that the final redactions of the Yahwist and Priestly traditions were roughly contemporaneous—in the sixth century BC; see A. Lacoque, *The Trial of Innocence: Adam, Eve and the Yahwist* (Eugene, Oreg.: Cascade Books, 2006), 17–21, 52–60.

[5] H. Wallace, 'Adam', *ABD* i. 62–4, at 63.

activities are given to 'the man' and only to him among all living creatures: namely, to cultivate the earth, to 'keep' or guard the Garden, and to name the animals—an act which suggests his unique wisdom and intelligence (Gen. 2: 15, 19–20). A psalm echoes the Genesis account and celebrates the wonderful share in his own dignity that God has granted human beings by giving them authority over the rest of creation: 'You have given them dominion over the works of your hands; you have put all things under their feet, all sheep and oxen, and also the beasts of the field, the birds of the air, and the fish of the sea' (Ps. 8: 6–8).

Humanity collectively enjoys a favoured status vis-à-vis the rest of creation, but relies totally upon God for this status and indeed for life itself. Humanity is likewise responsible collectively in its obedience to God, and should obey the commands of God—in particular, the command not to eat any fruit 'of the tree of the knowledge of good and evil' (Gen. 2: 16–17). Hence when 'the man' and 'the woman' disobey the divine command, their rebellion affects universally the whole human community. 'The man' and 'the woman' eat the forbidden fruit, and lose both their innocent relationship with one another and their trusting relationship with God. The story vividly portrays their loss of innocence and urge to redress their self-image: 'The eyes of both were opened, and they knew that they were naked; and they sowed fig leaves together, and made loincloths for themselves' (Gen. 3: 7). They now 'know' through their experience the difference between 'good' and 'evil' (Gen. 3: 5). In their guilt they try to hide 'themselves from the presence of the Lord God' (Gen. 3: 8). They had hoped that eating the forbidden fruit would make them even more 'like God' (Gen. 3: 5); now they anxiously try to get away from God. Sin has disrupted their basic relationship with their divine Lord.

The story of the first sin brilliantly presents what everyman and everywoman do: their instinct is to put the blame on someone else. 'The man' blames 'the woman' and even God: 'the woman whom you gave to be with me, she gave me fruit from the tree' (Gen. 3: 11). 'The woman' blames the crafty serpent who has tempted her: 'the serpent tricked me, and I ate' (Gen. 3: 13). But 'the man' and 'the woman' have deliberately disobeyed the divine will and must suffer the consequences. Their transgression has a tragic outcome.

The Genesis story picturesquely tells what follows the sinful loss of their first innocence, when 'the man' and 'the woman' were un-ashamedly naked (Gen. 2: 25)—in a guiltless relationship with one another and with God, which traditional Christian language was to call 'original justice'. The biblical text appeals to an ancient explanation for the pain of childbirth, when God says to the woman: 'I will greatly increase your pangs in childbearing; in pain you shall bring forth children' (Gen. 3: 16). In place of an ideal relationship of joyful equality and mutual dependence intended by the creator (Gen. 2: 18–23), the woman finds herself 'ruled over' by her husband (Gen. 3: 16) and named by him 'Eve' (Gen. 3: 20). Where pain now characterizes the woman's experience of giving life through childbearing, something similar holds true of the man. His work in cultivating the garden should have been normal and natural (Gen. 2: 15), but sin turns work into distressing toil (Gen. 3: 17–19). In bringing life, in his case by gaining bread from the ground and its crops, the man too will have to suffer pain. In language that is as fresh as ever, the Genesis story drives home the point: far from enhancing their life, sin leaves everyman and everywoman less than they should really be, and ushers in destructive consequences.

The most distressing consequence concerns death. Fashioned from dust (Gen. 2: 7), 'the man' and 'the woman' are by nature mortal; their death should have been like that of Abraham, who will die surrounded by his family in 'ripe old age'—a death that peacefully completes a life spent in faithful obedience to God (Gen. 25: 1–11).[6] But disobedience to God has changed the experience of death for sinful human beings: death has become a troubling, inexorable fate (Gen. 3: 19), a distressing sign of sin. Flanked by suffering and pain, death signals the radical change that sin brings to the human condition.

Having made a decision unworthy of those created in the divine image (Gen. 1: 26–7), the man and the woman are banished from the garden of Eden into a foreign place. Cherubim and a flaming sword now guard the entrance into the garden and 'the way to the tree of

---

[6] For the Yahwist tradition, physical death is humanity's return to dust and the handing back of life's breath to God. The OT expresses a firm belief in afterlife only in the post-exilic times.

life' (Gen. 3: 24). Other books of the Bible will use exile and suffering in a foreign land to symbolize sin and the lot of sinful human beings: Jesus' parable of the lost son, for example, pictures the boy who will become a dissolute sinner as leaving his parental home for 'a distant country' (Luke 15: 13). The last book of the Bible will portray final damnation as 'the second death' to which the damned will be banished and final redemption as entering a heavenly Jerusalem and receiving God's abundant blessings from the 'tree of life'. For humanity, paradise regained will mean re-entering the garden and being given access to the final 'tree of life', which will be watered by the river of life coming from the Lamb (Rev. 22: 1–2).

Despite the sad consequences of sin, God does not curse the first two human beings and continues to cherish them; their disobedience cannot render void the special relationship between God and the human race. Eve will remain 'the mother of all the living' (Gen. 3: 20). The curse upon the serpent in Genesis 3: 15 ('I will put enmity between you and the woman, and between your seed and her seed; he shall strike your head, and you shall strike his heel') seems to recall an ancient explanation of why serpents crawl rather than walk and why human beings instinctively fear serpents. Yet this curse also suggests the future possibility of human salvation: 'once admitted that the serpent symbolizes sin, death and the power of evil, it becomes much more likely that the curse envisages a long struggle between good and evil, with mankind eventually triumphing'.[7] Starting with Justin Martyr (d. around 165) and Irenaeus (d. around 200), many Christian commentators were to interpret this verse as 'the first Gospel (Protoevangelium)' conveying the first divine promise of salvation to come through 'the woman' (identified as Mary) and 'her seed' (Christ).[8] Moreover, even in the immediate aftermath of their sin, God actively cares for disobedient human beings by clothing and protecting them with 'garments of skin' (Gen. 3: 21). God does something similar after the murder of Abel, by putting a protective 'mark on Cain, so that no one who came upon him would kill him' (Gen. 4: 15). Human sin does not do away with divine mercy.

---

[7] G. J. Wenham, *Genesis 1–15* (Waco, Tex.: Word Books, 1987), 80.
[8] Ibid., 80–1.

When the Priestly tradition returns in the Genesis narrative, it teaches firmly that, despite the presence of sin, human beings remain created in the image of God. The divine 'likeness' and 'image' are transmitted to the descendants of Adam and Eve: 'When God created humankind, he made them in his likeness. Male and female he created them, and he blessed them.' When Adam begets Seth, he 'becomes the father of a son in his likeness [the divine likeness] and according to his image' (Gen. 5: 1–3).

We can sum up this vision of all humanity with which the Bible starts. Even after their sin, human beings continue to display the divine image and likeness and to experience the loving concern of God. They must rely on God for everything, and hope for a redemption to come. The universal benevolence of God brightens a situation darkened by human sin. While human guilt is universal, the divine love and concern are also universal.

NOAH AND HIS FAMILY

The Genesis story sees the disobedience of Adam and Eve as initiating an avalanche of sin. Cain murders his brother; this fratricide paves the way for a terrifying increase of violence and the unbridled revenge killings practised by Cain's descendant, Lamech (Gen. 4: 8, 23–4). Violence also brings a breach of boundaries between heaven and earth. 'Beings of the heavenly court' take human wives, even though their offspring remain mortal and do not become semi-divine (Gen. 6: 1–4). Whatever the source of this fragment of mythology, lustful practices contribute to the steady advance of sin that degrades the human condition. Described earlier as 'good' (Gen. 1: 31), the earth itself has now become corrupt through the violent and wicked deeds of human beings (Gen. 6: 11–13). In their colourful way, the opening chapters of Genesis show human beings opting against God and one another. Evil decisions coalesce and shape a whole situation of sin, which needs 'cleansing' to allow for a new beginning (Gen. 9: 1–2).

Although God's judgement takes the form of a catastrophic flood, the merciful love of God still operates. As we saw above, earlier in the

Genesis story God provides garments of skin to replace the flimsy clothing of fig leaves, and dresses up 'the man' and 'the woman' after they sin. He likewise puts a 'mark' on their son, the first murderer, so as to protect Cain. Then, the biblical authors use Babylonian traditions of prehistoric floods to highlight God's faithful mercy that sharply contrasts with the stubbornness and sinful inclinations of the human heart. Before the flood, God respects human freedom and offers all people the option of avoiding the impending doom. He then rescues Noah and a remnant of human beings and animals; they are the ones who have accepted God's offer (Gen. 6: 5–8: 22).

When the account of the flood ends, the Priestly tradition takes up the story and tells of the covenant that God establishes with humanity and with all creatures through the person of Noah and his descendants. The fundamental interconnectedness of all creation means that it has only one *history*, which finds in God its source and goal. While human beings bring about the birth of *culture*, they give rise to two conflicting forces which, in the flood story of Genesis, come to a head: the one force that seeks God and the other that tries to construct a world which allows no place for the creator. Human sin turns work into toil, and life into a burdensome struggle against 'thorns and thistles' that ekes out an existence from the soil (Gen. 3: 17–19). The flood accounts strikingly portray the close link between human sin on the one hand, and creation on the other.

But a new age opens after the flood. The blessing originally given to both human beings and non-human creatures (Gen. 1: 22, 28) is now renewed: 'Be fruitful and multiply and fill the earth' (Gen. 9: 1; see 8: 17). While God promises the divine blessing, he also calls on human beings to observe the law—in particular, by showing reverence for life. They may now eat the flesh of animals, but not 'with its life, that is with its blood' (Gen. 9: 3–4). Life is *the* divine gift, symbolized by blood and always to be reverenced (see Lev. 17: 11). Here God's covenant with Noah goes beyond dietary regulations to include a law against taking away life by murder. To kill another human being is to shed the blood of someone created in the divine image (Gen. 9: 5–6; see 4: 10–11).

The renewed relationship between God and human beings takes the form of a covenant, which will guarantee the preservation of the natural order against the powers of chaos: 'never again shall all flesh be cut off by the waters of a flood, and never again shall there be a flood to destroy the earth'.[9] Unlike the later covenants to be made with Abraham and Sarah (Gen. 17) and with the people of Israel at Mount Sinai (Exod. 24), the covenant with Noah is *universal* in its scope. As we shall see, the three sons of Noah are regarded as the ancestors of all peoples. This covenant is also made with every living creature and with the earth itself. The permanent symbol of this cosmic covenant with God will be the rainbow that in the sky unites heaven and earth (Gen. 9: 8–17). God will faithfully sustain the whole world, and will always show concern for the well-being of all creatures. In the words of a psalm, 'the Lord is good to all, and his compassion is over all he has made ... satisfying the desire of every living thing' (Ps. 145: 9, 16).

The meaning given to the rainbow seems a striking innovation, since many people in ancient times regarded the rainbow as a characteristic weapon of the Divine Warrior who used it to shoot the arrows of lightning.[10] Such symbolism turns up in the OT itself (e.g. Ps. 7: 12–13; Hab. 3: 9–11). In Genesis 9, however, the sign of the rainbow ceases to express the divine anger. God says: 'the bow in the clouds' is 'the sign of the covenant that I have established between me and all flesh that is on the earth' (Gen. 9: 1–17). This meaning is more in line with the 'natural' symbolism of the rainbow, in that it signals the *end* of a rainstorm.

The universality of this covenant is also signified by Shem, Ham, and Japheth: 'these three were the sons of Noah, and from these the whole earth was peopled' (Gen. 9: 18). To drive home the universal relevance of Noah, his family, and the covenant God made with him, Genesis provides a table of the nations (Gen. 10: 1–32), and so uses ancient traditions to illustrate that all humankind originated from Noah and his family.[11] This means that the entire human race has

---

[9] Even before Genesis speaks of the covenant with Noah, God has already promised the stable and regular course of nature: 'As long as the earth continues, seedtime and harvest, cold and heat, summer and winter, day and night shall not cease' (Gen. 8: 22).

[10] See Wenham, *Genesis 1–15*, 105–6; R. B. Y. Scott, 'Rainbow', *The Interpreter's Dictionary of the Bible*, iv (New York: Abingdon, 1969), 6–7. The entry 'Rainbow' by M. H. Pope in the supplementary volume of 1976, 725–6, goes to extremes in detecting real or possible sex symbolism.

[11] H. D. Preuss observes: 'According to the Table of the Nations in Genesis 10, a type of literary document that is without analogy in the ancient Middle East, Israel

inherited the divine blessings of the new age that follows the flood, and is understood to share in the covenant made with Noah. As C. Westermann puts it: 'the whole of humankind in all its members is created, preserved, and blessed by God'.[12]

The universalism developed here in Genesis seems even more astonishing when we recall that the Jahwist and Priestly traditions that feed into the final text come from times when the Israelites were long settled in Palestine and understood themselves to be the chosen people of God. Along with (or despite?) a profound sense of their own special election, they *also* endorsed—through their inspired writers—a conviction that God's loving care extended to everyone.

Noah, the central human character in the flood story and in the subsequent making of a cosmic covenant with God, is acknowledged to be 'a righteous man, blameless in his generation' (Gen. 6: 9). This legendary figure enjoys the status of a holy human being, who long predates the call of Abraham and the making of the Sinai covenant. Noah's blameless righteousness does not depend on his belonging to the chosen people. The ancient narrative presents some aspects of his contacts with God. Initially, it tells of God communicating through commands to prepare the ark which will save Noah, his family, and an assortment of animals and birds (Gen. 6: 13–22). Before the great flood comes, God commands Noah to take his entire entourage aboard the ark (Gen. 7: 1–5).

When the flood subsides, further commands from God lead Noah to disembark, along with his wife, sons, daughters-in-law, and the 'families' of animals and birds. Once again Noah does what he is told. But he does something further by building 'an altar to the Lord' and making on it 'burnt offerings' of 'clean' animals and birds. When 'the Lord smells the pleasing odour', he 'says in his heart' that, despite 'the evil inclination of the human heart', he will never curse the ground and bring destruction (Gen. 8: 15–22). In building an altar and offering this sacrifice of thanksgiving, Noah does so spontaneously and, obviously, without intending to follow the prescriptions about

enjoys vis-à-vis the nations no pre-eminence due to creation, mythology, or prehistory': *Old Testament Theology*, ii (Edinburgh: T. & T. Clark, 1996), 285.

[12] On 'The Table of the Nations', see C. Westermann, *Genesis 1–11: A Commentary* (London: SPCK, 1984), 495–530, at 526.

burnt offerings and other offerings understood to have been introduced later by God through Moses (Lev. 1–7).

Some further OT and NT books develop and encourage such a large-
minded vision of this 'man for all peoples'. Ezekiel associates Noah with
Job (and, possibly, with Daniel) for their classical righteousness (Ezek.
14: 14). Sirach recalls Noah as the second founder of the human race
after the flood: 'Noah was found perfect and righteous; in the time of
wrath he kept the race alive' (Sir. 44: 17). The cosmic covenant with
Noah remains firmly in place in the list of seven covenants that ends
with that made with King David (Sir. 44–7) Among its seven historical
illustrations of the saving power of wisdom, the Wisdom of Solomon
lists Noah: 'when the earth was flooded', wisdom 'saved it, steering the
righteous man by a paltry piece of wood' (Wisd. 10: 4). The NT follows
suit by celebrating the holiness and faith of Noah. He serves to exemplify the watchfulness needed as Christians wait for the end of the age
(Matt. 24: 37–9). The Letter to the Hebrews puts into its roll call of
heroes and heroines of faith Noah, who 'became an heir to the righteousness that is in accordance with faith' (Heb. 11: 7). The First Letter
of Peter brings the story of the flood and the rescue of Noah and his
family into a comparison with the basic Christian sacrament: in the
former case water destroyed sinners, in the latter the water used in
baptism saves sinners (1 Pet. 3: 20–1).

The OT presents, to be sure, stories about other figures like Job
and Melchizedek who do not belong to the chosen people and yet are
blessed and honoured by God. Yet Noah stands apart even from Job
and Melchizedek Through him God gives human history a fresh
beginning and makes a covenant with all peoples and with the
earth itself. Noah and his sons are portrayed as being the ancestors
of the entire human race. The vivid narrative about Noah continues
to invite an appropriate response of faith. Through a cosmic covenant all people (along with all non-human creatures) form a single
family, share the same basic blessings from God, and are called to
observe a universal moral law.[13] Everything else is secondary to this
primary relationship with one another and with God.

---

[13] The non-canonical Book of Jubilees, dated between the third and first centuries
BC, portrays Noah as teaching his sons 'the ordinances, the commandments, and all
the judgements he knew': 'he exhorted his sons to observe righteousness, to cover the
shame of their flesh, to bless their Creator, to honour father and mother, to love their

The OT narrative about Noah conveys a universal vision of divine benevolence, and this universalism is 'decentralized', rather than 'centralized'. That is to say, it does not entail a vision of all 'other' people coming to Jerusalem and sharing there in the specific blessings of the chosen people. In a later chapter we will see that, even if 'centralized' universalism proves dominant, a sense of God's 'decentralized' benevolence does not disappear, even in the prophetic books. Thus Isaiah and Malachi picture the 'others' as knowing God and in their worship offering him valid sacrifices (Isa. 19: 21; Mal. 1: 11).

Along with Noah, the NT continues to acknowledge the exemplary faith of other 'ancient' figures who do not belong to God's chosen people. Thus the list in the Letter to the Hebrews includes the saintly Abel, whose faith 'still speaks' to us (Heb. 11: 4). This legendary character in the story of human origins is seen as the first martyr whose spilt blood prefigures the sacrifice of Christ (Heb. 12: 24). But the Letter to the Hebrews dedicates more verses to the faith of Abraham and Sarah (Heb. 11: 8–12, 17–19). We can turn to them and see how much they yield for those who want to glean a fuller account of what the Book of Genesis suggests about God's universal benevolence.

ABRAHAM AND SARAH

Notwithstanding the new beginning marked by God's covenant with Noah, the history of sin continues. The story of the tower of Babel expresses an arrogant attempt to overreach human limitations (Gen. 11: 1–9). The attempt ends in an insuperable breakdown in human communications; the people are scattered over the face of the earth and their one language is broken up into many. The biblical text takes an old legend about the origin of the different language groups and

neighbour, and to guard their souls from fornication, uncleanness, and all iniquity… Whoever sheds man's blood and whoever eats the blood of any flesh shall be destroyed from the earth' (7. 20–39). These commands were later systematized into a list of universal moral laws laid upon the descendants of Noah; see Greenberg, 'Mankind, Israel and the Nations', 20–2.

uses it to symbolize proud desires to procure fame and security, something that quickly proves self-destructive.

Against this background of a divided humanity, God calls Abraham and Sarah to play a decisive role in achieving the divine purposes. They are to become the ancestors of 'a great nation', and their relationship with God will benefit other human families: 'in you all the families of the earth will be blessed' (Gen. 12: 1–9). Abraham, Sarah, and their descendants, the people of Israel, are elected to serve God in leading other people to God. The theme of the family of Abraham and Sarah becoming a conduit of blessings for all nations recurs in Genesis (Gen. 28: 14) and is echoed by the prophets (e.g. Isa. 19: 23–5; Jer. 4: 2).[14] Abraham and Sarah, responding obediently to the summons from God, accept their call and typify forever outstanding persons of faith (Heb. 11: 8–12), wherever such persons are found.

Many features of the stories about Abraham and Sarah show how the Israelites, when recalling this ancient couple and their family, reflected on the religious situation of 'others' who intersect with these stories. First of all, Melchizedek, a priest-king, abruptly appears to meet and bless Abraham, and does so in the name of 'God Most High (El Elyon)' (Gen. 14: 19–20). Like Adam, Eve, Cain (Gen. 4: 9–10), Enoch (Gen. 5: 21–4), Noah, Abraham, and Sarah, Melchizedek enjoys intimate contact with God. A priest of a Canaanite sanctuary, Melchizedek conveys a blessing to Abraham. He does so in the name of the deity whom he worships and who is at once identified as 'the maker of heaven and earth' (Gen. 14: 22). Later books will identify 'God Most High' as the Lord (YHWH) or God of Israel (Num. 24: 16; Ps. 46: 4).

In the nomadic or semi-nomadic world of Abraham, different epithets are applied to the supreme God 'El' (Divinity): 'El Bethel' ('God of Bethel'; see Gen. 35: 7), 'El Elyon' ('God Most High'), 'El Olam' ('Everlasting God'), and 'El Shaddai' ('God, the One of the Mountains').[15] These various names for God indicate not only

---

[14] On the chosen people of God and the nations, see Preuss, *Old Testament Theology*, ii. 284–307.

[15] See E. R. Dalglish, 'Bethel', *ABD* i. 706–10; M. Rose, 'Names of God in the OT', *ABD* iv. 1001–11; M. S. Smith, *The Memoirs of God: History, Memory and the Experience of the Divine in Ancient Israel* (Minneapolis: Fortress, 2004); id., *The Early History of God* (Grand Rapids, Mich.: Eerdmans, 2nd edn., 2002).

intense familiarity with God but also a vibrant trust and hope. They belong to different sanctuaries or places where God is worshipped. History as well as geography also enters in: God maintains a special relationship with some particular group from the time of being revealed to the group's ancestor or ancestors (see Gen. 46: 3; Exod. 3: 6). Eventually the 'God of Abraham, Isaac, and Jacob' will be identified as 'the Father of Our Lord Jesus Christ' (Rom. 15: 6; Eph. 1: 3). But the story of Abraham and Sarah, and not least the account of Abraham's encounter with Melchizedek, a mysterious Canaanite priest, suggests a world in which different religious groupings provide places where human beings experience God. Certainly Abraham and Sarah do not separate themselves rigidly from their neighbours, as if everything about the religious belief and practice of those 'others' were simply error, superstition, and downright idolatry.

Melchizedek, an ancient priest-king of Jerusalem, will be pictured by a royal psalm as a forerunner to the king of Israel. The new king, who also bears the dignity of priesthood, will be deemed 'a priest forever according to the order of Melchizedek' (Ps. 110: 4). The Letter to the Hebrews goes much further by interpreting the priesthood of Christ 'according to the order of Melchizedek' (Heb. 5: 10; 6: 20). Hebrews pronounces the mysterious priest-king to be superior to Abraham and his descendant Levi (the ancestor of the Levitical priests). The Levitical priests are mortal, and so their priesthood is temporary and provisional. Melchizedek, however, 'lives': the scriptures do not record his ancestors, birth, or death. He neither inherits his priestly office nor transmits it to his offspring. In such ways he prefigures the immortal Son of God who holds his priesthood permanently and through a divine oath ('the Lord has sworn, "You are a priest forever"') (Heb. 7: 1–28). This means assigning a unique importance to a Canaanite priest, who turns up briefly in the story of Abraham but mysteriously points ahead to Christ, the High Priest who will bring to perfection all sacrifices (Heb. 9: 11–10: 18). Thus a major NT book interprets and explains the priesthood of Christ through an 'outsider' and not through some figure in the story of the chosen people themselves.

It is hard to imagine how a priest from 'the outside' could have received a better biblical press. In Genesis, the mysterious

Melchizedek was honoured by receiving a tenth part of the goods that Abraham, the progenitor of the chosen people, had just recovered. In Psalm 110, Melchizedek served as a model for the priestly privileges of the Davidic king. In Hebrews, he prefigured the priesthood of Christ himself. It is no wonder then that from the time of Clement of Alexandria (d. around 200), the bread and wine offered by Melchizedek were understood to prefigure the Eucharist. He was introduced into the Roman Canon (which seems to go back to the fourth century): 'Look with favour on these offerings and accept them as once you accepted the gifts of your servant Abel, the sacrifice of Abrahahm our father in faith, and the bread and wine offered by your priest Melchizedek.'

The Genesis narrative moves on from the encounter with Melchizedek, and gives two versions of a divine covenant with Abraham (15: 7–21; 17: 1–27). In the second account, 'God, the One of the Mountains (El Shaddai)' gives Abraham a new name ('Abraham' instead of 'Abram') to express his new relationship with God, guarantees him an exceedingly numerous posterity, and promises that the covenant will be everlasting. But this covenant, unlike the everlasting covenant with Noah (Gen. 9: 1–17), applies only to the descendants of Abraham and Sarah. When recalling the covenant with Abraham, the Priestly version of the call of Moses will indicate that God, venerated by Abraham and others in the patriarchal period as El Shaddai, is now adored by Israel as YHWH ('the Lord') (Exod. 6: 2–4). Inevitably the situation of oppression by the Pharaoh brings a deterioration in relations with the 'others' that does not apply in the days of Abraham, even after the special covenant is made with him and Sarah.

Abraham and Sarah come to live in the land of Gerar. The local king, Abimelech, is led to believe that Sarah is Abraham's sister, not his wife. After Abimelech 'takes' Sarah but before he has sexual relations with her, he is visited by God in a vision by night. When God explains that Sarah is Abraham's wife, Abimelech becomes fearful about the religious implications of what has happened and restores Sarah to Abraham. He also makes some generous gifts of slaves, livestock, and silver to Abraham. Thereupon, through Abraham's prayers, Abimelech is blessed by God with abundant offspring (Gen. 20: 1–18). In this episode Abimelech, an 'outsider', behaves with sensitivity to the will of God and is blessed accordingly. The story presents him as more pious and respectful of God than Abraham himself.

After residing for 'many days in the land of the Philistines', Abraham and Sarah once again meet Abimelech, now identified as king of the Philistines. This identification seems anachronistic, since the arrival of the Philistines in Canaan happened after 1200 BC, centuries later than the supposed period of Abraham and the patriarchs. Interestingly, the story involves an ancient divine name, 'El Olam (the Everlasting God)' (Gen. 21: 22–34). Once associated with the pre-Israelite sanctuary of Beersheba, this title, as we see in Isaiah 40: 28, will be adopted by Israel as a name for the Lord. Abraham makes a treaty with the Philistine king, and plants a sacred tree (a tamarisk) in Beersheba. In that shrine belonging to 'outsiders', he calls 'on the name of the Lord', identified as 'El Olam'. Thus Abraham recognizes the divine presence in a sanctuary created by others, and prays there to God.

If we sum up what we have gleaned from the Book of Genesis, we should acknowledge the universal benevolence of God found in the stories of Adam, Eve, and Noah. Abraham's encounter with Melchizedek strikingly witnesses to the status the biblical text can give to a religious figure from among the 'outsiders'. Even after the special call of Abraham and Sarah and the covenant made with them, the story of Abraham's treaty with Abimelech testifies to the value of the shrines of 'others', their naming of God, and their sacred ceremonies. The protagonists whom we have recalled from Genesis, from Adam and Eve to Abimelech, illustrate how all human beings, even murderers like Cain, enjoy access to God and can converse with him in prayer. An intimacy with God blesses human beings everywhere.

2

Exodus, Deuteronomy, Ruth, and Naaman

As we continue the process of discerning how the OT evaluates the religious situation of 'others', we need to find our way around, or rather through, Exodus and Deuteronomy. At first sight, we can feel discouraged by much we read there. Let us begin with the anti-idol polemic.

IMAGES PROHIBITED

In the ancient world worshipping God *without images* set the faith of Israel apart. This and other cherished beliefs of the Israelites conflicted radically with those of 'others'. The peoples of the Middle East (and elsewhere) normally personified the powers of nature, made statues of them in a human or an animal form, and worshipped them.[1] The Ten Commandments, however, reflect a very spiritual understanding of YHWH and begin by imposing imageless worship: 'You shall not make for yourself an idol, whether in the form of anything that is in the heaven above, or that is on the earth beneath, or that is in the water under the earth. You shall not bow down to them and worship them' (Exod. 20: 4–5; see Deut. 5: 8–9). Idols are dismissed as mere 'gods made by human hands, objects of wood or stone that neither see, nor hear, nor eat, nor smell' (Deut. 4: 28).[2]

---

[1] See E. M. Curtis, 'Idol, Idolatry', *ABD* iii. 376–81; S. D. McBride, 'The Essence of Orthodoxy: Deuteronomy 5: 6–10 and Exodus 20: 2–6', *Interpretation* 60 (2006), 133–50.

[2] Jeremiah elaborates such a dismissal of idols (Jer. 10: 1–16), and so too does a satirical passage from Deutero-Isaiah (Isa. 44: 9–20). See also Pss. 115: 3–8; 135: 15–18.

Idolatry brings terrible moral corruption (e.g. Deut. 12: 31). Image-less worship is a fundamental tenet of Mosaic faith.

Israel will move beyond mere monolatry (or the worship of one deity) to monotheism or the belief that there is only one God, YHWH. At this point the move is not yet complete. The first commandment asserts that Israel should have no other gods, since the Lord is a jealous God who will not tolerate any rivals for the devotion of the people: 'you shall have no other gods before [or besides] me' (Exod. 20: 3, 5; see Deut. 5: 6). In the promised land, the Israelites meet, however, others whose forms of worship involve 'pillars' or upright stones that stood near the shrines of Baal and 'sacred poles' or 'Asherim' that symbolize Asherah, the mother goddess of the Canaanite religion (see Judg. 2: 13).[3] The chosen people of God must not tolerate such other forms of worship and their seductive idols: 'Take care not to make a covenant with the inhabitants of the land to which you are going, or it will become a snare among you. You shall tear down their altars, and cut down their sacred poles [Asherim]. For you shall worship no other god, because the Lord whose name is Jealous, is a jealous God' (Exod. 34: 12–14; see 23: 23–4). YHWH makes a total claim upon the loyalty of his people. In an exclusive way they must confess the saving power of the Lord and practise fidelity towards him. Such polemic against 'other' gods, we should recall, was in the ancient Middle East a standard way for exalting the specific divinity worshipped by a particular group and for affirming their own religious identity.[4]

THE COVENANT

The Book of Exodus describes vividly the ceremony through which the Israelites and their leaders seem to have been sharply separated from 'the others': the special covenant with God which was ratified at Mount Sinai (Exod. 24: 1–18). Through this gratuitous act of God,

[3] See J. Day, 'Asherah', *ABD* i. 483–7.
[4] See H. D. Preuss, *Verspottung fremder Religionen im Alten Testament* (Stuttgart: Kohlhammer, 1971).

the people are set apart to share the divine life. The structure of the ceremony resembles that of adoption and marriage.⁵ In his special role as covenant mediator, Moses first reads the 'words of the Lord' (the Ten Commandments) and 'all the ordinances'. He sets up twelve pillars, one for each tribe of Israel; the pillars symbolize how all the people share in the covenant. Then the ritual of dashing the blood (drawn from sacrifices) on the altar and on the people dramatizes the union between the two parties, the people and the Lord whose presence is symbolized by the altar.⁶ Blood is understood to be the efficacious means for establishing community between God and human beings. Peculiarly sacred to God, blood is constantly taken to be the place of the mystery of life and hence the powerful means for expiating sins and uniting people with God.

YHWH is now 'the God of Israel' (Exod. 24: 10). The tribal God, who has appeared to their ancestor, Abraham, and created a special relationship with him, has now delivered the people from captivity, given them the great gift of the law (Torah) (Deut. 6: 1–25; Ps. 119), and entered a special communion of covenanted life with them. As a 'holy nation' (Exod. 19: 6), they are all drawn near to God and are called to a life of holiness: 'You shall be holy; for I the Lord God am holy' (Lev. 19: 2). Along with the command to practise imageless worship, the Sinai covenant seems to disengage the Israelites from all 'others' in the divine plan of salvation and from the life and worship of 'others'. The disagreement seems to be irresolvable. Yet such a disengagement is by no means complete.

Jethro, the father-in-law of Moses, was a Midianite priest. After the exodus from Egypt, he visited Moses in the wilderness, gave him advice on the administration of the law, and offered a sacrifice to God (Exod. 18: 1–27). This tolerance in cultic practice hints at similar items that will turn up as the story unfolds. When Solomon dedicates the Temple in Jerusalem, it will be open to foreigners who come from distant countries (1 Kgs. 8: 41–3). As we shall see in later chapters, Isaiah and other prophetic books show here and there a similar cultic 'openness' to Gentiles who will come to Jerusalem.

⁵ See G. E. Mendenhall and G. A. Herion, 'Covenant', *ABD* i. 1179–202.
⁶ The awesome presence of God symbolized by the altar comes through strongly in the story of Isaiah's call (Isa. 6: 1–13). Even the seraph could not take a live coal with his own hands from the altar but had to use tongs.

In the story of the Exodus itself, one should not overlook a 'mixed multitude' who joined the Israelites when they left Egypt (Exod. 12: 38). Such non-Israelites were to be allowed to share in the future passover celebrations, provided the males among them were circumcised (Exod. 12: 43–9). According to the Book of Deuteronomy, 'strangers' shared in the covenant ceremony that preceded the death of Moses (Deut. 29: 11). They were also permitted to attend the ritual of covenant renewal that took place every seven years (Deut. 31: 12).

ASTRAL RELIGION

The Song of Moses (Deut. 32) has this to say about the divine beings who belong to the heavenly court: 'When the Most High (*Elyon*) apportioned the nations, when he divided humankind, he fixed the boundaries of the peoples, according to the number of the gods; the Lord's own portion was his people, Jacob his allotted share' (Deut. 32: 8–9). This polytheistic picture presents the High God with a court of lesser divine beings. When translating Deuteronomy 32: 8, the LXX demotes these divine beings to 'angels'. But the original (Hebrew) text of these two verses appears to assign various gods from the heavenly court of YHWH to be patrons of the different nations.[7]

In Deuteronomy 4: 19 this idea has already been applied to the religions of the nations. While astral cults are strictly forbidden in Israel, they are said to have been granted to various nations by YHWH. Thus Deuteronomy represents the religions of the nations as divinely approved, even if inferior to the religion of Israel. Let us see the details.

In the conclusion (Deut. 4: 1–40) to his first great address, Moses again warns against image worship and idolatry by reminding the people that, when the Lord spoke to them out of the fire, they 'heard the sound of words but saw no form; there was only a voice' (Deut. 4: 12). Thus the imageless worship of the invisible God is grounded in

---

[7] See M. S. Smith, *The Memoirs of God: History, Memory and the Experience of the Divine in Ancient Israel* (Minneapolis: Fortress, 2004), 108–9.

the self-revelation of the Lord at Horeb (Sinai) and the covenant made with him:

Since you saw no form when the Lord spoke to you at Horeb out of the fire, take care and watch yourselves closely, so that you do not act corruptly by making an idol for yourselves, in the form of any figure—the likeness of male or female, the likeness of any animal that is on the earth, the likeness of any winged bird that flies in the air, the likeness of anything that creeps on the ground, the likeness of any fish that is in the water under the earth. (Deut. 4: 15–18)

Three 'areas' are named ('the air', 'the ground', and 'the water under the earth') which could supply images. The Israelites are forbidden to take up any of these possibilities. Yet the same address by Moses goes on at once to allow a certain legitimacy to astral religion, along with a command to the Israelites not share in that religion.

The relevant text states: 'when you look up to the heavens and see the sun, the moon, and the stars, all the host of heaven, do not be led astray and bow down to them and serve them, *things that the Lord your God has allotted to all the peoples everywhere under heaven*' (Deut. 4: 19; see 29: 6). Commenting a century ago on the italicized words, S. R. Driver wrote: 'The God of Israel is supreme. He assigns to every nation its objects of worship; and the veneration of the heavenly bodies by the nations (other than Israel) forms part of his providential order of the world.'[8] Significant recent studies have shared the same view: 'YHWH has distributed the stars to all the peoples under heaven as objects of adoration.'[9] In his Anchor Bible commentary, M. Weinfeld endorses the same explanation of the verse: 'The heavenly bodies as objects of worship were assigned to the nations by God himself.'[10]

Such interpretations do not detract from the sovereign dominion of YHWH. His unique position is at once reaffirmed: 'The Lord has taken you and brought you . . . out of Egypt, to become a people of his very own possession' (Deut. 4: 20). As Dietrich Knapp puts it, the

---

[8] S. R. Driver, *A Critical and Exegetical Commentary on Deuteronomy* (Edinburgh: T. & T. Clark, 1903), 71.

[9] D. Knapp, *Deuteronomium 4: Literarische Analyse und theologische Interpretation* (Göttingen: Vandenhoeck & Ruprecht, 1987), 72.

[10] *Deuteronomy 1–11: A New Translation with Introduction and Commentary* (New York: Doubleday, 1991), 206.

Lord 'stands above the astral divinities, disposes of them, and with sovereign power assigns them' to their places.[11] Just as YHWH and Israel are bound together by a mutual relationship, so other peoples belong to the astral divinities assigned to them by YHWH. While the Lord has allotted to the peoples the cult of the stars, he has directly taken for himself Israel and called them to share, through a special revelation, in his own life.

Several significant conclusions follow from Deuteronomy 4: 19–20. First, what YHWH has assigned to the peoples means that their religious situation somehow belongs within the universal divine plan and hence cannot be dismissed as simply a matter of superstition and unbelief. Likewise the vision of these verses from Deuteronomy also rules out another view: namely, that the religious situation of the other peoples is *merely* the result of a human search, which has reached true conclusions about the existence of God and the need to worship him. Even such a view cannot be reconciled with the statements from Deuteronomy.

Second, even though they remain unaware of this, the 'others' exist in some living relationship with YHWH through the religious experience that occurs in the context of their own religion. To the extent that their religion authentically develops the basic gift of YHWH, the things he has 'allotted to all the peoples everywhere', it will prove a road to the true experience of salvation. Our Deuteronomy text interprets such an astral religion as a gift of the Lord and sign of his all-loving concern for all peoples and nations.[12]

A third important conclusion to be drawn from the Deuteronomy passage concerns the motivation given for the prohibition against adopting the religious forms that YHWH has assigned to the other peoples. Such a prohibition is not based on a negative evaluation of the other religions and their forms of worship but on the covenant made with God at Sinai. Verse 20 presents concisely the three key moments in the covenant: the divine election of Israel ('the Lord has taken you'), the liberation ('brought you out of Egypt'), and the

---

[11] Knapp, *Deuteronomium 4*, 73.

[12] This universal benevolence of YHWH suggests the title 'lover of the peoples'—an alternative reading in the penultimate chapter of Deuteronomy (Deut. 33: 3).

constitution of Israel as belonging essentially to YHWH (or as those who have 'become a people of his very own possession'). This sense of belonging to and of communion of life with YHWH forms the very heart of the covenant, as Deuteronomy understands it.

Fourth, we see here how Israel has developed a richer understanding of the religions of other peoples. It is precisely their faith in YHWH that allows Israel to recognize what God has done for 'all the peoples everywhere under heaven' and to appreciate that through living their religions these peoples are receiving a gift from God. One may not then interpret these religions as a mere preparatory step which will reach its goal only when the peoples renounce their own religions to embrace explicitly faith in YHWH. Our Deuteronomy passage maintains that, just as YHWH is at the origin of the saving experience of Israel, so he is at the origin of the religious pilgrimage of every people.

Fifth, the unique greatness of Israel's election by God and religious experience must be understood then in relationship to the 'others'. On the one hand, this election and religious experience are simply unparalleled since the time human beings were created (Deut. 4: 32). On the other hand, fidelity to the covenant will make the Israelites witnesses to non-Jews, who will acknowledge in them 'a wise and discerning people' (Deut. 4: 6). Thus, far from bringing disengagement from 'others', Israel's unique privilege should spread knowledge of the true God and prompt 'dialogue' with foreign peoples. By recognizing the spiritual wisdom and intelligence of Israel, at least indirectly they too can enjoy communion with YHWH. As we shall see in Chapter 4, Second Isaiah develops this theme: for instance, in the mission to the nations of the 'servant' of God. Israel's election and closeness to God belong to the divine plan and purpose for all 'others'.

PSALM 19

What we can glean from Deuteronomy 4 about the universal benevolence of YHWH finds analogues in the psalms: for instance, when the whole 'earth' is described as being filled by 'the steadfast love of the Lord' (Ps. 33: 5). A fascinating parallel to Deuteronomy's view of what can be called 'astral religion' comes in Psalm 19, which begins as a hymn to God as the creator of nature: 'the heavens are telling the glory of God; and the firmament proclaims his handiwork'. The phenomena of the heavens and, in particular, the power of the sun manifest the divine glory. The sky and the constant succession of days and nights are pictured as members of a choir who sing God's praises ceaselessly. The sun, like a champion athlete, runs its daily course along the track provided by the skies (Ps. 19: 1–6).

This divine revelation provided by the heavens and the heavenly bodies fills out some of the implications of the concise Deuteronomic language about the astral bodies that God has 'allotted to all the peoples everywhere', so as to inspire their religious worship and practice (Deut. 4: 19). The first part of Psalm 19 may have seemed to some an undue emphasis upon the self-manifestation of God in the works of nature. Hence some verses follow that praise the revelation of God's 'law' and 'ordinances' through Moses (Ps. 19: 7–13). The result is that the psalm embodies a tension that resembles that of Deuteronomy 4: 19–20: the tension between God's benevolent concern for all peoples and his unique election of Israel.

However, this bold attempt in Deuteronomy to place the other nations, their religions, and their gods within the one plan of God was flawed. Its scheme of the lesser divinities of the astral cults looked unacceptably polytheistic. The imagery of the divine court of lesser deities and the (subordinate) legitimacy of astral religion were not pursued in the OT. These two connected lines of approach do not recur. Apropos of the passages in Deuteronomy we have discussed, H. D. Preuss remarks: 'YHWH's assignment of the nations to other gods or, vice versa, the stars as gods to other nations... represents one of the few systematic attempts to give theological expression to Israel's and YHWH's relationships to the nations and their gods.'[13] The attempt was gallant, but jeopardized by its polytheistic picture.

---

[13] *Old Testament Theology*, ii (Edinburgh: T. & T. Clark, 1996), 285.

RUTH

Thus far this chapter has focused on the religious situation of the people of Israel and of other peoples in general. The OT also invites us to interpret religiously the situation of specific individuals and individual families, and not merely those we find in Genesis. I start with the Book of Ruth, which tells a family story and, in particular, of the mysterious ways God worked in the lives of Naomi, Ruth, and Boaz, three models of loyal commitment to the God of Israel.[14] The story is set in the days before the Davidic monarchy began. The two main characters are Naomi, an Israelite woman, and her Moabite daughter-in-law, Ruth, who eventually becomes an emigrant seeking welcome, food, and protection in Israel.

Some scholars date the composition of Ruth to a time before the Exile in Babylon, while others date its composition to a date after the Exile. The later date would support the case for holding that the anonymous author intended to show that a non-Israelite, Ruth, could become a faithful worshipper of the God of Israel. Nevertheless, whatever the date of the composition and the intentions of the author, the book was read after the Exile and in this context professed that the loving concern of YHWH extended beyond the chosen people to those of every nation.

The story opens with a famine which leads Naomi, her husband, and two sons to leave Bethlehem and go to the land of Moab. There the two sons marry Moabite wives. Tragedy strikes when Naomi's husband and two sons all die. When she hears that the famine has eased in Bethlehem, she decides to return home and encourages her two daughters-in-law not to come with her but to stay in Moab and re-marry there. Ruth, however, insists on going with her mother-in-law and says: 'Where you go, I will go; where you lodge, I will lodge; your people shall be my people, and your God my God. Where you die, I will die—there will I be buried' (Ruth 1: 16–17).

Back in Bethlehem, a new character enters the story, Boaz, a member of the family of Naomi's dead husband. When she takes

---

[14] See E. F. Campbell, *Ruth* (New York: Doubleday, 1975); P. Trible, 'Ruth, Book of', *ABD* v. 842–7.

advantage of a provision in Israelite law by gleaning the fields after the reapers have done their work, Ruth attracts the attention of Boaz. Behaving in a friendly and gracious manner towards this foreign woman, he instructs the young workers to let Ruth glean some barley and wheat (Ruth 2: 1–23). Naomi wants to help her daughter-in-law find a new husband; she realizes that Boaz is the obvious choice. By following the instructions of Naomi, Ruth wins favour with Boaz. But there are difficulties in the form of a more closely related kinsman and his rights (Ruth 3: 1–18). Boaz deals with this problem at once, and does so firmly and honourably. He marries Ruth and they have a son, Obed, the grandfather of King David (Ruth 4:1–18).

Two NT authors pick up this last detail, and name Obed among the ancestors of Jesus (Matt. 1: 4–6; Luke 3: 32). The OT narrative justifies the status of Ruth as the daughter-in-law *par excellence* in world history and literature. Theologically speaking, her significance is decidedly remarkable. It is not merely that, with Esther and Judith, she is one of three women who give their names to books of the Bible. With three other women (Tamar, Rahab, and the wife of Uriah [Bathsheba]) and all of them non-Israelite, she is listed by Matthew in his genealogy of Jesus (Matt. 1: 1–17).

Tamar, a Canaanite woman and the widowed daughter-in-law of Judah, acted resourcefully in disguising herself as a prostitute and becoming pregnant by her father-in-law. She gave birth to twins (Gen. 38: 1–30), one of whom (Perez) was an ancestor of Boaz and hence of Jesus. Rahab, a prostitute of Jericho, sheltered and saved the two spies sent by Joshua to reconnoitre the situation (Josh. 2: 1–21). When Jericho fell, she and her family were spared; and some Israelites later claimed to be descended from her (Josh. 6: 22–5). David committed adultery with Bathsheba, the wife of Uriah the Hittite, and then married her after the death of her husband. David repented of his sin, and Solomon was born to him and Bathsheba (1 Sam. 11: 1–12: 25). Later, when David lay dying, Bathsheba played her role in ensuring Solomon's accession to the throne (1 Kgs. 1: 1–2: 25).

Tamar, Rahab, Bathsheba, and Ruth are all resourceful women. Since Bathsheba is the wife of a Hittite soldier, presumably she too, like Tamar, Rahab and Ruth, is not an Israelite. Ruth stands apart, for her human qualities and fidelity to God. Whatever our evaluation of their respective personalities and actions, we find God 'writing straight with crooked lines' in their very different stories. In the context of this book, the four non-Israelite women symbolize the universal benevolence of God, who not only cares for them in different ways but also turns them, through divine providence, into ancestors of Jesus. They may start as 'outsiders' but then become highly significant 'insiders' in the total saving plan of God.

NAAMAN THE SYRIAN

The historical books of the OT yield a series of foreign figures whom God blessed in extraordinary ways (or who clearly merit divine and human approval).[15] Before dealing with the case of Naaman, it is worth recalling two other cases. At the beginning of the story of Elijah, during a time of severe drought God acted powerfully through the prophet's words and actions in favour of a widow of Zarephath. She presumably worshipped the Canaanite (or Phoenician) god Baal. First, through the word YHWH spoke to Elijah, a tiny supply of meal and oil never failed. Thanks to this miracle the woman and her household remained alive. But then her son died, only to be brought back to life by Elijah, the worthy prophet of a powerful God. As the woman put it, 'now I know that you are a man of God, and that the word of the Lord in your mouth is truth' (1 Kgs. 17: 7–24). She acknowledged the power of Elijah and of his God (YHWH), but was not drawn, let alone obliged, to abandon her religion and worship the one God, YHWH.

To illustrate how God blesses 'outsiders', Luke's Gospel was to cite the story of this widow in part of a sermon by Jesus that ended with

---

[15] See e.g. Hiram, the king of Tyre, who was not only a friend of David (2 Sam. 5: 11–12) but also helped Solomon to construct the Temple (1 Kgs. 5: 1–18); the Queen of Sheba, who witnessed to the wisdom of Solomon and the great future of Israel (1 Kgs. 10: 1–13); Uriah the Hittite, who faithfully served David but was repaid with death (2 Sam. 11: 1–27). In the previous chapter we recalled other worthy 'outsiders' such as Abimelech and Melchizedek. To them we could add such figures as the pharaoh who ruled during the lifetime of Joseph (Gen. 41: 1–57; 47: 1–26); the daughter of the succeeding pharaoh who rescued Moses as a baby (Exod. 2: 5–10); Jael, wife of Heber the Kenite, who killed Israel's enemy Sisera (Judg. 4: 11–22); Cyrus, the king of Persia, who decreed the return to their own land of the Judeans exiled in Babylon (Isa. 45: 1–4; 2 Chron. 36: 22–3).

his audience in Nazareth becoming enraged: 'There were indeed many widows in Israel in Elijah's time, when for three and a half years the skies never opened and there was a severe famine over all the land. Yet Elijah was sent to none of them except to a widow of Zarephath in Sidon' (Luke 4: 25–6).

When Elijah was taken up to heaven, he was succeeded by Elisha, about whom some similar stories were told: for instance, two divine favours granted through him to a woman of Shunem, a minor settlement about thirty miles north-east of Samaria (2 Kgs. 4: 8–37). She had been barren, but Elisha announced the birth of a son—another example of the biblical theme of a child born later in life to a hitherto barren woman. Often such an unusual birth involved a son who went on to become important in the history of salvation: for instance, Sarah's son Isaac (Gen. 17: 16–19), Hannah's son Samuel (1 Sam. 1: 1–28), and Elizabeth's son John the Baptist (Luke 1: 5–17). This was not so in the case of the unnamed Shunammite woman and her unnamed child. In her case, however, something happened which did not happen to Sarah, Hannah, Elizabeth, and the other hitherto barren women blessed with a child. After some years the little boy of the Shunammite woman fell ill and died. But Elisha returned to her home and in a dramatic scene brought her dead boy back to life.

Shunem had been a Philistine settlement, but apparently belonged to Israel at the time envisaged by this story about Elisha. Nevertheless, it seems to have been only a minor settlement on the edge of the territory of the tribe of Issachar. Even if she was not strictly an 'outsider', through Elijah God did two remarkable things in favour of the Shunammite woman.

Clearly, however, we read of a great blessing granted by God to an 'outsider' when Naaman was cured of his leprosy (2 Kgs. 5: 1–27). He was a successful commander of the army for the king of the Arameans (i.e. the Syrians who had their capital in Damascus). At the time they held the upper hand over the Israelites. Yet Elisha used his God-given powers to cure a Gentile enemy, by telling Naaman to bathe seven times in the river Jordan.[16] When Naaman was cleansed

---

[16] See R. L. Cohn, 'Form and Perspective in 2 Kings V', *Vetus Testamentum* 33 (1984), 171–84.

of leprosy and returned to Elisha, he declared: 'Now I know that there is no God in all the earth except in Israel.' The prophet refused to accept a gift offered by the Syrian general; to do so could have implied that the cure had been effected through the power of Elisha himself. With the prophet's blessing, Naaman took home to Damascus 'two mule-loads of earth' from Israel; he shared the ancient conviction that a deity could not be worshipped apart from his own land. Back in Damascus, Naaman would have to make a compromise—continuing to bow down officially to Rimmon (another name for Haddad Ramman, 'Haddad the Thunderer', the chief god of the Syrians) but now able to worship YHWH since he possessed a tiny part of his domain, Israel. Through the prophet Elisha, Naaman the Syrian leper was transformed physically and spiritually. Naaman accepted the supremacy of the Hebrew God. Through some soil from Israel he maintained his newly found faith in YHWH, even if publicly he continued to be involved in pagan worship.

The story sets Naaman, a noble 'outsider', over against Gehazi, Elisha's own servant, who proved blatantly greedy and dishonest. When the prophet declined to accept any gift, Naaman left on his return journey. Gehazi ran after him and invented a message from Elisha about the need to help two prophets who had just turned up. Although Gehazi asked for only one talent of silver and two changes of clothing, Naaman generously provided not only the clothing but also two talents of silver and two of his own servants to carry the presents home for Gehazi. When they had done so, Gehazi dismissed them and went to see Elisha. Being asked by the prophet where he had been, Gehazi lied and maintained that he had not gone anywhere. But he was caught out by Elisha. Through some kind of second sight, he knew what his servant had done and he punished the culprit by inflicting him with leprosy. An 'insider', the guilty servant of a great prophet, was infected with the very same disease from which his master had delivered a worthy 'outsider'.[17]

One of the most dramatic OT stories about divine blessings being extended to foreigners, the cure of Naaman is also cited by Luke

---

[17] The story of Uriah the Hittite (2 Sam. 11: 1–27) works similarly to contrast the rectitude and loyalty of an 'outsider' with the treachery and moral failure of a most distinguished 'insider'. Uriah, who has been deliberately intoxicated by David, behaves with more sexual self-control than the sober King David.

when he tells how Jesus challenged the people in the synagogue at Nazareth: 'there were many lepers in Israel in the time of the prophet Elisha, and none of them was cleansed except Naaman the Syrian' (Luke 4: 27). In Luke's narrative the reaction to that sermon became increasingly hostile, even to the point of the enraged townsfolk trying to do away with Jesus.

Later chapters will present what the Gospel of Luke and his Acts of the Apostles offers about God's dealings with 'outsiders'. But in the context of this chapter it is worth observing how the stories of such divine dealings with two 'outsiders', the widow of Zarephath and Naaman the Syrian, could prove so offensive to the 'insiders' or members of God's chosen people. We will see further examples of this tension between 'outsiders' and 'insiders' in the chapters to come.

3

Balaam, Amos, and Jonah

In scrutinizing what the OT scriptures suggest about the religious experience of 'others' and God's saving plan for them, we come next to the prophets. But before tackling some of the great prophets, like Jeremiah and Isaiah, it seems useful to reflect on certain valuable items that we can glean from three prophetic figures: Balaam, Amos, and Jonah. Without imposing our contemporary categories on this material, we ask: what do they offer for the overall theme of this book—either blatantly or in more subtle ways? I begin with Balaam, who was a foreign priest-diviner. While not belonging to the community of Israel, he showed himself obedient to the will of YHWH and delivered divinely inspired oracles.

BALAAM

The story of Balaam and the Moabite king, Balak, injects some fascinating material into any biblical reflection on the religious situation of those 'outside' (Num. 22: 1–24: 25).[1] Alarmed at the threat of the triumphant Israelites, Balak invited Balaam, a diviner from Mesopotamia, to come and put a curse on the invaders. In the ancient world and, often enough later, it was believed that a curse would set in train negative forces that could shape future events. Balak's message to Balaam was this: 'Come now, curse this people for me, since they are stronger than I. Perhaps I shall be able to defeat them and drive them from the land; for I know that whomever you

---

[1] See B. A. Levine, *Numbers 21–36* (New York: Doubleday, 2000), 160–240.

bless is blessed, and whomever you curse is cursed.' Balaam rejected
the officials sent on the first mission from Balak: 'Go to your own
land, for the Lord (YHWH) has refused to let me go with you.'

Balak was not discouraged and sent another more numerous and
distinguished group of officials to invite Balaam: 'Do not let anything
hinder you from coming to me. I will do you great honour, and
whatever you say to me I will do; come, curse this people for me.' The
night after this second group of officials arrived, God spoke to
Balaam (apparently in a dream): 'if the men have come to summon
you, get up and go with them. But do only what I tell you to do.' On
their way to Balak, Balaam's donkey, which three times reacted at the
sight of an angel of the Lord and then miraculously spoke to its
master, featured in a comic interlude that ended with the angel of the
Lord repeating the divine command Balaam had already received:
'Go with the men, but speak only what I tell you to speak.'

After arriving, Balaam met Balak and they performed a sacrificial
ceremony, just as ancient diviners did when seeking omens. Then the
Lord put into the mouth of Balaam an oracle which recognized that
Israel was a nation set apart for a special destiny. The oracle ended with
Balaam praying that, since he had not cursed the people of God, he
might himself die as a righteous person (Num. 22: 41–23: 10). Naturally Balak was shocked that Balaam had blessed the Israelites. But,
unwilling to defy God, he took Balaam to another place where he could
see the Israelites from a different perspective and, after some appropriate sacrifices, hopefully come up with a vigorous curse. However,
once again Balaam delivered from the Lord an oracle that favoured the
Israelites: 'the Lord their God is with them, acclaimed as king among
them'. God had brought them out of Egypt and could not be coerced by
techniques of divination into altering their destiny (Num. 23: 11–26).

Balak made a further attempt to secure a suitable curse after
making the necessary sacrifices. This time, however, Balaam refrained
from his usual rites of divination and did not look for omens. 'The
spirit of God came upon him' and he uttered a third oracle, which
celebrated what God did for the chosen people and their king.[2] In
anger Balak dismissed Balaam and ordered him to go home.

---

[2] Here Balaam acted like the ecstatic, charismatic prophets who were overcome by
the divine spirit (see 1 Sam. 10: 5–6, 10–11; 19: 18–24).

But Balaam defied this order and, without any preliminary rites of divination, delivered a fourth oracle. It announced that Israel would be victorious over Moab: 'a star shall come out of Jacob, and a sceptre shall rise out of Israel; it shall crush the borderlands of Moab... Edom will become a possession... while Israel will do valiant deeds' (Num. 23: 27–24: 19). The symbols of the star and sceptre referred to a royal leader, and the prophecy was understood to have been fulfilled at the time of David, who conquered both Moab and Edom (2 Sam. 8: 2, 13–14; see Gen. 49: 8–12). The star in the story that Matthew wrote centuries later about the wise men led by a star to visit the Child 'born king of the Jews' (Matt. 2: 1–2) has often been understood to refer to or even draw on the fourth oracle of Balaam. From the time of early Christianity, the 'star' and 'sceptre' of the Davidic ruler foretold by Balaam were applied to Jesus himself, 'the Son of David'. Balaam was numbered among the prophets for having predicted the birth of Christ.

Other books in the OT recalled what Balaam did by blessing and not cursing the people of God (Deut. 23: 5–6; Josh. 13: 22; 24: 9–10; Mic. 6: 5; Neh. 13: 2). The story of his oracles was widely received, and in no way confined to three chapters in the Book of Numbers. In this story Balak offered him an honorarium (Num. 22: 7)—a standard practice when calling on the services of a diviner or seer (e.g. 1 Sam. 9: 7; 1 Kgs. 14: 3; 2 Kgs. 8: 8). Yet Balaam insisted that not even a great stipend would dissuade him from doing and saying what God wanted. From the outset he made that clear to the servants of the king: 'Although Balak were to give me his house full of silver and gold, I could not go beyond the command of the Lord my God, to do less or more' (Num. 22: 18). In the NT, however, Balaam received a bad press, almost as if he had been ready to trim his words to the honorarium he would receive (2 Pet. 2: 15; Jude 11).[3]

---

[3] The NT authors clearly read Balaam in terms of the folk-story of his donkey (Num. 22: 21–35), another tradition which was inserted into the main narrative and which begins by asserting that it was against the divine will that Balaam travelled to meet Balak (Num. 22: 22) and presumably did so in search of an honorarium. Thomas Aquinas followed the lead of the NT authors and listed Balaam among 'the prophets of demons', but had to admit that sometimes they speak 'through divine revelation' (*Summa theologiae* II-II, q. 172, a. 6 ad 1).

Balaam deserved a better press than that. He was not a worshipper of YHWH, and yet a range of OT books agreed that the God of Israel had spoken and worked through this foreign seer or diviner. By means of a foreign prophet, God was understood to have legitimated the reign of David and his conquest of Moab. In the light of the sacrificial ceremonies in which Balaam was involved with Balak, we should call Balaam a priest/prophet. He proved faithful to the divine will when his career as an outsider intersected with a critical moment in the story of Israel and their struggles against the Moabites.

Thus Balaam illustrates not only that God can communicate true oracles or prophecies through 'outsiders', but also that the prophetic activity of such an outsider can impinge on the history of God's chosen people. In such terms Balaam is highly significant in showing how there is no sharp division between 'outsiders' and 'insiders' among those to whom God relates in the one great story of revelation and salvation. It leaves us with the question: even after the incarnation, could or does God ever speak and act through such a prophetic 'outsider' as Balaam?

AMOS

Called by God in the mid-eighth century BC to leave his work as a shepherd in the small village of Tekoa and play the prophet, Amos did so but was soon expelled from the royal sanctuary at Bethel and ordered not to prophesy there again. Apparently he and/or his disciples then wrote down the substance of his public preaching. The book begins with oracles against the neighbours of Israel (Amos 1: 3–2: 3). But then follow five chapters that indict Judah and, even more, Israel for their sin and injustice (Amos 2: 3–6: 14). The Book of Amos ends with three chapters that contain visions of God's judgement against Israel and a prophecy of the restoration of the Davidic dynasty and the glorious age to come (Amos 7–9).

Amos maintains the special election of the Jewish people. Israel has been chosen from 'all the families of the earth' (Amos 3: 2; see Exod. 19: 4–6; Deut. 7: 6). Yet both Israel and her neighbours are to be judged by the same standards. The elect should not suppose themselves to be exceptional, uniquely favoured objects of divine favour. The children of Israel do not enjoy some privileged relationship to YHWH that exempts them from proper behaviour. Amos anticipates what St Paul would write centuries later: simply because they possess the Mosaic covenant and the law, the Israelites have no favoured security and status (Rom. 2: 17–24). Ultimately they are no more important to YHWH than the other peoples. All nations are accountable before God. Thus the universalism espoused by Amos complements the doctrine of election that he endorses. The election of Israel does not mean that God has rejected the other nations of the world. God behaves as Saviour towards all people, and has no honoured favourites—either geographically or ethnically. In other words, Amos connects the special election of Israel to the rule of God that is universal.

In making this point, Amos picks out three peoples: the Nubians or Ethiopians (called in Hebrew the Cushites), the Philistines, and the Arameans. Through the prophet God questions Israel: ' "Are you not like the Ethiopians to me, O people of Israel?", says the Lord. "Did I not bring Israel up from the land of Egypt, and the Philistines from Caphtor and the Arameans from Kir?" ' (Amos 9: 7). The Nubians are a distant population who live 'at the end of the earth'; the Philistines (along the Mediterranean coast) are the traditional enemy of Israel to the West; the Arameans or Syrians, to the East, have been in conflict with Israel only a few decades before Amos begins his prophetic activity.

The prophet proclaims that the Nubians, even if distant and different, are not therefore inferior in the divine plan. God's saving actions reach everyone, including enemies of Israel (the Philistines and the Arameans). All peoples are blessed by God. The election of Israel is not a preferential privilege that discriminates against others.

What God says here through Amos puts the story of the Philistines and the Arameans on a similar level with that of the Israelites. The Philistines entered Canaan shortly after the Israelites and competed with them for dominance in the region. Like Amos, Jeremiah identified Caphtor (probably Crete) as the place from which they came (Jer. 47: 4). Kir was understood to be the place from which some at least of the Syrians came and to which they would be exiled (Amos

1: 5; 2 Kgs. 16: 9).[4] Amos 9: 7 ranks together in the saving activity of God both the invasions of the Philistines and the Arameans and the foundational, religious event for the Israelites: their exodus from Egypt. Their deliverance from Egypt was not unique and affords them no special assurance. The divine involvement in the story of *all* peoples could hardly be expressed more clearly than this. Despite the fact that YHWH has chosen and granted special status to Israel, it is not a superior status; the divine care and guidance, as well as God's sovereign rights, extend to all peoples.[5]

In effect, Amos asks the question: What emotions are appropriate vis-à-vis these 'others'? The prophet is confident that it is appropriate to recognize God's hand in their history. Feelings of compassion and solidarity towards the Ethiopians, the Philistines, and the Arameans of our world are called for. The teaching of Amos is strikingly universal. Yet, one must admit, this universal teaching turns up almost incidentally. In the Book of Jonah, however, the 'others' and the merciful love God exercised towards them are central to the plot.

JONAH

The universal benevolence of God comes through the very short Book of Jonah, which proves intriguingly different from another, slightly longer book which also concerns Nineveh, that of the prophet Nahum. In 612 BC the Medes and the Chaldeans destroyed the infamous city of Nineveh and so sealed the end of the domination by the Assyrians. For centuries they had been feared from the Mediterranean to Mesopotamia. The Book of Nahum, to be dated shortly after the overthrow of Nineveh, vividly celebrated the destruction of the wicked city as YHWH's judgement on a cruel and defiant people. Nahum and his generation remembered how the Ninevites had destroyed Samaria in 722–721 BC and had in other ways oppressed and victimized the Israelites.

[4] See R. S. Hess, 'Caphthor', *ABD* i. 869–70; on the difficulties of locating Kir, see H. O. Thompson, 'Kir', *ABD* iv. 83–4.

[5] See F. I. Andersen and D. N. Freedman, *Amos* (New York: Doubleday, 1989), 867–85; S. M. Paul, *Amos* (Minneapolis: Fortress, 1991), 282–4.

The author of Jonah seems to have lived a couple of hundred years later, and wanted to picture relations between God and Nineveh very differently.[6] Some of the earlier material in this book may have been associated with an obscure prophet who advised the King Jeroboam II in a successful clash with the Syrians (2 Kgs. 14: 23–9). Unlike the other prophetic books, Jonah contains no collection of oracles pronounced against foreign nations or against Israel. Instead it tells the story of God's word to a foreign nation coming through an obstinate and narrow-minded prophet.[7] He runs away from the mission that YHWH has given him, is miraculously saved from drowning, preaches repentance to the people of Nineveh, and then sulks when his hearers repent. Jonah has to learn that God's saving love extends to everyone, even to the horrendous and hated Ninevites. This is the theological lesson that the book aims at (through an extended parable or piece of didactic fiction), rather than providing the reader with an historical account.[8]

The Book of Jonah opens by recognizing the 'wickedness' of Nineveh, the city to which God sent Jonah to preach repentance. Jonah rejected the divine commission and tried to flee 'away from the presence of the Lord'. He went on board a ship bound for Tarshish, a port perhaps to be located in southern Spain. It was the farthest point to which Jonah could sail in the West, in order to avoid his mission to Nineveh in the East. God 'hurled' upon the sea a 'mighty storm' and 'the ship threatened to break up'. Led by their captain, the sailors discovered that it was Jonah who had been responsible for the threatening calamity. He encouraged the crew to throw him into the sea. The sailors made one last attempt to reach safety by 'rowing hard to bring the ship back to land', instead of resorting to the drastic action proposed by Jonah himself. But they failed and 'the sea grew more and more stormy against them'.

---

[6] For whatever reason(s), both the Masoretic text of Hebrew Scripture and the Greek translation (LXX) place Jonah *before* Nahum in the roster of the twelve 'minor prophets'. See J. M. Sasson, *Jonah* (New York: Doubleday, 1990), 13–15.

[7] Ironically Jonah, who is 'son of Amittai' (= trustworthy), proves at once untrustworthy by shirking his responsibility as a prophet.

[8] See T. E. Fretheim, *The Message of Jonah* (Minneapolis: Augsburg, 1977); J. Magonet, *Form and Meaning: Studies in Literary Techniques in the Book of Jonah* (Sheffield: Almond Press, 1983); U. Simon, *The JPS Bible Commentary: Jonah* (Philadelphia: Jewish Publication Society, 1999).

Then the sailors 'cried out to the Lord (YHWH): "Please, O Lord (YHWH), we pray, do not let us perish on account of this man's life. Do not make us guilty of innocent blood; for you, O Lord (YHWH), have done as it pleased you." ' Then they picked up Jonah and 'threw him into the sea; and the sea ceased from its raging'. This physical rescue brought at once a spiritual result, when 'the men feared the Lord (YHWH) even more, and they offered a sacrifice to the Lord (YHWH) and made vows' (Jonah 1: 1–16). In spite of himself, Jonah had become a missionary to a bunch of sailors. At the start of the story they had 'each cried to his god'; at the end they came to know and worship YHWH.[9] Yet the sailors did not 'convert' to Judaism.

Meanwhile God had arranged to save Jonah through a large fish, which swallowed the prophet and then three days later deposited him on dry land, apparently back at the place from which he had started (Jonah 1: 17; 2: 10). Once again the Lord despatched Jonah to Nineveh. This time Jonah went and proclaimed his message ('Forty days more, and Nineveh shall be overthrown'), apparently hoping that the Ninevites would reject the message and receive their just punishment from God. But in a sudden and total conversion, the whole people and the king of Nineveh 'believed God'. They proclaimed a fast and put on sackcloth, traditional signs of mourning and repentance. The king (who removed his royal robe and 'sat in ashes') and his nobles issued the decree: 'Human beings and animals shall be covered with sackcloth, and they shall cry mightily to God. All shall turn from their evil ways and from the violence that is in their hands.' When 'God saw what they did, how they turned from their evil ways, God changed his mind about the calamity that he said he would bring upon them; and he did not do it' (Jonah 3: 1–10).

This instant and wholesale conversion of Nineveh involved 'turning from violence and evil ways', a moral change of life, rather than doing what the sailors did in converting from their gods (or at least ignoring them for the moment) to worship YHWH. Thus the section about the preaching to Nineveh and their conversion uses the generic

---

[9] When rabbis of the first millennium described the 'conversion' of the sailors, they embellished the story by having them undergo circumcision; see Sasson, *Jonah*, 24 n. 22. But the text of Jonah does not indicate that the sailors permanently discontinued their previous religious activities to embrace the Mosaic law and practices.

name of *Elohim* when referring to God (Jonah 3: 5, 8, 9, and twice in v. 10). In its switches between *Elohim* (the universal God or God of the universe) and YHWH (who is in a particular relationship with Israel),[10] the whole Book of Jonah shows no 'overall pattern'.[11] Nevertheless, within Jonah 3: 4–10, the section that describes the Ninevites and their reaction to the prophet's preaching, significantly only Elohim is used. A shift to belief in and worship of YHWH as such, along with the adoption of the Mosaic law and practice, was not the issue. God was content to let the Ninevites remain what they were religiously, provided they underwent a moral conversion from 'their violence and evil ways'—a reasonable summary of Ninevite behaviour until their domination ended at the close of the seventh century BC.

It was Jonah who needed to change his *religious* views. Unlike the prompt moral conversion of the Ninevites, his conversion took time and called for repeated actions of God. The last chapter of the book is devoted to him. He began by being 'angry' that his preaching in Nineveh had instantly brought moral results.[12] He did not want that to happen. He explained to God that he had fled by ship because he refused to become the human instrument of the divine mercy towards the hateful Ninevites: 'I knew that you are a gracious God and merciful, slow to anger, and abounding in steadfast love, and ready to relent from punishing.' Jonah did not want to see the Assyrians spared by a loving, gracious God. He shrank from his prophetic obligation to care about their interests, and showed no concern or compassion for Nineveh. But God made it clear to him that the divine love extended beyond any covenant, to embrace every creature in the universe (Jonah 4: 1–11).

The Gospels recall the story of Jonah in a saying of Jesus, who favourably contrasted the Ninevites with his own audience and their

[10] According to the Priestly tradition, the name YHWH was revealed to Moses (Exod. 6: 2–8). According to the Yahwist tradition, however, that sacred name was invoked by all humanity from the time of the grandson of Adam and Eve (Gen. 4: 16); this tradition would exclude in advance all particularism.

[11] Sasson, *Jonah*, 18 n. 15.

[12] Jonah became angry also when the bush that had sheltered him abruptly withered—something of much less consequence than the fate of 120,000 inhabitants of Nineveh (Jonah 4: 6–11).

failure to respond: 'The men of Nineveh will appear in court when
this generation is on trial and ensure its condemnation; for they
repented at the preaching of Jonah; and what is here is greater than
Jonah' (Luke 11: 32; New English Bible trans.). Evidently for Jesus
'the sign of Jonah' concerned preaching and its impact. Jonah's
audience repented; those who were listening to Jesus did not do so.
Matthew's version maintains the contrast between successful and
unsuccessful preaching but adds a reference to the burial and resurrection of Jesus: 'just as Jonah was three days and three nights in the
belly of the sea monster, so for three days and three nights the Son of
Man will be in the heart of the earth' (Matt. 12: 40).

Matthew's reference to the deliverance of Jesus from death had a
large and lasting impact in early Christian iconography. For centuries
paintings and manuscripts featured this symbol of Jesus' resurrection
from the dead. This use of the Jonah story distracted Christians
somewhat from the central teaching of the book: the merciful love
of God which knows no frontiers. Much worse was the way some or
even many Christians have allowed themselves to be led astray by silly
debates about the survival of the prophet inside the great fish. The
Book of Jonah provides plenty of clues for a reader to spot that it is
not 'real history' but an extended parable, driving home a central
point about the universal nature of the divine love by using legendary
and other fictional material. The book describes Nineveh as being 'an
exceedingly large city, a three days' walk across' (Jonah 3: 3). It is only
in modern times that cities have grown to those dimensions. Then,
both the bush which God causes to spring up miraculously overnight
and the worm sent to attack it (Jonah 4: 6, 10) are clearly the stuff of
folklore, used to feed into a story about God's educating a bigoted
prophet. As the all-powerful creator, God uses a fierce storm, a great
fish, a castor bean plant, and a worm to achieve his purpose: helping
a small-minded and disobedient prophet to share his vision of
humanity and do the divine will. Debates, which have started from
the false presupposition about the historical character of Jonah, have
sidetracked readers into missing the moral of the book: the universal
scope of God's merciful love.

Have Christians backed away from this lesson, fearing that it
would make their belief in God's mercy less likely to be true if that
mercy is more widely shared? Should they have appreciated rather

that the example of the Ninevites could have enhanced their own faith life? After all, those hateful Ninevites instantly repent en masse, even though they do not know God as YHWH but only in a 'generic' way as *Elohim.* One can esteem and admire them, without deciding to abandon faith in YHWH and share their belief system.

4

Isaiah, Jeremiah, and Malachi

This chapter takes up passages from three prophetical books of the Bible and examines what they can suggest about the religious situation and destiny of other nations. The polemic against idols and the oracles against the nations that we find in these books should not distract readers from some positive teaching on God's plans and activity on behalf of the 'others'. We begin with Isaiah.

ISAIAH

As is well known, Chapters 40–66 of Isaiah are usually divided into 'Second Isaiah' (40–55) and 'Third Isaiah' (56–66). These two sections take at times a very positive view about the religious situation and future of the other nations. Yet such an open-minded attitude is not lacking in Chapters 1–39. The prophet announces a new age when the nations will 'stream' to Zion and say: 'Let us go to the mountain of the Lord, to the house of the God of Jacob; that he may teach us his ways and we may walk in his paths. For out of Zion shall go forth instruction, and the word of the Lord from Jerusalem.' The prophet promises a new age of peace: The Lord 'will judge between the nations, and he shall arbitrate for many peoples; they shall break their swords into ploughshares, and their spears into pruning hooks; nation shall not lift up sword against nation, neither shall they learn war any more' (Isa. 2: 2–4). The prophet Micah uses identical language to proclaim a coming age of peace; Jerusalem will enjoy a glorious future and become a centre of worship for the nations (Mic. 4: 1–3).[1]

To be sure, many chapters in First Isaiah contain oracles concerning foreign nations: against Babylon, Assyria, Moab, Egypt, and so on (Isa. 13: 1–23: 18). Yet wedged into this predominantly negative section several verses foretell a coming relationship of Egypt and Assyria with YHWH. The text of Isaiah announces the day when 'there will be five cities in the land of Egypt that speak the language of Canaan [= of the Jewish settlements] and swear allegiance to the Lord of hosts. One of these will be called the City of the Sun [probably Heliopolis]' (Isa. 19: 19).[2] The prophet announces that 'on that day there will be an altar to the Lord in the centre of the land of Egypt, and a pillar to the Lord at its border'. Blenkinsopp explains: 'The prohibition of regional sanctuaries in Deuteronomy may not have been thought to apply outside the land of Israel, or it may simply have been disregarded.'[3] The Egyptians will experience deliverance from oppression through the power of God, just as Israel did (Isa. 19: 20). Without going to Jerusalem, 'the Egyptians will know the Lord on that day, and will worship with sacrifice and burnt offering, and they will make vows to the Lord and perform them' (Isa. 19: 21). At this time 'the Egyptians will worship with the Assyrians' and Israel will be a blessing to the nations. 'Israel will be third with Egypt and Assyria, a blessing in the midst of the earth, whom the Lord of hosts has blessed, saying, "Blessed be Egypt my people, and Assyria the work of my hands, and Israel my heritage"' (Isa. 19: 24–5).

These last two verses are a remarkable statement of universal divine benevolence. They put Egypt and even Assyria (both denounced elsewhere in Isaiah and other OT texts for cruelly oppressing Israel) on a par with Israel, as 'my people' and 'the work of my hands'. Such expressions are elsewhere reserved for Israel itself (e.g. Isa. 60: 21; 64: 8). Yet there is no question here of Egypt and Assyria

---

[1] See J. Blenkinsopp, *Isaiah 1–39* (New York: Doubleday, 2000), 190–1.

[2] This 'alludes to the spread . . . in Egypt' of 'the Yahveh cult involving the use, at least for liturgical purposes, of Hebrew and of the name of Yahveh in forensic affairs and in sealing contracts—a situation amply illustrated in the Elephantine papyri' (ibid., 318).

[3] Ibid., 319.

joining themselves, or being assimilated, to Israel; they keep their own cultural and religious identity. The LXX translation betrays embarrassment, for it felt the need to modify the text, making it refer not to two foreign nations but rather to 'my people who are in Egypt and who are in Assyria' (i.e. the Israelite diaspora in Egypt and Assyria). The passage at the end of Isaiah 19 looks like a corrective inserted in the midst of polemic against Egypt and Assyria. The positive view about the future of these 'others' inevitably reminds one of the divine promise to Abraham and to his people that in them 'all the families of the earth shall be blessed' (Gen. 12: 3). More of this optimistic scenario for the 'others' recurs a little later in the Book of Isaiah.

Several chapters (Isa. 24–7), often called the 'Isaiah Apocalypse', develop various eschatological themes that will be found in later apocalyptic books, including the theme of a final banquet for all peoples: 'On this mountain [Zion] the Lord of hosts will make for all peoples a feast of rich food, a feast of well-aged wines, of rich food filled with marrow, of well-aged wines strained clear.' It is also promised that YHWH will 'destroy on his mountain' the 'shroud/ sheet of mourning' (or perhaps 'ignorance') that is 'cast over all peoples' and 'spread over all nations'. Then 'the Lord God will wipe away the tears from all faces' (Isa. 25: 6–8). This promise of divine benevolence to be exercised towards all peoples when gathered in Jerusalem complements what we find at the very end of Third Isaiah. There it will be more a question of what human beings do for God by raising a universal chorus of praise; here it is rather a question of how God will feed, illuminate, and comfort all peoples.

In Second Isaiah, some passages predict the gathering of the nations. Their wealth will pour into Jerusalem, and they will acknowledge the God of Israel: 'God is with you alone, and there is no other; there is no god besides him' (Isa. 45: 14). God calls on the nations: 'Turn to me and be saved, all the ends of the earth! For I am God, and there is no other' (Isa. 45: 22). Jeremiah presents the conversion of the nations in a similar light. All peoples will recognize the useless-ness and falsity of idol worship, and will join Israel in worshipping the one, all-powerful YHWH (Jer. 16: 19–21).

One of the most strikingly universalist texts about foreign peoples to whom divine salvation is extended and who join themselves to

Israel occurs in a poem in Third Isaiah that pictures the glorious restoration of Jerusalem: 'Arise, shine, for your light has come, and the glory of the Lord has risen upon you...Nations shall come to your light, and kings to the brightness of your dawn. Lift up your eyes and look around; they all gather together, they come to you' (Isa. 60: 1–4).

God has called his 'Servant' (either the whole covenant people, Israel, or a faithful remnant of Israel, or an individual) to bring 'light to the nations' who fumble in the darkness of ignorance (Isa. 42: 6–7). The language concerning 'the Servant' in Isaish 40–55 oscilllates between portraying the Servant as an individual or as a corporate figure. The Israelites who have survived the Babylonian captivity or an individual will have this new mission, that of being 'a light to the nations' (Isa. 49: 6).[4] In the NT, Luke will pick up this language—for instance, in the prayer of old Simeon: 'For my eyes have seen your salvation, which you have prepared for all nations, the light to enlighten the Gentiles and give glory to Israel your people' (Luke 2: 30–2). In the Acts of the Apostles Luke applies this language to the mission of Paul and Barnabas (Acts 13: 47) and echoes it in Paul's testimony to the resurrection of Jesus from the dead (Acts 26: 23).

In Isaiah 42: 1–4, we read the first of the four 'servant songs' (see 49: 1–6; 50: 4–11; 52: 13–53: 12). The 'servant' is probably to be identified here, at least primarily, with the nation itself. Israel, the 'chosen' of God, has a mission to bring the divine teaching and justice to all peoples and to do so with great patience (Isa. 42: 1–4). Thus Second Isaiah opens with Israel chosen by God for its special mission and called to be a blessing to the nations. Both during the Babylonian Captivity and earlier, Israel had every chance to observe the differences between their own beliefs and those of others. Yet, so far from following the line of Jonah and avoiding at all costs these 'others', they find themselves called by God to share the divine teaching and justice with them.

---

[4] K. Baltzer comments: 'Light is the quintessence of justice and righteousness, and means deliverance, help, [and] salvation for the nations too.' Baltzer understands this 'light' to be 'nothing other than the Torah that has been given to Moses on Sinai, but that is now valid for the whole world' (*Deutero-Isaiah: A Commentary on Isaiah 40–55* (Minneapolis: Fortress, 2001), 311.

The closing chapter of Third Isaiah (Isa. 66: 18–23) shows, however, YHWH and not his 'servant' exercising a saving mission towards the nations. In an eschatological scenario, these final verses offer a classic message about God's active love towards all peoples.[5] The passage begins by God announcing: 'I am coming to gather the nations of every language. They shall come and see my glory.' This promise might tempt us to translate it in terms of our modern world and imagine God saying: 'I am coming to gather the nations of every language, those who speak Mandarin, those who speak Hindi, those who speak English, those who speak Arabic, and so forth.' The passage from Isaiah lists some of the nations: Tarshish, Put, Lud, Meshech, Tubal, and Javan.[6] It is a list of exotic names for ancient places, from which the triumphal procession will set out for Jerusalem on a kind of new and final exodus. We might modernize the list and substitute other names: Beijing, Tokyo, Washington, Khartoum, and so on. God is very upbeat about the divine plan to show all nations his glory and bring all nations together. In the language of this section from Isaiah, God is going to bring the nations to Jerusalem where they will make their offerings in the Temple. They will arrive in Jerusalem on horses, mules, or camels, or riding in chariots, or being carried on litters. For all these strangers and outsiders, the divine plans are very inclusive and open-minded. As our text from Isaiah says, God even intends to select some persons from among the Gentile nations and make them serve in the Temple as 'priests and levites'—an expression typical of Israel but now applied to non-Israelites.[7]

For some or even many Israelites when the final part of Isaiah was composed, this was subversive and even intolerable talk. How could their God reveal himself to all those outsiders? How could God

[5] See J. Blenkinsopp, *Isaiah 56–66* (New York: Doubleday, 2003), 308–17.

[6] On their location see the entries in *ABD* by D. W. Baker: 'Javan', iii. 650; 'Lud', iv. 397; 'Meshech', iv. 711; 'Put', v. 560; 'Tarshish', vi. 331–3; 'Tubal', vi. 670.

[7] For other cases of theological expressions typical of Israel being applied by OT prophets to non-Israelites, see W. Gross, 'YHWH und die Religionen der Nicht-Israeliten', *Theologische Quartalschrift* 169 (1989), 34–44, at 35. Another (more limited) interpretation is possible here: God intends to select for Temple duty some of the exiled Israelites whom the nations will bring home to Jerusalem. Beyond question, the return of the 'diaspora' Jews bulked large in OT hopes (e.g. Isa. 43: 5–6; Ps. 107: 3; Baruch 4: 37).

gather those outsiders together in Jerusalem, open the Temple to them, and accept their offerings and sacrifices? How could God go so far as to make some of them priests and levites to serve in the Temple alongside the Israelite priests and levites?[8] For many Israelites of the sixth century BC, it was a shocking message which the prophetic text communicated from God—a message that could have seemed to threaten their own faith. How could God be so inclusive and welcoming to all? What had happened to the exclusive privileges of the chosen people? The controversial picture of the Temple being open to all people and of Gentiles (seemingly proselytes) being authorized to serve in the Temple has been, at least partly, anticipated at the start of Third Isaiah (56: 7). It describes the Temple as the 'house of prayer for all nations'; the foreigners who embrace faith in YHWH may join the congregation in worship—a situation also envisaged in 1 Kings 8: 41–3.

The author(s) of the last part of Isaiah never suggested that the special gifts and privileges God had given to his chosen people were now in doubt. The prophetic author(s) did not waver in his/their faith that God had established a unique covenant with the Israelites. God would not revoke the special graces that he had revealed and given to the chosen people. But the prophetic writer(s) knew that God was greater than any of his gifts. The Lord was not limited by what he had done, even by what he had done and was doing for a unique community, his chosen people. Through them YHWH aimed to create a new community for all people. The divine love was shockingly universal and generous.

In this way the last chapter of Isaiah can prove a classic role model in a balancing act. It maintains loyal faith and is grateful for all that the God of Abraham, Isaac, and Jacob has done and continues to do for the chosen people. But the text also looks beyond all those extraordinary gifts to the wider reality, to the way in which the same God is at work in bringing revelation and salvation to all the nations. God has blessed amazingly the prophetic writers and the other members of the chosen people. Yet the same God also cares

[8] This would have been a radical departure from the prescriptions of Numbers, which limits the exercise of priesthood to the descendants of Aaron (Num. 4: 1–29; 8: 1–26; 18: 1–32).

most lovingly for everyone else in the world, and will reveal to them the divine glory. As far as God is concerned, there are no outsiders. With Israel, the nations will assemble in Jerusalem, and a great chorus of praise will ceaselessly rise to the throne of God (Isa. 66: 22–3). The scene evokes a psalm that celebrates God's enthronement as king of all the nations. The whole world is assembled to praise YHWH, who 'sits on his holy throne' as 'king of all the earth' (Ps. 47: 7, 8).

The closing chapter of Isaiah brings to mind the prophet Jonah. He is not asked to play down his Jewish faith. What he must do is recognize that God's love is active everywhere and treats everyone with mercy and forgiveness. Jonah moves towards seeing this, but pretty reluctantly. He is a kind of anti-role model, but nonetheless effective in that role.

Yet there is a significant difference between Isaiah 66, with its vision of centralized universalism, and Jonah. According to Isaiah 66, the nations will come to Jerusalem, acknowledge the supremacy of YHWH, and share in a great chorus of praise to God. All humanity will join Israel in worshipping YHWH, the one true God, in Jerusalem. Psalm 87 reflects a similar vision of 'centralized' universalism: Babylon, Rahab (= Egypt), Ethiopia, and Philistia will become 'children' of 'the City of God' and 'find their home' in Jerusalem. In another psalm a sufferer prays for deliverance and vows to offer thanksgiving 'in the midst of the congregation' at the Temple. The hymn that will then be sung envisages all the nations sharing in the worship of YHWH (Ps. 22: 22–31, at 27). In Jonah, however, there is no question of the Ninevites accepting the worship of YHWH and taking part in a great procession to Jerusalem. What God expects of them is moral conversion, and that is instantly forthcoming. Thus the model for the Book of Jonah is rather non-centralized universalism or, what we might call, decentralized benevolence of God.

JEREMIAH

Just as we saw in Isaiah, Jeremiah includes chapters of oracles against the foreign nations (chs. 46–51); and so too does Ezekiel (chs. 25–32). These judgements against the Egyptians, the Philistines, the Moabites, and the rest are not only religious but also inspired partly by political hostility towards invaders and military enemies. The prophets also have hard things, at times equally hard things, to say about and against Israel itself.

The Book of Jeremiah has scarcely started before it moves to denounce the apostasy of Israel (2: 1–37). Comparing the Sinai covenant to marriage vows, God remains faithful to his spouse, despite her infidelity and rebellion. God calls on the heavenly assembly to witness such unprecedented folly: 'cross to the coasts of Cyprus and look, send to Kedar and examine with care; see if there has ever been such a thing. Has a nation changed its gods, even though they are no gods? But my people have changed their glory for something that does not profit. Be appalled, O heavens, at this, be shocked, be utterly desolate' (Jer. 2: 10–12). Cyprus is in the west, and 'Kedar' refers to a desert tribe who live to the east of the Transjordan in northern Arabia. From east to west one finds nothing like the infidelity of Israel. Across the face of the earth, other peoples remain loyal and dedicated to their gods. The fidelity of the 'others' towards their gods ('even though they are no gods') is contrasted with the failure of the Israelites.[9]

Beyond question, we are dealing here with a passing comparison and criticism. But these verses do imply that there is something positive and even admirable about the way other peoples remain faithful to their gods. This theme is even more explicit in another prophet, Malachi.

MALACHI

The person of Malachi remains shrouded in mystery; at best we can say that this prophet probably lived some time after 500 BC. His emphasis on fidelity to the covenant and high view of the Jewish priesthood led him to condemn strongly the priests for failing in their vocation, misleading the people, and corrupting the worship of God (1: 6–2: 9; 3: 3–4).

---

[9] See W. L. Holladay, *Jeremiah* (Philadelphia: Fortress, 1986), 90–1; J. R. Lundblom, *Jeremiah 1–20* (New York: Doubleday, 1999), 266–7.

This involved a sharp comparison with the pure worship of God offered by the Gentiles. So far from being a threat to Malachi, diversity (here the diversity in actual practices of cult) offered the prophet a source for criticizing the situation in Israel. Malachi did *not* ask about 'the nations': are they (totally) reliable guides in their version of God? Should their beliefs shape our beliefs? But he admired the way they 'reverenced' and worshipped God, finding in their practice a standard to imitate.

The famous statement about this worship offered by Gentiles comes as an oracle from 'the Lord of hosts': 'from the rising of the sun to its setting my name is great among the nations, and in every place incense is offered to my name, and a pure offering; for my name is great among the nations' (Mal. 1: 11). This oracle seemingly describes what is actually happening among the nations around the world who pay homage to YHWH everywhere from East to West ('from the rising of the sun to its setting'), without a hint of this worship being centralized in Jerusalem. Hence this description differs from a psalm which announces the future glory of Jerusalem, when 'the nations will fear the name of the Lord, and all the kings of the earth' the divine glory (Ps. 102: 15). A few verses further on, Malachi reiterates this very positive description of the Gentiles, when 'the Lord of hosts' says: 'my name is reverenced among the nations' (Mal. 1: 14).

The prophet is clearly outraged by the current corrupt practices of the Jewish priests and hence is ready to contrast them very unfavourably with 'others'. This important prophet, who treasures the special divine covenant with the chosen people, looks at 'the nations' around the world and sees them not only reverencing the name of YHWH but also making pure offerings to him in their worship. Whether they are aware of this or not, the cult of the Gentiles 'in every place' entails true reverence for the God of Israel and a 'pure offering' to his name. It is hard to imagine a more positive view of the religious faith and cultic practices of the 'others'. Nevertheless, given the eschatological emphasis of the Book of Malachi as a whole, the prophet may intend 'the future establishment of the kingship of God over all the earth'.[10]

---

[10] See A. E. Hill, *Malachi* (New York: Doubleday, 1998), 219. G. Habets also understands Malachi 1: 11 to refer to the future: 'Verbild und Zerrbild. Eine Exegese von Maleachi 1,6–2,9', *Teresianum* 91 (1990), 5–58.

Zephaniah, a prophet who was active around 630 and so earlier than Malachi, announces the *future* conversion of the nations and does so in terms of cultic worship: 'From beyond the rivers of Ethiopia my suppliants, my scattered ones, shall bring my offering' (Zeph. 3: 10).

Fairly quickly in their story, Christians were to apply Malachi 1: 11 to the Eucharist, its sacrificial dimension, and its celebration by various communities of believers meeting from east to west ('from the rising of the sun to its setting'). Thus, apropos of the Sunday celebration of the Eucharist, the anonymous author of the *Didache* (from around the end of the first century AD), when instructing some early community, connected the purity of this sacrifice (Malachi's 'pure offering') with reconciliation within the community:

On the Lord's own day gather together, break bread and give thanks, having first confessed your sins so that your sacrifice may be pure. Let no one who has a quarrel with a companion join you until they have been reconciled, so that your sacrifice may not be defiled. For this is the sacrifice concerning which the Lord said: 'In every place and time offer me a pure sacrifice, for... my name is marvellous among the nations' (no. 14).[11]

About a century later Irenaeus of Lyons called on the same passage from Malachi to vindicate his faith in the Eucharist as the 'pure sacrifice' for all nations (*Adversus Haereses* 4. 17. 4). Many centuries later the Council of Trent would appeal to the same, now classical, passage when expounding the sacrificial character of the sacrament. In the late twentieth century, the post-Vatican II Third Eucharistic Prayer includes a clear echo of the same verse from Malachi when addressing God the Father in its opening paragraph: 'from age to age you gather a people to yourself, so that from east to west a perfect offering may be made to the glory of your name'. The original Latin text of this Eucharistic Prayer comes closer to the words of Malachi: 'ut a solis ortu usque ad occasum oblatio munda offeratur nomini tuo (so that from the rising of the sun to its setting, a pure offering may be made to your name)'.

In its teaching on the Eucharist in 1562, the Council of Trent referred to our text from Malachi, understanding it to prefigure 'the clean oblation/offering' of the Eucharist. Then the Council

---

[11] See K. Niederwimmer, *The Didache* (Minneapolis: Fortress, 1998), 194–9.

spoke of the eucharistic offering being 'prefigured by various types of sacrifices under the regime of nature and of the law. For it includes all the good that was signified by those former sacrifices; it is their fulfilment and perfection' (DzH 1742; ND 1547). This was a generous evaluation not only of the Jewish sacrifices (under the law) but also of sacrifices offered in other religions ('under the regime of nature'). Clearly such sacrifices included a variety of 'good' elements, which in the divine plan not only 'prefigured' the Eucharist but also reached their 'fulfilment and perfection' in the Eucharist.

Both in itself and in its later 'reception' in Christian teaching, our passage from Malachi evaluates positively the worth of sacrifices offered by 'the nations' who did not live 'under the law' but, as Trent put it, 'under nature'. Trent did not dismiss such cult as something simply superseded by Christianity but saw it as being open to being perfected and fulfilled in the central sacrament of the Eucharist.

Here one should recall something that had been happening for well over fifty years before the session of Trent in 1562—what has been euphemistically called 'the expansion of Europe'. The discoveries initiated by Christopher Columbus in 1492 had revealed the existence of millions of human beings living in societies that had gone on for many centuries without the slightest chance of hearing about Jesus Christ and joining the Church. The arrival of Europeans in the Americas decades before the Council of Trent began its work in 1545 raised with new vigour the issue of universal participation in the benefits of Christ's redemption. How could he have been the Saviour for the indigenous peoples of the Americas? How could they have shared in his redemptive grace without ever hearing his name?[12]

The context of the discovery of the Americas provided a fresh context for reading and applying the text from Malachi about the 'incense offered' in 'every place' to God's name. It offered too a new way of interpreting the text through the distinction between 'nature' and 'law', inspired by St Paul and his recognition that there are Gentiles who are morally insightful and responsible: 'When Gentiles,

[12] In *Salvation Outside the Church* (London: Geoffrey Chapman, 1992), 69–81, Frank Sullivan describes how Columbus's discoveries raised questions about the salvation of those who for long centuries had no contact with the Christian message.

who do not possess the law, do by nature what the law requires, these, though not having the law, they are their own law. They show that what the law requires is written on their hearts' (Rom. 2: 14–15). In this section of Romans, the Apostle is expounding the basis for divine judgement. Gentiles, while not blessed with the law of the covenant from Sinai, can, in fact, do what the law (above all, the Ten Commandments) require. Paul laments that many Jews, while possessing the written law, do not even live up to ordinary morality (Rom. 2: 17–24). His contrast, between many Gentiles who 'by nature' live up to the requirements of the law of Sinai and many Jews who do not, resembles somewhat the contrast made centuries before by Malachi: between the 'nations' who make 'a pure offering' to God and the Jewish priests who corrupt the worship of God.

Trent, reflecting on the human situation *before* the birth of Christ, associated Malachi's recognition of the 'pure offerings' made around the world among the nations of his day with Paul's distinction between 'law' and 'nature'. There is no hint that members of the Council of Trent thought of the regime of 'nature' persisting in parts of the world (e.g. in the Americas) down to their own day. But their teaching is at least open to that possibility.

To adapt Paul's scheme of thought, we could say that the 'law' was available *geographically* around the Mediterranean world and ended *chronologically* at the coming of Christ. But other, distant parts of the world (e.g. the Congo, the Americas, and Japan) were inaccessible for those who practised and advocated the Jewish 'law'. Hence the regime of the 'law' could not be present, but only that of 'nature' (the regime of the Gentiles). Hence the regime of 'nature' might be understood to prevail there until the preaching of the gospel began in the fifteenth (the Congo and the Americas) and the sixteenth (Japan) centuries.

In Romans Paul links those under 'the law' with those who live 'by nature'. In the Bible this link had already been made by wisdom literature. We turn now to the wisdom books of the OT, which have much to contribute to our theme.

5

Wisdom and the 'Others'

The wisdom literature of the OT is particularly rich for those who pursue our theme.[1] This literature is international in character, reflects a general orientation to human life, and pictures individual persons in their everyday existence in a world created by God, and not individual Israelites who tackle issues of faith and life on the basis of their particular history and identity as Israelites. Such a 'particular' approach in the light of God's actions in the history of Israel surfaces in such later sapiential books as Sirach and Wisdom, but only in the concluding chapters of those books (Sir. 44–50; Wisd. 11–19). For the most part, wisdom literature remains general and non-specific in its religious approach, and so helps us to appreciate the one, long story in which no group or individual is forgotten by God. There are blessings for everyone, coming from the God who cherishes and seeks out all human beings. Let us begin, however, with a story which has many mysterious and painful aspects, that of the holy 'outsider' *par excellence*, Job.

JOB

Written perhaps in the sixth century BC, the Book of Job draws on an ancient folktale about a saintly person called Job (Ezek. 14: 14, 20), a blameless man from Uz (somewhere in north-west Arabia, connected

[1] See J. L. Crenshaw, *Old Testament Wisdom: An Introduction* (London: SCM Press, 1982); D. F. Morgan, *Wisdom in Old Testament Traditions* (Oxford: Blackwell, 1987); R. E. Murphy, 'Wisdom in the OT', *ABD* vi. 920–31; id., *The Tree of Life: An Exploration of Biblical Wisdom Literature* (New York: Doubleday, 3rd edn., 2002).

either with Aram or Edom[2]), who was tested terribly by unexpected and unmerited suffering. This holy person loses his wealth, posterity, and health, and becomes an outcast from society (Job 30: 1–8). While remaining totally committed to God, he is torn between feelings of despair and faith. This dramatic book which features Job's long discussions with three friends (3: 1–31: 40) reaches what looks like a later insertion, four discourses by Elihu the Buzite (32: 1–37: 24). Finally, the Lord speaks out of the whirlwind (one of the settings in the Bible for divine appearances), puts 'impossible' questions to Job, and draws him deeper into the divine mystery (38: 1–41: 34), until Job experiences an intimate communion with God: 'now my eye sees you' (42: 5).

In this dramatic testing of Job, a non-Israelite, God reveals himself in his cosmic power and responsibilities: he is the God who 'brings rain on a land where no one lives' (38: 26) and not the God of the exodus from Egypt (and of any other key episodes in Israel's history). Yet this God of cosmic majesty shows himself personally involved with the life and destiny of human beings. God respects human freedom and wants to have the free obedience of human beings. Under a terrible testing, Job perseveres and the restoration of his life and family matches his integrity and shows the divine generosity (42: 7–17).

In this awesome dialogue with Job, a non-Israelite, God emerges as both majestically transcendent and caringly close. God is mysteriously involved in the whole of creation (38: 1–40: 2), the maker and conserver of all things who eludes the imagination of Job. Yet this same God cherishes the one whom he calls 'my servant Job' (42: 7–8). The Book of Job is a unique paradigm of how God relates, in good times and bad times, to devoted 'outsiders'.

The OT contains no other story like this: the long story of a blameless non-Israelite. It drives home for us the lesson: the just person is not necessarily an Israelite. It is not difficult to connect this ancient piece of OT folklore and the truth it expresses with our present reality: an 'outsider' can be a believer of eminent obedience towards God. Along with Noah, Melchizedek, Balaam, Ruth, and

[2] See E. A. Knauf, 'Uz', *ABD* vi. 770–1.

Jonah, the figure of Job challenges any small, closed version of where holiness can be found.

Here and there in the Christian tradition, Job was acknowledged for his sanctity. Thus a church bears the name of 'St Job' in Venice, and a village in Flanders has the same name. Even more significant is the way that Job proved one of the impulses behind the medieval representations of 'Christ on a Cold Stone'. Late-medieval piety in Northern Europe created the image of Christ seated naked on a cold stone awaiting his crucifixion. He wears nothing but the crown of thorns, and seems totally exposed and vulnerable. The Gospels do not mention such an event in the passion story, but medieval devotion found in this scene a moment for contemplating the depth of Christ's physical and psychological suffering at the hands of violent and brutal men. The mournful image has many references, including that of Job suffering cruelly on a heap of ashes and scratching his sores with a potsherd (Job 2: 7–8).

At the end of the 1980s I was working in the German city of Nuremberg when a controversial modern bronze statue of Job was placed right outside a late Gothic church. Naked and hunched up, Job sat alongside a main street that cuts across the city from the railway station. His gaunt shoulders showed how pain had got the better of him. Handsome, well-fed people moved briskly past Job on their way to spend money at sales in those temples of consumer society, the huge department stores. Some paused to look at Job and catch a sense of the mysterious meaninglessness that can envelop our lives and paralyse our activity. Why should an innocent and good person like Job suffer the way he did? And why did the all-holy Jesus, prefigured by Job, endure the brutality of his passion and crucifixion?

Job and Christ rightly force those questions on us. But, in the context of this book, it is the holiness of Job, a non-Israelite, that matters primarily. Like Job, his three friends (Eliphaz the Temanite, Bildad the Shuhite, and Zophat the Naamathite) were also non-Israelites who seem to have come from north-west Arabia. Unlike these friends, Job addresses God directly (e.g. Job 7: 7–11). He will do so frequently, but they never do so. The holiness of Job also manifests itself in the way he persistently struggles in prayer to face the awful suffering that has swept over him. He proves himself an outstandingly holy and *wise* person.

The OT understood Wisdom, along with Word and Spirit, to serve as personified agents of divine activity. As personifications that were not yet formally recognized as persons, they operated with personal characteristics, and this was particularly so in the case of Wisdom. Our interest here focuses on Wisdom.

Hokmah or wisdom and its Greek equivalent, *Sophia,* occur over three hundred times in the OT. Nearly 75 per cent of these occurrences turn up in Job, Proverbs, Ecclesiastes (Qoheleth), Sirach, and Wisdom. Wise counsels are also found elsewhere: for example, Tobit 4: 3–21; 12: 6–13; and Baruch 3: 9–4: 4. Personified Wisdom or Sophia becomes increasingly related to the divine work of creation, providence, and salvation, and this in relation not only to the chosen people of God but also to all peoples.

The Book of Job abruptly introduces Wisdom at the end of a long dialogue between Job and his friends—in a poem that scholars have variously called an interlude, a bridge, or a later insertion (28: 1–28). The poem stresses the mysterious inaccessibility of divine Wisdom, which is quite beyond the reach of human beings (Job 28: 12–14, 20–1), utterly precious (Job 28: 15–19), and accessible only to God (Job 28: 23–7). At this early stage of reflection, the Book of Job celebrates and does not formally personify Wisdom. Here Wisdom appears as related to the works of creation, yet distinct from any particular work of creation. God, who controls the wind, the sea, the rain, and the thunderbolts, alone knows the way to Wisdom. Although many of the subsequent characteristics of Wisdom do not show up in this poem from Job, one feature appears persistently: her mysterious inaccessibility. Wisdom will be seen constantly as divine gift rather than primarily human achievement. The books of Proverbs, Sirach, and Wisdom may represent the availability of Sophia, who invites all to her feast, dwells in Jerusalem, and graciously presents herself to those who love her. Yet the initiative remains hers.

What the presence of that chapter in Job celebrating Wisdom signals is her role in the life of 'outsiders'. Some sapiential literature (e.g. Sirach) clearly emerges from the life of the Jewish people. What the presence of Wisdom in the Book of Job, a long work about a non-Israelite and his non-Israelite friends, establishes is that the same divine Wisdom also illuminates and shapes their lives. Wisdom and her teaching forms a bridge between the people of God and 'others'.

This bridge-building function of Wisdom also emerges from Proverbs, a book which consists of several collections of proverbs attributed to 'Solomon, son of David, king of Israel' (Prov. 1: 1). Some of these sayings may well pre-date the sixth-century Babylonian Exile, while others are post-exilic; the whole book was put together after the exile. One section is particularly relevant for the theme of Wisdom and 'outsiders'. Most scholars agree that Proverbs 22: 17–24: 34, a second collection of proverbial sayings, depends in some way on an Egyptian sage, Amen-em-ope. Entitled 'the Words of the Wise' (Prov. 22: 17), this collection in Proverbs includes many parallels to the work of that famous sage. Thus the Book of Proverbs stands against any sharp separation of the place of Wisdom within Israel and beyond Israel. The 'others' not only can receive Wisdom but can also prove a source of Wisdom teaching for Israel itself. This example from Proverbs is a further (in this case, spectacular) instance of how the people of God learned from outsiders about the appropriate life of human beings and their relationship with God.[3]

THE WISDOM OF BEN SIRA

Among the earliest deutero-canonical books and longest books of the Bible, Sirach contains the most extensive example of Jewish wisdom literature we have.[4] It was originally written in Hebrew about 180 BC and two generations later translated into Greek. Around 66 per cent of the original Hebrew text has now been recovered from finds in Cairo, Qumran, and Masada. Wisdom appears at the beginning of Sirach (1: 1–30), at the halfway mark (24: 1–34), and at the end

[3] See R. J. Clifford, *Proverbs: A Commentary* (Louisville, Ky.: Westminister John Knox, 1999); B. K. Waltke, *The Book of Proverbs*, 2 vols. (Grand Rapids, Mich.: Eerdmans, 2004–5). A further interesting example of learning from 'outsiders' comes from the celebration of Yom Kippur, the Day of Atonement. For fifteen hundred years or more, Jews have read on the afternoon of that feast the Book of Jonah. The mercy God exercised towards the Ninevites gave and gives Jewish worshippers hope that they too will experience divine mercy. See J. M. Sasson, *Jonah* (New York: Doubleday, 1990), 28.

[4] See P. W. Skehan and A. Di Lella, *The Wisdom of Ben Sira* (New York: Doubleday, 1987).

(51: 1–27). In the heavenly court, Sophia proclaims her divine origin and *universal presence*:

I came forth from the mouth of the Most High and covered the earth like a mist. I dwelt in the highest heavens, and my throne was a pillar of cloud. Alone, I compassed the vault of heaven and traversed the depths of the abyss. Over waves of the sea, over all the earth, and *over every people and nation, I have held sway*. Among all these, I sought a resting place. In whose territory should I abide? (Sir. 24: 3–7; italics mine)

Sophia came forth 'from the mouth of the Most High' as divine Word, dwells like God 'in the highest heavens', and is enthroned like God 'on a pillar of cloud'. Like God, she is present everywhere (from 'the vault of heaven' to 'the depths of the abyss') and has universal dominion ('over all the earth' and 'over every people and nation'). She covered 'the earth like a mist', just as the divine Spirit or Breath covered the waters at creation (Gen. 1: 2).

Wisdom looked for a permanent home ('a resting place'). In a dialogue with her (that has no counterpart in the case of Word and Spirit), God chose a place for her to dwell:

The Creator of all things gave me a command, and my Creator chose the place for my tent. He said, 'Make your dwelling in Jacob, and in Israel receive your inheritance.' Before the ages, in the beginning he created me, and for all ages I shall not cease to be. In the holy tent I ministered before him, and so I was established in Zion. Thus in the beloved city he gave me a resting place, and in Jerusalem was my domain. (Sir. 24: 8–11)

Existing with God from 'the beginning' and enjoying eternal existence ('for all ages I shall not cease to be'), Sophia followed the divine choice of Israel and has made her home in Jerusalem. Settled in the holy city, she sends out an invitation for her great banquet: 'Come to me, you who desire me, and eat your fill of my fruits. For the memory of me is sweeter than honey, and the possession of me sweeter than the honeycomb. Those who eat of me will hunger for more, and those who drink of me will thirst for more' (Sir. 24: 19–21). Here Sophia presents herself as food and drink, the source of nourishment and life.

At this point, Sirach innovates even further by identifying Sophia with that central symbol of YHWH's will and guidance for the people, Israel's Torah: 'All this is the book of the covenant of the

Most High God, the law that Moses commanded us' (Sir. 24: 23; see
Bar. 4: 1–4). Usually Wisdom literature did not appeal to the saving
history and covenant of Israel. Sirach (with the Book of Wisdom)
proves one of the two great exceptions, by introducing a long section
in 'praise of the ancestors' (chs. 44–50) and, even more, by identifying personified 'Lady' Wisdom with the Torah. Even for Israel this
identification seems a mixed blessing. On the one hand, it extends
the influence of Sophia into the most sacred realm of Israel's relationship with God. On the other hand, this identification can be seen
to curtail Sophia by confining her to 'the manageable limits of
a book'.[5]

Before leaving Sirach, we can observe two wonderful aspects in its
presentation of divine Wisdom. While Wisdom is present to 'every
people and nation' (Sir. 24: 6), by the divine choice she dwells in
Israel and finds her home in Jerusalem (Sir. 24: 8–11). On the one
hand, a universal presence does not preclude a special dwelling place
for Wisdom being chosen by God. On the other hand, such a
particular divine choice does not mean that Wisdom is absent elsewhere in the world and hence unavailable for the whole human race.

THE WISDOM OF SOLOMON

Probably written shortly before the birth of Jesus and, in any case, the
last of the OT books, the Wisdom of Solomon[6] yields much for our
central theme of God and 'the others', especially from its first half
(Wisd. 1: 1–11: 4), which in turn is divided into two sections. The
first (Wisd. 1: 1–5: 25) deals with retribution for good and evil and
with the immortality that Sophia can bring. Some vivid verses
describe how the ungodly urge one another to persecute and even
kill righteous people (Wisd. 2: 10–20). But after death the righteous
are forever safe and will share in the life of God (Wisd. 3: 1–9). This
promise of immortal life is held out to all just persons, and not

    [5] M. Scott, *Sophia and the Johannine Jesus* (Sheffield: JSOT Press, 1992), 54.
    [6] See H. Hübner, *Die Weisheit Salomons: Liber Sapientiae Salomonis* (Göttingen:
Vandenhoeck & Ruprecht, 1999); C. Larcher, *Le Livre de la Sagesse ou la Sagesse de
Salomon*, 3 vols. (Paris: Librairie Lecoffre, 1983–5).

merely to just Israelites. A reference to Genesis and to humanity being created in 'the image' of God's 'own eternity' (Wisd. 2: 23) brings out the universality of what is envisaged: God will bless with immortality all who have led righteous lives.

The second section from the first half of Wisdom describes Sophia and her operations in the world and explains how she is to be found (Wisd. 6: 1–11: 4). Although closely and remarkably identified with God, she makes herself accessible: 'One who rises early to seek her will have no difficulty, for she will be found sitting at the gate' (Wisd. 6: 14). Indeed, she herself 'goes about seeking those worthy of her, and she graciously appears to them in their paths, and meets them in every thought' (Wisd. 6: 16). The speaker, supposedly Solomon, while addressing kings and judges, seems to be speaking to the Jewish community in an exhortation to seek Wisdom. Yet no restrictions are placed on the general accessibility of Wisdom (Wisd. 6: 1–25). She will come to all who are 'worthy of her'.

Being present everywhere and 'the fashioner of all things', Wisdom is not limited to Israel. 'All-powerful' and 'overseeing all', she 'penetrates all things', and 'penetrates through all spirits that are intelligent'. In a classic passage, the Book of Wisdom sets out Sophia's relationship to God and her activity in the created universe: 'She is a breath of the power of God and a pure emanation of the glory of the Almighty.' Hence 'she can do all things, and while remaining in herself, she renews all things; in every generation she passes into holy souls and makes them friends of God and prophets'. This vision of Wisdom closes by declaring: 'she reaches mightily from one end of the earth to the other and she orders all things well' (Wisd. 7: 22–8: 1).

Identified with the divine 'spirit', Wisdom proves to be a saving power for 'those on earth', a guide to God for all humanity: as one might say, she is the universal self-revelation of God that brings true, spiritual life. A prayer for the gift of wisdom says this to God: 'Who has learned your counsel, unless you have given wisdom and sent your holy spirit from on high? And thus the paths of those on earth were set right, and people were taught what pleases you, and were saved by wisdom' (Wisd. 9: 17–18).

The Book of Wisdom then proceeds to list seven figures (from Adam to Moses) whose stories illustrate the saving power of Wisdom (Wisd. 10: 1–11: 4). After stating that Sophia was at work to save all human beings (represented by Adam and Noah), the biblical author reinterprets Israel's history by assigning to her the saving deeds normally attributed to YHWH. It was Sophia who was at work in protecting Abraham, Lot, Jacob, and Joseph. It was Sophia who through Moses delivered the chosen people in the Exodus; 'she brought them over the Red Sea, and led them through deep waters' (Wisd. 10: 15–18). In speaking thus of Wisdom, the biblical text portrays her as the saviour of the ancestors of Israel.

This involvement of Wisdom in the particular salvation history of Israel does not cancel her role in the lives of all 'those on earth', human beings at large who can know the light and saving power of Wisdom. She pervades all creation and the whole human story. Not surprisingly the list of seven stories opens with two 'universal' figures (Adam and Noah) and one through whom 'all nations will be blessed' (Abraham). Like Sirach, the Book of Wisdom respects both the universal function of Wisdom and her specific role in the history of Israel.

CONCLUDING QUESTIONS

This sampling of what seems to be the last book of the OT leaves us with two central questions. First, the NT will not only identify the incarnate Son of God with divine Wisdom in the creation and conservation of the world (e.g. 1 Cor. 8: 6; Col. 1: 16–17) but will also follow the lead of the Book of Wisdom by recognizing his role in the saving history of Israel (e.g. John 12: 41; 1 Cor. 10: 4). To what extent does this identification of Christ as divine Wisdom illuminate our quest for understanding about his active role (as creator and redeemer) in our world and, specifically, in the various cultures and religions of our world?

Linked with this first question is an even more difficult one. To what extent could or should the Book of Wisdom encourage us to interpret world religions as being, at least in part, the fruit of the activity of Wisdom? The long closing meditation on history (Wisd. 11: 5–19: 22) dismisses the cult of the stars and of other beautiful things in nature (Wisd. 13: 1–9), indulges in strong polemic against the folly of worshipping idols (Wisd. 13: 10–19), and singles out for ridicule the folly of those who trust in a wooden image on the ship's prow when they put to sea (Wisd. 14: 1–14). Idolatry not only entails ignorance of God but also proves 'the beginning, cause and end of every evil': a section on the evil results of idolatry spells out in detail this argument (Wisd. 14: 22–31). The writer contrasts the folly and wickedness of worshipping idols with the positive results of worshipping the true God: essentially, 'complete righteousness' here and now and 'immortality' to come (Wisd. 15: 1–17).

After some luminous chapters on the universal accessibility of Wisdom, the later chapters of this book pass a sombre judgement on what happens widely among non-Israelites: the worship of idols and the evil results of this. Nevertheless, an exception is partly made in the case of those who worship the forces of nature, the least culpable form of false worship (Wisd. 13: 1–9). Such idolatry can arise from an honest search for God: 'these people are little to be blamed, for perhaps they go astray, while seeking God and desiring to find him' (Wisd. 13: 6–7).[7] Even so, such a gentler judgement highlights the human search for God rather than the primary divine 'search' for human beings, which is indicated by the universal activity of Lady Wisdom. This issue will recur when we take up the books of the NT.

[7] Those who search for God do not show a 'control mentality'—unlike those who make idols and keep them 'under their control'.

6

Provisional Conclusions from the Old Testament

How then are the God of Israel and Israel as the people of YHWH related to other peoples? Looking at the broad picture, we might sum matters up as follows. The relationship of YHWH, God of Israel, and of his divine personification, Wisdom, to other peoples remains in a state of unresolved tension in the OT. On the one hand, YHWH is presented as the God of Israel in an altogether special way. On the other hand, some prophetic, sapiential, and other texts propose that YHWH is also the God of all peoples and all individuals and has saving plans for 'the nations'. The two sets of ideas coexisted in a dialectic tension, without ever being examined and related in any full-scale fashion. We can express this tension in another way.

It seems accurate to state that many OT texts which refer to the relations between YHWH and nations other than Israel are antagonistic in nature. The Israelites often lived in a constant state of threat; that was no setting for generating fully 'balanced' thoughts about the 'others'. Those nations were seen as hostile to the God of Israel and to Israel, the people of YHWH. Nevertheless, a strong nationalist identity of Israel did not rule out an awareness of YHWH as the God of the entire world. If these general conclusions seem justified, let us see some details.

THE DIVINE BENEVOLENCE TO ALL

Earlier chapters have documented the concern that God exercises towards all peoples and individuals.[1] The Hebrew Bible—and, in

---

[1] Let me emphasize that in these chapters dealing wtih the OT, for the most part I take up the 'final form' of the biblical texts and do not ask either about their literary

particular, Genesis—witnesses to this universal benevolence. We saw how the Genesis stories about the creation of human beings and the fall into sin of human beings apply to all men and women in their origin and life in the presence of God (Chapter 1). 'Adam' and 'Eve' depict everyman and everywoman, and not merely two individual human beings. Each man and each woman is made in the divine image and likeness (Gen. 1: 26–7)—something that defines all human beings in their primordial relationship to God. Despite the tragic consequences of sin, God continues to cherish Adam and Eve. Sin does not render void the special relationship between God and the whole human race. The universal benevolence of God brightens a situation darkened by human sin. Thus the story of Adam and Eve teaches something that touches every man and woman: human happiness depends on a personal relationship with a loving God; sin frustrates this relationship; one needs God's action to restore the relationship.

In the Genesis narrative the disobedience of Adam and Eve initiates an avalanche of sin that brings divine judgement in the form of a catastrophic flood. This flood 'cleanses' an evil situation and gives the human race a fresh start (Gen. 9: 1–2). Through Noah, the new founder of the human race, God establishes a covenant with all humanity and the whole of creation. The three sons of Noah are regarded as the ancestors of all peoples, and all peoples are regarded as the beneficiaries of this cosmic covenant. To illustrate the universal relevance of this covenant, Genesis provides a 'table of the nations'— an elaborate list to show that all human beings originated from Noah and his family (Gen. 10: 1–32). Thus the entire human race shares in the covenant made with Noah and in the divine blessings of the new age.

The Book of Genesis moves to the story of Abraham and Sarah, who receive the call to become ancestors of 'a great nation' (Israel) and the promise: 'In you all the families of the earth will be blessed' (Gen. 12: 1–9). This theme of the family of Abraham becoming a channel of blessings for all nations not only recurs in Genesis (28: 14) but also is echoed by the prophets (e.g. Isa. 19: 23–5; Jer. 4: 2). God elects in a special way Abraham and Sarah, but their election does not

and historical status (for instance, as incorporating ancient legends, as didactic fiction, or as popular history) or about their origins.

occur without a universal reference. (We return below to this theme of Israel being a conduit of blessings for others.) Abraham himself is blessed by a Canaanite priest-king, Melchizedek (Gen. 14: 18–20), a mysterious 'outsider' who will serve as model for the priestly privileges of the Davidic king (Ps. 110: 4) and for the priesthood of Christ himself (Heb. 5: 10; 6: 20). Melchizedek is the most striking example of the status before God that a biblical text can give to a religious 'outsider'.

The OT goes beyond Melchizedek to present other figures who do *not* belong to the chosen people and yet are blessed and even honoured by God. As we saw in Chapter 5, Job is the holy 'outsider' *par excellence.* He is tested terribly by unexpected and unmerited sufferings. He is questioned by God, and comes to experience an intimate communion with God (Job 42: 5). In this testing of Job, a non-Israelite, God reveals himself in his cosmic power and not through the exodus from Egypt nor through other key episodes in Israelite history. The Book of Job drives home two lessons: the just person is not necessarily an Israelite nor even visibly related to Israel; the revelation of God can be mediated through creation and is not limited to particular historical events.

Another individual 'outsider' whom God remarkably blessed is the widow of Zarephath. Through the actions of Elijah, God sees to it that she and her household remain alive in a time of severe drought and then that her dead son is brought back to life. Blessed in these two remarkable ways, the widow acknowledges the power of Elijah and of his God (YHWH). But she is not drawn, let alone obliged, to abandon her religion and worship the one God, YHWH (1 Kgs. 17: 7–24).

It is the same in the Book of Jonah. God sends a reluctant prophet to preach repentance to the people of Nineveh. The Ninevites instantly do penance for their violent and evil ways, and so are saved from destruction. They undergo a moral change of life, but are not called to worship YHWH as such and adopt the Mosaic law and practice. God blesses the Ninevites and makes it clear to Jonah that his divine love embraces every creature in the universe (Jonah 4: 1–11). The merciful concern of YHWH knows no frontiers.

The prophet Amos has a similar message (Chapter 3 above): God behaves as Saviour towards all nations, and all nations are accountable to God. Israel has been elected to be the people of God, but that does not discriminate against other nations. God has sovereign sway over all the nations and does not indulge any favouritism—either geographically, ethnically, or historically. In making this point, Amos picks out the Nubians (or Ethiopians), the Philistines, and the Arameans. Through the prophet God indicates that he has been present both in the history of the distant Ethiopians, and in that of enemies of Israel who live nearby: the Philistines and the Arameans. YHWH was involved not only in the Israelites' exodus from Egypt but also in the migrations of the Philistines and the Arameans (Amos 9: 7). YHWH has chosen Israel and guided its history, but the divine care and guidance, as well as the sovereign rights of God, extend to all peoples. The hand of God is found in the history of the Ethiopians, Philistines, and Arameans, even if Amos says nothing about these nations being incorporated into the chosen people and accepting the obligations of the Mosaic law. They are 'peoples of God', alongside Israel, the people of God. The teaching of Amos militates against restricting the meaning of 'people of God'.

Two individuals began as 'outsiders' (Naaman and Ruth), and in their different ways ended as 'insiders' (Chapter 2 above). Both found faith in the God of Israel, but the first foreigner (Naaman) returned to his own country, whereas the other foreigner (Ruth) came to live in Israel. Naaman, the commander of the Syrian army, was greatly blessed by God when he was cured of his leprosy and accepted the supremacy of YHWH. By taking home to Damascus some soil from Israel, he planned to maintain his newly found faith in the Israelite God, even if officially he would continue to be involved in the cult of Haddad the Thunderer, the chief god of the Syrians. Through the prophet Elisha, Naaman the Syrian leper was transformed physically and spiritually, and came to share in the Israelite worship of YHWH (2 Kgs. 5: 1–27).

A Moabite widow, Ruth, exemplifies even more such a change when she arrives as a migrant 'from outside' seeking food and protection in Israel. She marries Boaz and has a son who is the grandfather of King David. Presumably she embraces the religion of Israel (Ruth 4: 1–18). Thus an 'outsider' from Moab becomes an ancestor of Jesus; with three other women (also non-Israelites), she is listed by Matthew in his genealogy of Jesus (Matt. 1: 1–17). Of these four women, Ruth stands apart for her human qualities and fidelity to God. She and the other non-Israelite women symbolize the universal benevolence of God, who not only cares for them in different ways but also turns them, through divine providence, into ancestors of Jesus. They may start as 'outsiders', but then become highly significant 'insiders' in the total plan of God.

Lastly, the divine benevolence towards all people and, specifically, towards 'outsiders', shines through God's presence in creation (Prov. 8: 22–31; Job 38–41) and in the experience of the human condition. The Wisdom literature of the OT, both the sapiential books themselves and sections in other books, testify to the way in which non-Israelites (e.g. Job) can receive the gifts of Wisdom (through the works of creation and their personal experience) and respond in faith. God's life-giving self-communication is not limited to particular events of salvation and revelation in history (e.g. the exodus from Egypt and the captivity in Babylon). Non-Israelites or 'outsiders' (e.g. those righteous persons who are not Israelites of Wisd. 2: 10–20; 3: 1–9; 4: 7–19) can respond in faith to the revelation of God mediated through human life and the works of creation. Lady Wisdom, according to Sirach, proves a universal source of nourishment and life. According to the Book of Wisdom, she promises immortal life to truly righteous persons, whoever they are. In short, as the self-revelation of God, 'Lady Wisdom' is available to all people; she teaches, saves and *brings life* (Chapter 5 above). In the words of Proverbs, 'she is a tree of life to those who lay hold of her; and those who hold her fast are called happy' (Prov. 3: 18). Later in this book I will take up themes of OT Wisdom literature which wonderfully illuminate the religious situation of 'outsiders'.

THE PROPHETIC AND PRIESTLY ACTIVITY OF OUTSIDERS

The OT also positively assesses some prophetic and priestly activity of non-Israelites and pre-Israelites. As regards words of *prophecy*, Balaam provides the supreme example of prophetic activity coming from an 'outsider' (Chapter 3 above). A diviner from Mesopotamia, he pronounces four oracles which recognize that Israel is a nation set apart for a special destiny. His fourth oracle, which speaks of a 'star' and a 'sceptre' refers to a royal leader, initially understood to be King David and later applied to Jesus himself (Num. 22: 1–24: 25).

Balaam was not a worshipper of YHWH, and did not embrace the Mosaic faith and practice. After delivering his four oracles in favour of Israel, he returned home to Pethor on the Euphrates (Num. 22:5; 24: 25). Numbers and a range of other OT books, as we saw in Chapter 3, agree that the God of Israel had spoken through this foreign seer or diviner. By means of this 'outsider', God was understood to have legitimated the reign of David and his conquest of Moab. The prophetic career of Balaam intersected with a critical moment in the story of the Israelites and their struggles with the Moabites. Thus Balaam illustrates not only that God can communicate true oracles through 'outsiders', but also that the prophetic activity of such an 'outsider' can impinge dramatically on the history of God's chosen people. Prophecies delivered by this outsider are even incorporated in the inspired text of Numbers. Balaam is highly relevant in showing how there is no sharp division between 'insiders' and 'outsiders' among those whom God uses in the one great story of revelation and salvation.

Several OT books display positively some *priestly* activity of 'outsiders' and 'predecessors': for instance, Noah, Melchizedek, and Abraham (Chapter 1 above). When the flood subsides, Noah follows the divine command to lead the disembarkation from the ark. But Noah does something further by building 'an altar to the Lord' and making on it 'burnt offerings' of 'clean animals and birds'. When building the altar and offering this sacrifice of thanksgiving, he does so spontaneously and without following any prescriptions about offerings understood to have been introduced later by God through Moses. The priestly gestures of Noah 'please' God (Gen. 8: 15–22). By performing a priestly act of cult, this new founder of the human race has done something that Adam never does either before or after the fall.

An ancient priest-king of Jerusalem, Melchizedek, brings out 'bread and wine'—presumably to make a cultic offering—before he blesses Abraham in the name of 'God Most High (*El Elyon*)'. A priest of the Canaanite cult, Melchizedek imparts this blessing in the name of the deity whom he worships (Gen. 14: 19–20) and who is at once identified as 'the maker of heaven and earth' (Gen. 14: 22). Later books in the OT, as we saw in Chapter 1, identify 'God Most High' as the Lord (YHWH) or God of Israel. This episode of a priestly offering and blessing coming from an 'outsider' (Melchizedek) enjoys a very positive press in the scriptures, culminating in the Letter to the Hebrews. This NT book sees Melchizedek, a Canaanite priest, as prefiguring the high priesthood of the incarnate Son of God (Heb. 5: 10; 6: 20). Thus a major NT book explains the priesthood of Christ through the model of an 'outsider', and not through some figure in the story of the chosen people themselves.

Before leaving Abraham and the Book of Genesis, we should recall what Chapter 1 set out about the treaty Abraham made with the Philistine leader Abimelech (Gen. 21: 22–34). This episode involves a divine name, *El Olam* ('the Everlasting God'), which was associated with the pre-Israelite sanctuary of Beersheba and would be adopted by Israel as a name for the Lord (YHWH). In making his treaty, Abraham plants a sacred tree in Beersheba. In a shrine belonging to 'outsiders', he calls 'on the name of the Lord'. Thus Abraham recognizes the divine presence in a sacred shrine created by 'others' and prays there to God. Thus the story of Abraham's meeting with Abimelech testifies to the value of the shrines of 'others', their naming of God, and their sacred ceremonies.

Three more OT passages also positively evaluate sacrificial, cultic actions of 'outsiders'. The first is from Jonah (Chapter 3 above) and concerns the sailors. They find that Jonah's disobedience had prompted the storm that threatened to destroy the ship and everyone on board. Before throwing him into the sea—a dramatic solution proposed by Jonah himself—they cried out to YHWH: 'Please, O Lord (YHWH), we pray, do not let us perish on account of this man's life. Do not make us guilty of innocent blood; for you, O Lord (YHWH), have done as it pleased you.' Then they threw Jonah overboard, and 'the sea ceased from its raging'. Their physical rescue brought at once a spiritual result: 'the men feared the Lord (YHWH) even more, offered a sacrifice to the Lord (YHWH), and made vows' (Jonah 1: 1–16). At the start of this segment of the story in the Book of Jonah, 'each sailor cried to his own god'. At the end, they came to make a sacrificial offering to YHWH. Even so, the sailors are not said to have discontinued their own religious activities in favour of the Mosaic law and practice. An emergency situation prompted their cultic worship of YHWH—obviously a good, if transitory, episode in their lives.

In Chapter 4 we recalled two further instances of cultic, priestly rites practised outside Israel. The Book of Isaiah announces that 'there will be an altar to the Lord in the centre of the land of Egypt'. Without going to Jerusalem, 'the Egyptians will know the Lord on that day, will worship with sacrifice and burnt offering, and will make vows to the Lord and perform them' (Isa. 19: 21). The text goes even further: 'the Egyptians will worship with the Assyrians'. At that time 'Israel will be the third with Egypt and Assyria, a blessing in the midst of the earth, whom the Lord of hosts has blessed, saying: "Blessed be Egypt my people and Assyria the work of my hands, and Israel my heritage"' (Isa. 19: 24–5). There is no question here of Egypt and Assyria being assimilated religiously to Israel; yet they are put on a par with Israel. The worship that they will offer will clearly be acceptable.

The most famous statement about worship offered to YHWH by 'outsiders' comes from a divine oracle in Malachi: 'from the rising of the sun to its setting my name is great among the nations; and in every place incense is offered to my name, and a pure offering; for my name is great among the nations' (Mal. 1: 11). This statement seemingly describes what is currently happening among the nations around the world. They celebrate sacrificial rites in homage to YHWH, without a hint of any need to centralize this worship in Jerusalem. The cult of the nations 'in every place' entails true homage to the God of Israel and a 'pure offering' to his name. Given the eschatological thrust of the Book of Malachi as a whole, the prophet may be pointing to the future kingship of God established over all the earth. Nevertheless, the text expresses a very positive view of the religious faith and cultic practices of the 'others'. Like Isaiah (see above), Malachi pictures the 'others' as knowing God and in their worship offering him valid sacrifice, without going up to Jerusalem to do so.

JERUSALEM THE CENTRE

Israel constantly experienced the nations militarily and religiously as a threat to its existence and way of life. The Philistines and the Assyrians endangered the very survival of Israel, while other groups, like the Canaanites, threatened the way the Israelites lived out their faith in YHWH. In such a situation it is not surprising that any recognition of the universal benevolence of YHWH that we have documented earlier could recede at times into the background.

Nevertheless, as we have seen above, some OT texts reveal a more open outlook. YHWH is God not only of Israel but also of the whole world, and displays benevolence towards non-Israelites as well as towards Israelites. Yet such texts generally envisage the nations being associated in some way with Israel. God extends salvation to 'the ends of the earth', but 'the ends of the earth' must come to Jerusalem. Salvation for the nations does not bypass Israel or occur without the involvement of Israel. It is only in a relatively few cases (e.g. the Ninevites in Jonah) that the nations experience the blessings of YHWH while retaining their own identity. Even in those cases where the OT texts reflect positively on the nations as such (e.g. the Ethiopians, Philistines, and Arameans in Amos 9: 7), these texts do so normally without focusing on their religious practices and beliefs.

In general—and, in particular, in the Book of Isaiah—an Israel-centred and Jerusalem-centred outlook prevails. YHWH is the creator and ruler of all (e.g. Isa. 45: 5–7, 21); yet his universal dominion is to be publicly inaugurated and consummated in Jerusalem. Knowledge of the one true God, who is present in a special way in Jerusalem, will be shared with the peoples of the world. The future Jerusalem is envisaged as the religious centre of the world and the goal of pilgrimage for the nations. The nations will 'stream' to Zion and say: 'Let us go to the mountain of the Lord, to the house of the God of Jacob, that he may teach us his ways and we may walk in his paths' (Isa. 2: 2–3). The gloriously restored Jerusalem will attract all nations (Isa. 60: 1–3). At the end-time the Gentiles will come to be included among the people of God (e.g. Zech. 8: 2–3).

What will the nations do when they arrive in Jerusalem? They will turn away from their false and impotent idols to share in the community of God's people and worship the one true God (Jer. 16: 19–21). The curse of a multiplicity of languages (Gen. 11: 1–9) will be removed, the people will share in one 'pure' speech, and will worship God together.[2] The Temple will be open to all people and will become 'the house of prayer for all nations'—for the foreigners who embrace faith in YHWH and join the congregation of Israel in worship (Isa. 56: 6–7). God may even make some of these 'outsiders' into 'priests and levites' to serve in the Temple (Isa. 66: 18–23). The chapters added later to Zechariah do not picture those who survive from the nations as remaining in Jerusalem but as going up year after year to 'worship the King, the Lord of hosts'. On their yearly visits they will keep 'the festival of the booths'. If they fail to come to this yearly festival, they will be punished by drought and plague (Zech. 14: 16–19). At the end, according to Isaiah, there will be a final banquet for all peoples (Isa. 25: 6–8).

Yet much of what will happen when the nations 'stream' to Jerusalem is left unstated. Will the foreigners become proselytes and so be incorporated into the Jewish people? Will the normal obligations be placed on them about keeping the Sabbath, about avoiding some food, and about practising circumcision?

ISRAEL AS MEANS OF SALVATION

What of the role of Israel for the final salvation of humanity? Israel is obviously not to be a barrier between YHWH and the nations, and not to behave like Jonah, who is reluctant to function as the divine instrument in prompting the Ninevites to repent. If God makes possible salvation and mediates it by calling the nations to participate in the community of his chosen people, what part does Israel play in all this?

First, when YHWH acts on his people's behalf, this activity exemplifies his intentions for the entire world. Thus divine activity on

[2] See Zephaniah 3: 9–10: 'I will change the speech of the peoples to a pure speech, that all of them may call on the name of the Lord and serve him with one accord. From beyond the rivers of Ethiopia my suppliants, my scattered cities, shall bring me offering.'

behalf of Israel *also* has the goal of other nations coming to know and acknowledge him as God. Thus the experience of Israel illustrates the divine intentions for every people. Let me offer two examples. The exodus from Egypt, the foundational event for the Israelites, also serves as a pattern when Amos interprets what God has done in the migrations of the Philistines and Arameans (Amos 9: 7). Then the final return of the Jewish diaspora to Jerusalem mirrors YHWH's desire to call all the nations there and let them find in the Temple their 'house of prayer' (Isa. 56: 6–7).

Second, the Israelites are meant to be agents through whom others can know God. Elisha brings this about when Naaman's cure from leprosy becomes the occasion for the Syrian commander to find faith in YHWH (Chapter 2 above). In the same chapter we saw how fidelity to the covenant will turn the Israelites into witnesses to the 'others', who will acknowledge in them 'a wise and discerning people' (Deut. 4: 6). By recognizing the spiritual wisdom and intelligence of Israel, at least indirectly the 'outsiders' can enjoy communion with Israel. Through different terminology Second Isaiah makes a similar point. The 'Servant' of YHWH has a mission not only to Israel, but also to foreign peoples as 'a light to the nations' (Isa. 49: 6). The 'Servant' is to bring to all people the divine teaching and righteousness (Isa. 42: 1–4).

The Book of Daniel exemplifies Jewish people being the means of others coming to know God. In Babylon Daniel interprets for Nebuchadnezzar a troubling dream. Through Daniel, the Babylonian king came to know that YHWH is God over all other gods and King over all other kings: 'Truly, your God is God of gods and King of kings and a revealer of mysteries' (Dan. 2: 47). Yet this recognition does not stop the king from making a huge golden statue and ordering his people to worship it. When three friends of Daniel (Shadrach, Meshach, and Abednego) refuse to pay homage to the statue, they are thrown into a fiery furnace but emerge unscathed. Nebuchadnezzar recognizes that the God of these young men has the power to deliver (Dan. 3: 29) and enjoys a sovereignty that exists now and forever (Dan. 4: 2–3; see 4: 31–2). After suffering from a strange form of insanity, the king recovers his reason and blesses 'the Most High God' and 'king of heaven' (Dan. 4: 34–5, 37).

Darius, a successor of Nebuchadnezzar, plans to appoint Daniel as his grand vizier. But some jealous officials conspire against Daniel and, on the basis of his fidelity to the God of Israel, have him flung into a den of lions. Daniel comes out alive and unharmed. This prompts King Darius to issue a decree for his whole royal dominion that 'people should tremble and show fear before the God of Daniel. For he is the living God, enduring forever. His kingdom shall never be destroyed, and his dominion has no end. He delivers and rescues; he works signs and wonders in heaven and on earth; for he has saved Daniel from the power of the lions' (Dan. 6: 26–7). Both the story of the deliverance of the three young men from the fiery furnace and that of Daniel from the den of lions are traditional tales that point a moral. They show how fidelity to YHWH brings divine aid to faithful Jews and enables them to triumph over their enemies in Babylon. But these tales *also* illustrate how these loyal followers of God can bring others (specifically, Nebuchadnezzar and Darius) to know and confess the God of Israel. It is not surprising to find the Book of Daniel moving at once to a vision, in which the 'saints of God' will include all nations and people of every language (Dan. 7: 14, 18).

The concern that the Israelites should show for the welfare of 'outsiders' belongs among the basic laws attributed to Moses. Practical norms covering the harvest of grain, olives, and grapes make provision for food being available not only for orphans and widows among the Israelites but also for resident 'aliens' (Deut. 24: 19–22). As H. D. Preuss points out, in 'ancient Near Eastern legal collections' there were 'many stipulations' for the protection of widows and orphans. But such protection was never extended to strangers. The protection of 'aliens' was a unique feature of Israel.[3] Such concern for the bodily welfare of aliens would seem to imply some concern for their moral and spiritual welfare. It was, after all, something profoundly religious, Israel's consciousness of being elected and liberated by God, that gave rise to 'some of the most sensitive ideas

---

[3] H. D. Preuss, *Old Testament Theology*, ii (Edinburgh: T. & T. Clark, 1996), 402. For the defence of the rights of resident aliens, see also Exod. 22: 21; Lev. 19: 10; Deut. 10: 18–19; 16: 11; 24: 14, 17; 27: 19.

concerning the treatment of aliens and foreigners found anywhere in the ancient world'.[4]

DIALOGUE WITH THE NATIONS

Contemporary versions of inter-religious dialogue speak of a giving and a receiving: the people of God receive from 'others', as well as giving them a chance of sharing in a life shaped by Christ. In the story of Israel and its contacts with the nations, one would need to torture the data before proposing the existence or even the concept of such inter-religious dialogue.

Even in Second and Third Isaiah, what Israel was to receive from the nations is their wealth and service. Foreigners were to bring their wealth to Zion, and build the new Jerusalem and its glorious Temple (Isa. 60: 4–14). Nevertheless, such passages on the future relationship between Israel and the nations should not lead us to overlook another form of 'receiving', the many instances in which Israel assimilated (and transformed) non-Israelite religious phenomena (cultic practices, beliefs, and various concepts and images). We have seen already two examples: some names for God (Chapter 1 above) and a collection of proverbial sayings from Egypt echoed in a section of Proverbs (Chapter 5 above). The biblical texts do not explicitly acknowledge this process of assimilation; it largely took place, without any conscious sense of being engaged in inter-religious dialogue and/or borrowing. Obviously one persistent venue for dialogue and assimilation came through Israelite men marrying foreign wives.[5]

The absence of any strong awareness about inter-religious dialogue is not surprising, given the persistent antagonism towards the nations. Right through to the conclusion of the OT, biblical texts speak of the punishment and even annihilation that the nations will suffer

---

[4] J. S. Kaminsky, 'Did Election Imply the Mistreatment of Non-Israelites?', *Harvard Theological Review* 96 (2003), 387–425, at 408. For literature on aliens in Israel, see ibid., 411 n. 31.

[5] See V. P. Hamilton, 'Marriage: Old Testamaent and Ancient New East', *ABD* iv. 559–69, at 563–5.

(e.g. Zech. 14: 12–19). The Book of Daniel predicts the judgement and even destruction that will be visited upon the nations
(e.g. Dan. 7: 1–28).

To conclude. In the OT, the relationship both of Israel's God and of
his people to other peoples remains in a state of unresolved tension.
Prompted by the Holy Spirit, the inspired authors recorded in
writing the different ways in which they thought about and acted
towards 'outsiders'. The OT, even when it endorsed a positive attitude, continued to be of two minds in its expectations when it was a
question of the salvation of the nations and their destiny.

On the one hand, there are texts that picture YHWH as benevolent
towards the entire world (e.g. the covenant with Noah) and towards
individuals and groups, even towards such violently oppressive
groups as the Ninevites (Jonah). Genuine prophets (e.g. Balaam)
and true cultic worship (e.g. Mal. 1: 11) are acknowledged to exist
among the 'outsiders'. The 'outsiders' will find in Jerusalem their
place of worship and their final banquet with God. On the other
hand, the nations can be seen as irredeemably hostile, fit objects to be
judged, punished, and even destroyed by God.

There are troubling aspects to some texts, especially those directed
against such groups as the Canaanites and Amalekites. Passages
which describe Joshua's victory over five kings (Josh. 10: 1–43)
seem to imply a total destruction ordered by God—something that
evokes genocidal policies practised in modern times towards real or
supposed 'enemies'. But surely genocide is always morally wrong and
could never be decreed by God? Faced with such texts, one can and
should argue as follows. Certain Israelites, at a given point in their
history, imagined that God wanted such genocidal destruction of the
enemy. The biblical authors were inspired to record faithfully this
terrible conviction.

Yet there is more to be said than just that. As Kaminsky points out,
'even the harshest texts are more nuanced and ambiguous than some
would concede. Thus, while Joshua 10 implies that all the Canaanites
were killed in one fell swoop, all Canaanites were not in fact killed.
Not only do Rahab and her extended family survive (Joshua 2), but
so do the Gibeonites (Joshua 9), as well as other groups.'[6] One should

---

[6] Kaminsky, 'Did Election Imply the Mistreatment of Non-Israelites?', 401.

recall further biblical texts in which Israelites and Canaanites lived together amicably. Abraham peacefully purchased a family burial place (at Hebron) from 'the people of the land' (Gen. 23: 1–20, at v. 7). In Genesis 38 the wife of Judah was clearly a Canaanite (Gen. 38: 1–5). Kaminsky recalls this and further evidence to argue that the Canaanites 'were probably never purged in a genocidal campaign by Joshua'. He goes on to recall the common view that 'the majority of ancient Israelites were themselves the descendants of Canaanites'.[7]

Unquestionably, some of the OT texts against 'the nations' are troubling and in undeniable tension with other texts that see such peoples as belonging within a universal divine plan. A similar (if less important) tension prevails about the role that Zion will play in the salvation of the nations. On the one hand, the peoples will come in pilgrimage to Zion, hear the word of YHWH, and walk in his ways. The Temple will become a house of prayer for all nations (Isa. 56: 6–7). On the other hand, each nation will worship YHWH in its own place (Isa. 19: 21; Mal. 1: 11; Zeph. 2: 11). *Where* then will the nations find salvation? The total picture remains unclear and inconclusive.

Reading with gratitude the Hebrew Bible, I find myself as a Christian believer left at the end with an open-ended situation. These scriptures, drawing on more than a thousand years of experience, convey rich insights, beliefs, and expectations about the situation of 'outsiders'. But the truth, ultimately, is in the whole. As Hugh of St Victor, a twelfth-century Augustinian canon, put matters, 'the whole of scripture is one book, and that one book is Christ'.[8] Let me turn now to the NT, which completes the Christian canon of scripture and in which Christ clearly stands at the centre.

---

[7] Kaminsky, 'Did Election Imply the Mistreatment of Non-Israelites?', 403.
[8] *De Arca Noe Morali* 2. 8–9.

7

Jesus and the 'Outsiders'

Around AD 27 Jesus, a Galilean Jew from Nazareth, began his public ministry, which centred on the preaching of the kingdom or the saving rule of God already powerfully present but not yet fully consummated. He is remembered by Matthew as having said that his primary mission was to reform Israel and call Jews back to God: 'I was sent only to the lost sheep of the house of Israel' (Matt. 15: 24). This statement (which is probably based on a saying found in 10: 5–6) appears in an account of Jesus' encounter with a Gentile woman living in Gentile territory, 'the districts of Tyre and Sidon'—that is to say, beyond upper Galilee and in Phoenicia. Mark 7: 26 identifies her as Greek and Syro-Phoenician,[1] while Matthew calls her a 'Canaanite'. In this story the woman, even though a Gentile, asked help for her tormented daughter. While Jesus took his mission of salvation primarily to his fellow Jews, he was ready to respond to faith wherever he found it, and healed the woman's daughter instantly (Matt. 15: 21–8). When a Gentile dared to ask him for a miracle, he was willing to do so and began breaking down the barriers that separated Jews and Gentiles.[2]

---

[1] J. R. Donahue and D. J. Harrington comment: 'A "Greek" (used only here in Mark) does not [necessarily] mean someone who is ethnically Greek but can be used as a generic term for a non-Jew. It also suggests someone who had assimilated Greek culture and language' (*The Gospel of Mark* (Collegeville, Minn.: Liturgical Press, 2002), 233). On the story of the Syro-Phoenician woman, see D. A. Hagner, *Matthew 14–28* (Dallas: Word Books, 1995), 438–53; U. Luz, *Matthew 8–20* (Minneapolis: Fortress, 2001), 336–42; J. P. Meier, *A Marginal Jew: Rethinking the Historical Jesus*, ii (New York: Doubleday, 1994), 659–61, 674–6.

[2] Since this and the next chapter draw on the Gospels, I should make some points clear from the outset. (1) I use the scheme of *three stages* in the transmission of

This episode raises the questions: What did Jesus do and intend to do for 'others'? What did he teach about their salvation? Can we and how can we ground an outreach to 'the nations' already present in the ministry of Jesus?

SOME GENTILE INDIVIDUALS AND GROUPS

The Gospels record further episodes in which Jesus responded to the needs of non-Jews: both specific individuals and groups. In Capernaum a centurion, a non-Jewish military officer in command of 50 to 100 soldiers, appealed to Jesus for help when his son (*pais*, which could also be translated 'servant') fell desperately ill (Matt. 8: 5–13).[3]

---

testimony to Jesus' words and deeds: the initial stage in his earthly life when his disciples and others spoke about him, repeated to others his teaching, and began interpreting his identity and mission; the handing on, by word of mouth or in writing (including the use of 'notebooks'), of testimony about him after his death and resurrection; and the authorial work of the four evangelists later in the first century. (2) I agree that one can use a range of criteria when arguing that testimony to particular words or deeds derives substantially from the first stage: i.e. from Jesus himself. (3) When I draw on the Gospels, I will indicate whether I understand some passage to testify to what Jesus said or did at stage one, or whether the passage seems to illustrate rather what a particular evangelist at stage three (and/or the tradition behind him at stage two) understood about Jesus' identity or work. (4) I cannot stop every time to justify why with others I hold some saying or deed to have its historical origin in what Jesus said or did. (5) I welcome the case Richard Bauckham has developed in *Jesus and the Eyewitnesses: The Gospels as Eyewitness Testimony* (Grand Rapids, Mich.: Eerdmans, 2006): that the period between Jesus (stage one) and the final composition of the Gospels (stage three) was spanned by the continuing presence and testimony of those who had personally participated in the story of Jesus: namely, the original eyewitnesses (both the major ones like Peter, the Twelve, Mary Magdalene, and the beloved disciple, and minor ones like Bartimaeus and Simon of Cyrene).

[3] Since Roman troops were not yet stationed in Galilee, he probably belonged to the forces of Herod Antipas, who seemed to have 'employed foreigners in his service' (M. A. Chancey, *The Myth of a Gentile Galilee* (Cambridge: Cambridge University Press, 2002), 175–6). On the healing of the centurion's son, see D. A. Hagner, *Matthew 1–13* (Dallas: Word Books, 1993), 200–6; Luz, *Matthew 8–20*, 8–12; Meier, *A Marginal Jew*, ii. 718–27, 763–72. Impressed by the Roman military title 'centurion' and by the strategic importance of Capernaum, some commentators speculate that there 'must' have been a contingent of Roman soldiers stationed there, and that hence the centurion in question was Roman; see Hagner, *Matthew 1–13*, 203.

Apparently the centurion knew that, as a Jew, Jesus should not enter the house of a Gentile. But he was convinced that a word of command would be enough, since diseases obeyed Jesus just as soldiers obeyed their officers. Jesus was astonished at the way the centurion trusted his (Jesus') power to work the cure: 'Truly I tell you, in no one in Israel have I found such faith.' The faith of this Gentile put Israel to shame, in the sense that his faith went beyond anything Jesus had so far experienced in his ministry to Jews.

Before healing the centurion's son by a simple word of command, Jesus—at least in Matthew's account—used the image of God's eschatological banquet to warn what would happen at the end. Many 'outsiders' will enter the kingdom while many Israelites will be excluded: 'I tell you, many will come from east and west and will eat with Abraham and Isaac and Jacob in the kingdom of heaven, while the heirs of the kingdom will be thrown into the outer darkness.' This is a 'pointed threat rather than something irrevocable. It may well go back to Jesus.'[4] Thus the faith of the centurion, 'the first member of the gentile church',[5] signalled how the final gathering of the nations had already begun in the ministry of Jesus. Instead of streaming to Mount Zion (as Third Isaiah and other prophets had foretold), the Gentiles will find the goal of their pilgrimage in 'the kingdom of heaven'.

With the centurion, as with the Syro-Phoenician woman, Jesus healed someone at a distance. It is *only* in these two cases of Gentiles that the Gospels record such 'remote' healings.

Luke tells much the same story (Luke 7: 1–10) about a centurion's *doulos* or slave (but also called a *pais* (son or servant) in 7: 7).[6] The evangelist or his source includes a delegation of some 'elders' or leaders in the Jewish community who pleaded on behalf of the devout centurion and established his credentials: 'He loves our people, and it is he who built our synagogue for us.' In Luke's version Jesus praised highly the faith of this Gentile officer but did not promise the gathering of 'outsiders' at the final banquet (as in Matt. 8: 11). John's Gospel includes a similar story—about a 'royal

---

[4] Luz, *Matthew 8–20*, 9.   [5] Ibid., 11.
[6] See J. A. Fitzmyer, *The Gospel According to Luke I–IX* (New York: Doubleday, 1981), 647–54; J. Nolland, *Luke 1–9:20* (Dallas: Word Books, 1989), 312–19.

official' whose *son* was at the point of death (John 4: 46–54) and who 'believed' that Jesus' word would bring a cure. Despite some differences,[7] this healing story seems to be another version of what we read in Matthew and Luke. At all events it highlights the faith of a 'royal official', who in the Johannine tradition may have been a Gentile military officer.

Various exorcisms that formed a prominent part of the wonder-working activity of Jesus included one dramatic exorcism in favour of a demoniac who seems to have been non-Jewish (Mark 5: 1–20). Even if textual variants do not allow us to pinpoint the precise locality (Gerasa or Gadara), the area (the Decapolis) was Gentile and the non-Jewish identity of the possessed man 'is suggested by the presence of a herd of swine into which the demons flee'.[8] Jesus liberated this Gentile outcast from his evil condition and restored him to normal society.

Along with this exorcism and the healing of the Syro-Phoenician woman's daughter (Mark 7: 24–30), Mark includes two further miraculous deeds which Jesus performed in Gentile territory: the restoration of hearing and speech to a deaf-mute (Mark 7: 31–7) and the feeding of the 4,000 (Mark 8: 1–10). In Mark's narrative, crowds followed Jesus and/or joined him on his journey through the predominantly Gentile area of the Decapolis (Mark 7: 31). The deaf-mute, since he apparently belonged to that area, was presumably a Gentile. His cure, or at least the way Mark presents it, symbolized a new world being born—a world of plenitude and blessing 'springing into existence' through Jesus.[9] The crowds who followed Jesus were with him for three days and faced a long journey home. Jesus miraculously multiplied some loaves and fish to feed them (Mark 8: 1–10). Earlier Jesus had miraculously fed 5,000 fellow Jews (Mark 6: 36–44). Now in a separate episode in Mark's story, he provided an

---

[7] For instance, unlike the 'centurion' in Matthew and Luke who believed that Jesus could heal at a distance, the 'official' in John begs Jesus to 'come down' and heal his son. It is by the initiative of Jesus that the son is healed at a distance.

[8] Chancey, *The Myth of Gentile Galilee*, 178. A group of Hellenistic cities that lay east of Samaria and Galilee, the Decapolis contained predominantly Gentile communities; see ibid., 130–43. On the Gentile identity of the possessed man, see Joel Marcus, *Mark 1–8* (New York: Doubleday, 1999), 342, 347, and 353. See also Meier, *A Marginal Jew*, ii. 650–3, 664–7.

[9] See Marcus, *Mark 1–8*, 472–81, at 481; Meier, *A Marginal Jew*, ii. 711–14, 758–9.

abundance of food for a crowd who seem to have been Gentiles. At least in the scheme of the evangelist, whatever we decide about the intentions of Jesus himself, the second feeding substantially parallels the first, and shows Jesus providing an abundance of food for Gentiles, after having done so earlier for Jews.[10]

A healing story which includes an 'outsider', which is found only in Luke and bears the imprint of the evangelist's editorial work, is that of ten lepers being cleansed by Jesus (Luke 17: 11–19).[11] One of them, who unlike the other nine was not a Jew but a Samaritan, returned, 'praising God', 'prostrating himself' at Jesus' feet, and 'thanking him'. Jesus said to this man whom he called a 'stranger': 'your faith has made you well (saved you)'—words that he also used with two Jews, a woman cured of a long-standing haemorrhage (Mark 5: 34) and a blind beggar who received his sight (Mark 10: 52). In all three cases the verb conveys the idea of the divine power at work to rescue someone from an evil force. Spiritual, as well as merely physical, 'saving' or 'making well' was involved. The Samaritan 'saw' what his healing implied, came to faith, and received salvation. In this fuller way Jesus blessed a person who was doubly an outcast—as a leper and a 'foreigner'.

Samaria had come into existence when the kingdom of Israel was destroyed by the Assyrians in 721 BC. Sargon II deported the Israelites and replaced them with people from Babylon and elsewhere. The land was no longer called Israel but Samaria. The inhabitants were no longer called Israelites but Samaritans, a people whose worship of the Lord did not correspond to what was considered appropriate (2 Kgs. 17: 1–41). At the time of Jesus, Jews and Samaritans were not on speaking terms.[12] Hostile Samaritans would harass pilgrims going to keep a feast in Jerusalem (Luke 9: 51–6), since they considered a temple on Mount Gerizim and not on Mount Zion the primary place for worship (John 4: 20).[13]

[10] Marcus, *Mark 1–8*, 482–97. Some scholars argue that the two feedings are alternative versions of one and the same feeding miracle that the evangelist has incorporated in his text in two different places; see Meier, *A Marginal Jew*, ii. 950–66, 1022–38, at 956–8.

[11] See J. A. Fitzmyer, *The Gospel According to Luke X–XXIV* (New York: Doubleday, 1985), 1148–56; Meier, *A Marginal Jew*, ii. 701–6.

[12] In John's Gospel some Jews insult Jesus by alleging that he is a Samaritan and is possessed by a demon (John 8: 48).

[13] See Chancey, *The Myth of Gentile Galilee*, 153–4.

Luke and John, in particular, recall in different ways the openness Jesus showed to the Samaritans. A spectacular example was the parable that bears the name of 'the Good Samaritan'. A Jewish priest and a Levite (one of those designated to be lay-associates of the priests) fail to stop for a wounded traveller. It is a Samaritan, an outsider hardly expected to show much sympathy to Jews, who generously takes care of the wounded man (Luke 10: 29–37). John's Gospel pictures Jesus not as despising the Samaritans for being religious apostates but as ready to meet them (John 4: 4–42). Unlike other rabbis, Jesus did not avoid speaking in public with a woman and a Samaritan woman at that (John 4: 9, 27). By delicately encountering this woman who after running through five husbands was now living with another man, Jesus turned her into a witness to him. Through her testimony and their personal experience, many of the Samaritans came to express faith in Jesus as 'the Saviour of the world' (John 4: 42).[14] Whatever we decide about the historical status of this Samaritan interlude in the ministry of Jesus, it is of a piece with what Luke tells us of Jesus' outreach to the Samaritan leper and Jesus' picture of a Samaritan traveller as a role model for those ready to help people in terrible need.

BEYOND FRONTIERS?

Jesus' message of the kingdom reached beyond the frontiers of racial and religious separations. God's reign here and hereafter was for everyone. What we have seen above suggests that conclusion. Yet we may not forget that Jesus in many ways behaved like an observant Jew. Mark (along with the other Gospels) reports that shortly before the crucifixion Jesus came to Jerusalem to eat the Passover and keep the concurrent festival of Unleavened Bread (Mark 14: 12–16). John's Gospel recalls other times when Jesus went to Jerusalem to keep various Jewish feasts: for instance, the feast of the Tabernacles (John 7: 2–14).

---

[14] John Meier points out that this language of 'Saviour of the world' was 'very much at home in the Greco-Roman world' (*A Marginal Jew*, ii. 770).

Matthew's Gospel underlines the full fidelity of Jesus to the Jewish law and prophets (Matt. 5: 17–20).[15] When he healed a leper, Jesus told him to follow the provisions of the Jewish law (Lev. 13: 49): 'show yourself to the priest, and offer for your cleansing what Moses commanded' (Mark 1: 44). Jesus gave the same order when cleansing the ten lepers: 'go and show yourselves to the priests' (Luke 17: 14). In Jerusalem Jesus prayed in the Temple and venerated it as a special sign of the divine presence. His anger at the way this sacred place was being defiled by business dealings led him to 'cleanse' the Temple by driving out the dealers who had turned its precincts into a market-place (Mark 11: 15–17; John 2: 13–17). While remembered as having abolished the Jewish food laws by declaring all food ritually 'clean' (Mark 7: 14–23), Jesus never challenged the law of circumcision.[16] Nor did he aim at abolishing the Sabbath, even if he came under attack for violating laws concerning the observance of the Sabbath (e.g. Mark 2: 23–8; 3: 1–6).

The story of the Syro-Phoenician woman (Mark 7: 24–30) stands apart as being the *only example* in all four Gospels of an exorcism that takes place at a distance and the only example of someone who wins an argument with Jesus. But the episode also stands apart for its harsh, insulting language addressed to a sincere and suffering peti-tioner. It 'portrays a Jesus who is unusually sensitive to his Jewish countrymen's claim to salvation-historical privilege and unusually rude about the position of Gentiles: the Jews are God's children, and their needs come first; compared to them, non-Jews are just dogs'.[17] So where should we turn to establish that Jesus' preaching of the kingdom was not limited by the religious and racial frontiers hon-oured by devout Jews of his time but went beyond them to foreigners?

There is a hint of this broader outlook when apparently he fol-lowed Second Isaiah (56: 7) by declaring the Temple in Jerusalem to

---

[15] See Hagner, *Matthew 1–13*, 102–10.

[16] The letters of Paul and the Book of Acts show how valuable some saying against the obligation of circumcision coming from Jesus would have been for those con-cerned with admitting Gentiles into the Church. But they would not in that way 'massage' the traditions coming from Jesus' ministry and make them conform to the needs of the Gentile mission. On the contrary, they maintained the embarrassing saying from Jesus that we saw above: he was 'sent only to the lost sheep of the house of Israel'.

[17] Marcus, *Mark 1–8*, 470.

be 'a house of prayer' not just for Jews but 'for all nations' (Mark 11: 17). (We will come back to this text in the next chapter.) In responding to our question, some theologians could be tempted to follow generations of NT scholars who have perpetuated the myth that Galilee at the time of Jesus was not overwhelmingly Jewish but was inhabited largely by Gentile foreigners. In such a picture, when Jesus visited and preached in various Galilean communities, his audiences would have been partly or even in large part non-Jewish. But this picture exists 'despite the evidence, not because of it'. The 'image of Galilee that results from an integration of information provided by Josephus and the Gospels with the discoveries of modern excavations is entirely different. The vast majority of first-century CE [Common Era] Galileans were Jews.' Gentiles were 'a small minority'. Galilee was Jewish and, unlike surrounding territories, did not have numerous Gentile inhabitants.[18]

Some will inevitably bring up two counter-arguments: a passage from Matthew that quotes Second Isaiah about 'Galilee of the Gentiles' (Matt. 4: 15–16) and Mark's picture of a great crowd gathered to hear Jesus that came from Galilee, 'Judea, Jerusalem, Idumea, beyond the Jordan, and *the region around Tyre and Sidon*' (Mark 3: 7–8). Chancey musters the evidence to prove that the homeland of Jesus was called 'Galilee'. The 'belief that it was frequently called "Galilee of the Gentiles" in the first century' is a 'scholarly and popular misconception'. The phrase 'Galilee of the Gentiles', appearing only once in a first-century source (Matthew's Gospel), and 'that a quotation of an eighth-century' BC source, 'tells us nothing about the region's population in the Roman period'.[19] The phrase tells us about Matthew's recognition of God's outreach to the nations and not about Galilee in the first century. Apropos of the passage from Mark concerned with a large and diverse crowd gathering from all parts of Palestine and even beyond to hear Jesus, these verses reflect the growing popularity of Jesus. Yet Chancey rightly remarks: 'whether Mark has taken historically accurate traditions and adapted them to his own use or has created the story to illustrate his own themes is debatable. In either case, he *does not specify that the crowds are non-Jewish*; he only notes

---

[18] Chancey, *The Myth of a Gentile Galilee*, 167.
[19] Ibid., 170–4.

their places of origin.'[20] Mark has made one theme clear: the spreading impact of Jesus, who drew people from all points of the compass. Even though the 'region around Tyre and Sidon' was inhabited mainly by Gentiles, the emphasis is simply on the personal magnetism of Jesus—with perhaps a hint of 'the post-Easter expansion of the news about Jesus into Gentile areas'.[21] In general, the conclusion Chancey reaches seems justified: 'The evidence, both literary and archaeological, corroborates the Gospels' depictions of Jesus as a Jew preaching to and working primarily among other Jews.'[22]

A MESSAGE FOR EVERYONE

It is the content of Jesus' preaching that offers the clearest grounds for demonstrating his outreach to everyone. By and large he proclaimed the kingdom of God only to Jews, but his message was for everyone. Even if at times his message was addressed to a Jewish audience precisely as Jewish (e.g. Mark 12: 1–12), normally his words were directed to men and women precisely as men and women. It was that universal appeal which conveyed a sense that the divine kingdom and its claims knew no frontiers. Let us see some examples.

(1) First, in a controversy with certain Pharisees over divorce (Mark 10: 1–12), Jesus dismissed as secondary and a concession to the people's sinfulness the Mosaic legislation that allowed divorce. He expressed his ideal for marriage and his opposition to divorce in the light of the creation of humankind (Gen. 1: 29; 2: 24): 'the original will of God in creating man and woman was that they should constitute "one flesh" in an indissoluble union'. Jesus envisaged a 'restored creation in which unity and mutuality in marriage mirror God's original plan'.[23] That, of course, was to develop teaching which concerned not merely Jews but all human beings whoever they were.

---

[20] Ibid., 178.
[21] Marcus, *Mark 1–8*, 260.
[22] Chancey, *The Myth of a Gentile Galilee*, 182.
[23] Donahue and Harrington, *The Gospel of Mark*, 292–9, at 294 and 298.

(2) Second, Jesus set about founding a new family or new final community. Looking around at a group sitting near him, he solemnly declared: 'Whoever does the will of God is my brother and sister and mother' (Mark 3: 35). He did not specify as candidates for his new family 'all those Jews who do the will of God'. Any man or woman who did what God wanted to be done qualified for admission to this new community and became, whether he or she knew it or not, truly related to Jesus, a 'family member in the kingdom' of God.[24] They did not have to come from those who had accepted an explicit call to follow Jesus as disciples, as though he had said: 'Whoever among my disciples does the will of God is my brother and sister and mother.'

Other sayings that also took the form of 'whoever' did not make Jewishness a condition for this familial relationship. Jesus was recalled as settling a dispute about 'greatness' by remarking: 'whoever wants to be first must be last of all and servant of all'. Then, taking a little child in his arms, he said: 'Whoever welcomes one such child in my name welcomes me, and whoever welcomes me welcomes not me but the one who sent me' (Mark 9: 34–7). A startling example of these 'whoever' statements comes from a report of Jesus answering an objection to an unnamed exorcist. The man cast out demons in the name of Jesus, but did not belong to the circle of disciples who followed him. Jesus said: 'do not stop him, for no one who does a deed of power in my name will be able soon afterwards to speak evil of me. Whoever is not against me is for me' (Mark 9: 38–9). Anyone who experienced the power of Jesus, even someone who did not belong to the circle of the disciples, would speak well of him. Jesus looked beyond the particular case of an 'outside' exorcist to make this generalization.

In the case of the little child, Jesus did not specify any Jewishness. He did not say: 'if any Jews welcome one such Jewish child in my name, they welcome me'. The 'whoever' left matters quite open and could be applied anywhere to human beings who welcome and care for little children. In both the saying about little children and that about the unnamed exorcist, Jesus talked about things done explicitly

---

[24] Hagner, *Matthew 1–13*, 358.

in his 'name'. That condition was absent in the statement about doing the will of God. Here things were left totally open and could be applied to anyone, even to those who had never even heard of Jesus' name. This was also the case in the saying about being servant of all. It was left totally open and applied anywhere to anyone. Here Jesus challenged assumptions about rank and status that were/are to found in many, if not all, cultures. Once again no explicit condition was attached, as if Jesus had spoken of being 'servant of all' in his name. The teaching was for all people of any place concerned with issues of status in a world which, whether they knew it or not, was being reshaped by the presence of God's kingdom.

Beyond question, these 'whoever' statements are embedded in the differing contexts in which the Gospel writers present Jesus' proclamation of the kingdom to his Jewish audience. Yet the statements have a generalized form that lifts them above and beyond their specific setting to apply generally to people anywhere.

(3) Third, the *parables* formed a major element when Jesus preached the kingdom.[25] Unquestionably, Jesus addressed them to Jewish audiences. He also gave some of the parables a Jewish spin (e.g. that of the Pharisee and the Tax Collector in Luke 18: 10–14) and a setting in Palestine such as the road from Jerusalem to Jericho (the Parable of the Good Samaritan in Luke 10: 30–7). Yet characteristically the parables pictured situations repeated in indefinitely many places and times: a woman searching for a lost coin (Luke 15: 8–10) or a woman mixing yeast in the flour she is kneading for the oven (Matt. 13: 33). For nearly two thousand years readers around the world have drawn inspiration from the parables. Everywhere and for anyone they can generate insights about God and the reign of God. They have displayed a universal power that takes them far beyond Palestine, the original setting in which Jesus first preached them.They were and are stories told for everyone, not just for insiders.

---

[25] See J. D. Crossan, 'Parable', *ABD* v. 146–52; J. R. Donahue, 'The Parables of Jesus', in R. E. Brown, J. A. Fitzmyer, and R. E. Murphy (eds.), *The New Jerome Biblical Commentary* (London: Geoffrey Chapman, 1989), 1364–9; R. Etchells, *A Reading of the Parables* (London: Darton, Longman & Todd, 1998); L. Houlden, 'Jesus, Parables of', in L. Houlden (ed.), *Jesus: The Complete Guide* (London: Continuum, 2003), 430–3.

In his parables Jesus proved himself to be 'the' religious story-teller of all time. Much more than mere picturesque illustrations, his parables continue to question readers/hearers anywhere, to challenge their normal standards and securities, and to invite them to walk in radically different ways. His parables have revealed a new world and a new way of living for everybody—not merely for his fellow Jews. They did so and continue to do so through language and pictures that seem quite familiar and very ordinary, even if at times Jesus gave his story line unusual and even extraordinary twists.

Jesus tells us of two brothers, the younger one who runs away and the elder one who stays at home. He introduces day-labourers who work in vineyards and managers of large estates. He brings in women searching for lost property or preparing dough for baking. His stories present a lazy judge, a merchant hunting for precious jewels, a traveller robbed and left for dead, a rich man who does nothing for sick and hungry people on the street outside his door, and servants waiting up at night for their master to return. The parables continue to take people everywhere into the mind and heart of Jesus. The parables let them glimpse his vision of the world around him, a world in which the final reign of God is dawning. These stories by Jesus answer the universal questions: What is God like? How is God dealing with us? What does God expect from us? Let us see one classic example to illustrate the depth of parables in their universal appeal.

The Parable of the Prodigal Son, which could be better called that of the Merciful Father, vividly pictures a parent who is incredibly generous and loving toward two sons (Luke 15: 11–32).[26] This longest and loveliest of Jesus' parables opens up a vision of God's astoundingly merciful love towards sinful men and women. God is utterly glad to find and welcome home those who have gone astray and even become morally and religiously lost. The Parable of the Prodigal Son is the fullest answer Jesus offered to the question human beings raise at least sometimes in their lives: What is God like? Without using either the noun or the verb 'love', this parable portrays

---

[26] See Fitzmyer, *The Gospel According to Luke X–XXIV*, 1082–94; J. Nolland, *Luke 9:21–18:34* (Dallas: Word Books, 1993), 777–91; G. O'Collins, *Following the Way* (London: HarperCollins, 1999), 3–28.

God's love and its essential characteristics: forgiving, welcoming, life-giving, and the trigger of real and lasting joy. To be sure, there are Jewish touches in the parable: above all, the religious disgrace involved when the prodigal son begins working with unclean animals, the pigs, and so publicly abandons his commitment to the Mosaic law. Nevertheless, any Jewishness is incidental; the main thrust of the parable goes beyond any ethnic and religious frontiers to answer the universal questions: Who is God? And to whom does God show mercy?

When addressing these and other questions, Jesus significantly did not appeal much to the OT scriptures and to the history of the chosen people. He did appeal to 'the God of Abraham, Isaac, and Jacob' (Mark 12: 26), but never—at least explicitly—to God as the One who delivered his people from slavery in Egypt. He spoke of God not as the God of the exodus but as the loving Father (*Abba*) who constantly cares for all his creatures (Matt. 6: 25–34) and blesses with his rain and sunshine all human beings, even the wicked and the unjust (Matt. 5: 43–8). In filling out the identity and characteristics of 'Our Father' with whom the Lord's Prayer begins (Matt. 6: 9–13; Luke 11: 2–4), Jesus drew on wide experiences of all people rather than on the specific Jewish experience of God in their particular history of salvation.

(4) Fourth, we might cite other areas of Jesus' teaching which illustrate how it was expressed in ways that reached out to everyone: for instance, the beatitudes and the Lord's Prayer.[27] On the one hand, the language (e.g. the 'poor' of YHWH and God's name being 'hallowed') enjoy a rich OT background, as John Meier shows abundantly. Yet, on the other hand, this language speaks to everyone: for example, 'blessed are the peacemakers' and 'thy will be done'. Both here and in the other examples I have quoted above, major themes in the teaching of Jesus touched all human beings and not merely the Jewish audience to which he spoke. It is not plausible to claim that, when he taught, he never intended to reach beyond the religious

---

[27] For commentary and rich bibliography on the beatitudes and the Lord's Prayer, see Meier, *A Marginal Jew*, ii. 317–36, 377–89 (beatitudes), 291–302, 353–66 (Lord's Prayer).

and ethnic frontiers of his particular audience and to deliver a
message to others.

THE LOVE COMMAND

When questioned about 'the first commandment', Jesus responded
from within the Jewish tradition by first quoting the *Shema* ('Hear,
O Israel') on the love of God (Deut. 6: 4–5) and then adding another
OT text on the love of neighbour (Lev. 19: 18): 'Hear, O Israel: the
Lord our God, the Lord is one; you shall love the Lord your God with
all your heart, and with all your soul, and with all your mind, and
with all your strength. The second is this, You shall love your
neighbour as yourself' (Mark 12: 28–34).[28] In the context of the
Shema, faith in YHWH as 'the one and only God' provides the
motive for loving this God with total love and an undivided dedica-
tion which holds nothing back—that is, with all one's being ('heart',
'soul', 'mind', and 'strength'). Deuteronomy repeatedly introduces
the wider background and basis for this commitment: the story of
God's saving acts in delivering the people from Egypt and bringing
them to the promised land (e.g. Deut. 6: 20–5; 26: 5–10).

Jesus innovated in two ways: first, by combining the two classic OT
texts on love of God and love of neighbour, respectively. He distinguished but would not separate the vertical relationship to God and
the horizontal relationship to neighbour. Together they form one
commitment of love that transcends all the other commandments in
importance, summarizes the key values of the Jewish Torah, and
provides a basic framework for understanding and applying the law
of God.

The second innovation introduced by Jesus was to go beyond
defining 'neighbour' narrowly as one's kin and one's people. In
Leviticus 19: 18 'neighbour' meant one's fellow Israelite; a few verses
later 'neighbour' was slightly extended to include 'resident aliens'

---

[28] See Donahue and Harrington, *The Gospel of Mark*, 354–8; Fitzmyer, *The Gospel
According to Luke X–XXIV*, 876–82; U. Luz, *Matthew 21–28* (Minneapolis: Fortress,
2005), 75–87.

(Lev. 19: 33–4; see Job 31: 32 on hospitality to strangers). Jesus, however, defined 'neighbour' in a way that went beyond family and ethnic relationships and contacts with resident aliens. He spoke out on the need to love even one's enemies, whoever they were (Luke 6: 27–35). When Luke records the teaching of Jesus on love for God and neighbour, he at once has Jesus tell the story of the Good Samaritan in answer to the question: 'And who is my neighbour?' (Luke 10: 29). Even if this parable may not have belonged originally in that setting, it goes back to Jesus and lets us glimpse his universal application of neighbourly love. In this story the hero is neither the Jewish priest nor the levite but a despised and even hated outsider, a Samaritan. This compassionate person is held up as an example for everyone, a practical model for human conduct when faced with someone who is distressed and afflicted and to whom we should 'show pity and kindness, even beyond the bounds of one's own ethnic or religious group'.[29]

This teaching is also inculcated by a scene which Matthew draws from his special source: the great judgement scene in which 'all the nations' and, seemingly, every individual will appear before 'the Son of Man' (Matt. 25: 31–46).[30] He will bring the final blessings of the kingdom in all its fullness for the righteous, and will pronounce condemnation for the wicked. The two groups will be, respectively, approved for their deeds of mercy towards Jesus himself ('I was hungry and you gave me to eat') and faulted for their lack of loving deeds towards him ('I was hungry and you gave me no food'). Jesus lists six needs (being hungry, thirsty, a stranger, naked, sick, and in prison), which he repeats four times in the text, with a corresponding list of remedies ('I was a stranger and you welcomed me'). Yet the list is open-ended, represents needs of all kinds, and can be expanded (e.g. 'I was ignorant and you taught me'; 'I was dying and you gave me blood'). Jesus mentions various situations when, in a hidden way, he was in need and when, without recognizing him, the righteous met that need.

In the perspective of Jesus, those who were in desperate need belonged to him; he identified himself with them; they were members

[29] Fitzmyer, *The Gospel According to Luke X–XXIV*, 884.
[30] Hagner, *Matthew 14–28*, 737–47; Luz, *Matthew 21–28*, 263–84.

of his family. One's relationship to other people—above all, those in serious need—could not and cannot be divorced from one's relationship to Jesus himself. The scene of final judgement elaborated and universalized what Jesus said elsewhere about identifying himself with his disciples, with little children, and with others (Matt. 10: 40–2; 18: 5–6).

The passage leaves us with a question: How could all the people of the world be fairly judged by standards which they may never have heard of? If they had all known Jesus, acknowledged his identity as Son of God, and recognized that he took deeds of mercy towards the needy as done to himself, the reward and punishment of every individual at the final judgement would seem justified. But even if the disciples of Jesus were to have proclaimed rapidly 'the good news of the kingdom' literally 'throughout the world' and so brought their 'testimony to all the nations' (Matt. 24: 14), this missionary outreach would have taken some time. What of those who died in the mean-time without having heard the proclamation? Or those who, with the best will in the world, remained and remain unconvinced by this proclamation? Would the norms of the last judgement scene be fairly applied to all of them, as the words of Jesus imply? Yes, the standards were and are universal. All will be judged on the basis of their works of charity towards the needy.

Here it is worth recalling that the 'catalogue of charitable works' converges with 'statements from other religions. There is nothing specifically Christian about this list; it appears in similar language in other religions', and—one must add—in the OT and further Jewish sources.[31] In Jesus' picture of the judgement scene, those to be judged—that is, all human beings without exception—did not have to know that they were dealing with Jesus when exercising practical love towards the needy or failing to do so. In that sense the practice of love towards suffering men and women can fairly be *the* norm of universal judgement.

A further puzzle about the judgement scene arises from what Jesus says to the righteous: 'Just as you did it [some work of mercy] to one of these my lowliest brothers, you did it to me' (Matt. 25: 40; see 25: 45). Some scholars understand 'these my brothers' to be the needy

---

[31] See Luz, *Matthew 21–28*, 269–70, 266 n. 30, 278 n. 137.

disciples of Jesus—in particular, itinerant Christian missionaries. Elsewhere in Matthew's Gospel when the family of Jesus arrives to speak with him, Jesus points to his disciples and calls them 'my brothers' and 'my brother and sister and mother' (Matt. 12: 49–50). Nevertheless, what he says in Matthew 25: 31–46 occurs in a different context, the final judgement at which 'all the nations' will be present. In this context Jesus speaks of his 'brothers' (and sisters) as all those who need help, whoever they are and wherever they are—even one's enemies who are in any case to be loved (Matt. 5: 43–4). The language of brothers and sisters applies far beyond the small group of Jesus' disciples who were to go on mission to all the non-Jews, to 'all the nations'.

THE FINAL BANQUET

Matthew's scene of the last judgement (stage three) seems to go back through his special source (stage two) to the preaching of Jesus himself (stage one). It portrays the righteous as 'inheriting the kingdom' (Matt. 25: 34) and 'going away into eternal life' (Matt. 25: 34) but not as sitting at a final banquet. During his ministry Jesus not only attended numerous banquets (e.g. Mark 2: 15–17; Matt. 11: 18–19; Luke 7: 36–50; 14: 1–15; 19: 1–10), but also used such meals with his fellow Jews as a vehicle for his ministry. The table fellowship he celebrated with sinners conveyed to them the divine forgiveness (Luke 15: 1–2).

Banquets in great households, including wedding banquets (Matt. 25: 1–13),[32] caught the imagination of Jesus and provided material to express the final banquet to come—a banquet at which righteous people from 'the nations' would sit at table with the patriarchs of Israel (Matt. 8: 11–12). Through such an image Jesus conveyed his desire to create a new people who would include Jews and non-Jews. In picturing the final banquet as a feast 'for all peoples', Jesus

[32] Jesus used the imagery of a bridegroom and his wedding guests (or perhaps the groom's attendants) to characterize his ministry as a time of joyful fulfilment and celebration like wedding festivities. His presence made it just that (Mark 2: 19; see John 3: 29).

probably drew as well from the passage we recalled in the last chapter: 'the Lord of hosts will make for all peoples a feast of rich food' (Isa. 25: 6–10, at v. 6). As Luz points out, in Jewish tradition, the image of a banquet was already 'closely connected with the coming age'.[33]

Jesus proposed the Parable of the Great Dinner and of those who after accepting an invitation—surprisingly—made last-minute excuses for not coming. The host reacted by first sending a slave to bring in from the streets of the town some poor, crippled, blind, and lame people. The slave was sent out a second time to bring others from the roads and footpaths near the town and so fill up the house for the great dinner (Luke 14: 15–24). In this parable Jesus challenged those in his Jewish audience who considered themselves the elect and confidently 'took it for granted' that they would 'be present at the great eschatological banquet'.[34] By refusing to accept the message of Jesus, they excluded themselves 'from the joy of that festive meal, in which Abraham, Isaac, Jacob, and all the prophets will share'.[35] The parable related primarily to the actual moment of Jesus' ministry to his fellow Jews, the moment that offered them the chance to accept firmly and definitively an invitation to the messianic banquet. That ministry was also initiating the final kingdom, which would embrace the Gentiles. The parable hinted at the successive calls, first to Jews and then to Gentiles, by distinguishing betweeen the group invited off the streets of the town and the second group who came from roads and footpaths outside the town.

Matthew adapts the original form of this parable and presents a wedding banquet staged by a king for his son (Matt. 22: 2–14).[36] Matthew introduces, among other things, an invitation that goes out to everyone, 'good' and 'bad' alike, and a 'wedding robe' that the guests were expected to wear (22: 9–13). The invitation to all people does not exempt them from living righteously. To emphasize this theme, Matthew adds a saying of Jesus that apparently had no fixed context in the tradition: 'many are called, but few are chosen'—a Semitic way of saying that all (Jew and Gentile alike) are called, but not all will belong to the elect. The Book of Revelation also takes up

[33] Luz, *Matthew 21–28*, 50.
[34] See Nolland, *Luke 9:21–18:34*, 752–9, at 752.
[35] Fitzmyer, *The Gospel According to Luke X–XXIV*, 1048–59, at 1053.
[36] See Hagner, *Matthew 14–28*, 624–32.

the image of a final, wedding feast, 'the marriage supper of the Lamb', at which the dress will be 'fine linen', understood as 'the righteous deeds of the saints' (Rev. 19: 7–9). Matthew, while signalling the mission to the whole world, also wants to insist that to be called to the Christian community does not automatically mean to be saved. 'Inside the Church', one might say, 'there is not necessarily salvation.'

THE EVANGELISTS

The example of the great dinner (Luke) or the wedding feast (Matthew) illustrates the persistent difficulty of distinguishing between the theological programme of the evangelist (stage three) and/or their sources (stage two) and the historical record derived from the activity of Jesus (stage one). Here we might recall also the episode (discussed at the start of this chapter) involving the centurion in Capernaum. This led Matthew to insert into his account a free-floating saying from Jesus. Originally Jesus may have intended to refer only to the final gathering of scattered Jews (Luke 13: 28–9). In Matthew's text the saying is applied to Gentiles coming from the four corners of the earth to share in the final banquet with the long-dead patriarchs of Israel (Matt. 8: 11–12).[37]

Things Jesus did (e.g. the healing of the Syro-Phoenician's daughter) and said (e.g. the Parable of the Good Samaritan and his teaching on marriage) prefigured the Church's coming mission and message to the Gentiles. The Evangelists and other early Christians were justified in understanding their mission to Jews *and Gentiles* as continuing and expanding what Jesus had begun during his earthly ministry.

Matthew pictures Jesus reaching out to 'others' right from his birth. Admittedly, an 'angel of the Lord' instructs Joseph to give the name of 'Jesus' to the child to be born of Mary and explains the meaning of the name with reference to the *Jewish people*: 'he will save

---

[37] See Meier, *A Marginal Jew*, ii. 309–17, 371–7; Nolland, *Luke 9:21–18:34*, 735. Meier argues that Jesus did originally refer to the coming of the Gentiles to share in the final kingdom; the particular application of the saying comes from Matthew or the tradition on which he drew.

his people from their sins'. He is to be the Messiah of Israel, the OT
people of God. Matthew has already made that clear through the
genealogy of Jesus (Matt. 1: 1–17), and will reiterate the point by
having Jesus called 'the king of the Jews' (Matt. 2: 2). Nevertheless,
after the birth of Jesus some Gentiles, the 'Magi' or wise men, arrive
at once to pay him homage and leave their gifts of gold, frankincense,
and myrrh (Matt. 1: 21; 2: 1–12). Under the divine guidance provided by a star, these Gentiles come to worship the Messiah of
Israel—right at the start of his human history. In his version of a
discourse on the end of the age, the evangelist has Jesus say: 'this
good news of the kingdom will be proclaimed throughout the world,
as a testimony to all the nations; and then the end will come' (Matt.
24: 14; see Mark 13: 10). Whether or not the earthly Jesus ever
enunciated so clearly the mission to the Gentiles, Matthew obviously
understood the ministry of Jesus to lead (through the crucifixion and
resurrection) to a period when the followers of Jesus would bring to
'all the nations' their witness to him, and do so during times of great
suffering both within the community of those followers and in the
wider world (Matt. 24: 5–14).

In his version of the Parable of the Great Dinner, Luke may have
adapted its original form to add a separate sending of the servant
'into the streets and lanes of the town' and then onto 'the roads and
footpaths' (outside the town). The implication was clear: first of all,
Jesus successfully invited the outcasts of 'the town' (Jewish people of
'lower' religious standing), and then Gentile 'outsiders' were also
brought in to share in 'the banquet'. Later, in his second work,
Luke would develop this theme more explicitly in the aftermath of
Pentecost. The word of God would be addressed to Jews and Gentiles
right to the ends of the earth (e.g. Acts 13: 46).[38]

Apart from the meeting with the Samaritans (John 4: 4–42), John's
Gospel pictures Jesus as active among his own people and disengaged
from 'outsiders'. He does not record, for instance, such healing stories
(found in the Synoptic Gospels) as that of the Syro-Phoenician's
daughter (Mark and Matthew) or that of the son/servant of a Gentile
centurion (Matthew and Luke). Nevertheless, in the Fourth Gospel
Jesus frequently speaks a language that goes beyond his immediate

---

[38] See Fitzmyer, *The Gospel According to Luke X–XXIV*, 1053.

Jewish context and that continues to communicate universally: for instance, in such 'I am' statements as 'I am the Bread of Life' (John 6: 35) and 'I am the Light of the world' (John 9: 5). Towards the end of the Gospel, he reaches out to the Gentiles. When, like a grain of wheat, he goes down into the earth, his death will yield a rich harvest (John 12: 24). In the context of some Greeks wanting 'to see' Jesus (John 12: 20–2), this remark points to the gathering in of the Gentiles. A few verses later Jesus speaks of being lifted up on the throne of the cross and so drawing all people to himself (John 12: 32–3). The evangelist himself understood the death of Jesus to be both his dying for the Jewish people and his 'gathering into one' the children of God scattered through the world (John 11: 52).

What can we say about the intentions of Jesus himself when faced with death? Can we establish some data from stage one that allow us to reach conclusions about the redemptive intentions of Jesus vis-à-vis the Gentiles as well as the Jews?

8

Dying and Rising for All?

The main thrust of the last chapter was to establish some conclusions about the way Jesus understood his mission to involve not only Jews but also Gentiles. What of the passion, death, and resurrection with which his ministry ended? Are there any indications that he anticipated and interpreted his death in advance? Did he, for instance, suggest that his violent end would bring God's final reign and prove salvific for the whole human race?[1]

One can put the issue in terms of a possible continuity between the pre-Easter situation and the post-Easter situation. Is there any (even partial) continuity between the early Christian interpretation of Jesus' death and resurrection and what he himself intended when death closed in on him? St Paul, for example, wrote of God reconciling to himself the whole world through that death and resurrection (2 Cor. 5: 19). Does such a claim reach back, in some sense, to the earthly or pre-Easter Jesus himself?

In trying to determine Jesus' intentions as death loomed up, we should not wrongly suppose that these intentions—or rather what we can establish about them—provide the *only* criterion for acknowledging that Jesus died to save sinful human beings and for deciding how that death on behalf of others worked or works. There could have been and can be more meaning and efficacy in his death than he fully and clearly realized when he accepted that death. Nevertheless, we normally expect the value of important human actions to stem at least partly from the conscious intentions of the agent in question.

---

[1] For a well documented account of how Jesus seems to have understood his death, see S. McKnight, *Jesus and His Death* (Waco, Tex.: Baylor University Press, 2005).

ANTICIPATING A VIOLENT DEATH

At some point Jesus began to anticipate and accept his violent death. At least six points can be cited to establish this conclusion.

(1) He referred to himself as 'the bridegroom' whose presence gave joy to the wedding guests (or to the groom's close attendants) but who would be 'taken away' from them. This portrayal of himself as a tragic bridegroom alluded to his violent death (Mark 2: 18–20).[2] This reference is brief and unobtrusive but is filled out by sayings of Jesus that involve the fate of prophets and of the 'Son of Man'.

(2) Jesus saw his ministry standing, at least partially, in continuity with the prophets, right down to John, his prophetic precursor from whom he received baptism.[3] In his own prophetic role Jesus seemingly had a premonition that he would inevitably die a martyr's death and apparently expected that to happen in Jerusalem, the 'city that murders prophets and stones those sent' to it (Luke 13: 33–4; see 11: 47, 49–51).[4] There was a tragic tradition about various messengers of God being persecuted and killed in Jerusalem.[5] Apparently Jesus sensed that he would share the fate of those already done away with in that city. Not only past history but also contemporary events had their lesson to teach. The violent death of John, someone whose prophetic activity prepared the way for the ministry of Jesus himself, showed how perilous such radical religious activity was in the Palestine of that time. Jesus would have been remarkably naive not to have seen the danger.

(3) In this connection we should cite the Parable of the Vineyard and the Tenants (Mark 12: 1–12 parr.), which seems to have come

---

[2] See J. Marcus, *Mark 1–8* (New York: Doubleday, 1999), 232–9.

[3] On the historicity of Jesus' baptism by John, see J. P. Meier, *A Marginal Jew: Rethinking the Historical Jesus*, ii (New York: Doubleday, 1994), 100–4.

[4] See J. A. Fitzmyer, *The Gospel According to Luke X–XXIV* (New York: Doubleday, 1985), 941–53, 1027–38); D. A. Hagner, *Matthew 14–28* (Dallas: Word Books, 1995), 678–81; U. Luz, *Matthew 21–28* (Minneapolis: Fortress Press, 2005), 150–7; J. Nolland, *Luke 9:21–18:34* (Dallas: Word Books, 1993), 659–72, 737–44.

[5] For details see Fitzmyer, *The Gospel According to Luke X–XXIV*, 1032.

from a discourse of Jesus in controversy with some religious leaders.[6] It is the only parable in which Jesus speaks clearly about his own mission. The owner (who evidently symbolizes God) leases to some tenant farmers a vineyard (which, in the light of Isaiah 5: 1–7, inevitably evokes Israel), and eventually sends a series of servants to collect his share in the produce. But the tenants refuse to honour the claims of the owner; they mistreat his agents and even kill some of them. Finally, the owner sends his son, a fully accredited representa-tive, but the tenants murder him, throw his corpse out of the vineyard, and plan to seize the property for themselves. The original parable probably ended with a question and a response: 'What then will the owner of the vineyard do? He will come and destroy the tenants and give the vineyard to others.' Many scholars argue that the quotation from Psalm 118 about the 'rejected stone' becoming the 'cornerstone' was added in stage two of the tradition. Many also hold that the qualification of the 'son' as 'beloved' was likewise added in stage two. Some commentators maintain that Jesus originally ended his parable with the question: 'What then will the owner of the vineyard do?' Yet it has been argued convincingly that the transfer of the vineyard to others came from Jesus (at stage one).

What may we draw from the parable for this chapter? The 'servants' stood for the prophets who, on God's behalf, had over the centuries confronted the religious and political leaders of Israel. Jesus may have intended to include John the Baptist among these biblical figures. He thought of himself as 'the son' through whom 'the owner of the vineyard' made a final bid to 'the tenant farmers', the leaders of Israel. But a violent death overtook 'the son'—a clear pointer to the fate that Jesus anticipated for himself. Who were the 'others' to whom the property was to be given (and not merely leased)? Seemingly they were the Jewish disciples of Jesus and the Gentiles, who together would form the reconstituted Israel. Yet the identity of the 'benefici-aries' was not clarified, nor did any resurrection from the dead figure as the aftermath of the violent death endured by 'the son'. The major conclusions we draw should be limited to four. First, Jesus

---

[6] For details see J. R. Donahue and D. J. Harrington, *The Gospel of Mark* (College-ville, Minn.: Liturgical Press, 2002), 337–43; Fitzmyer, *The Gospel According to Luke X–XXIV*, 1276–88; Hagner, *Matthew 14–28*, 615–24; Luz, *Matthew 21–28*, 34–44; Nolland, *Luke 9:21–18:34*, 945–55.

understood himself to be in person the climax of God's dealings with the chosen people. Second, he found himself in dangerous controversy with some of the religious leaders of Israel. Third, the outcome of that unflinching conflict would be his own violent death, the nature of which was not specified. Fourth, there would be a dramatic change in God's relationship with his 'vineyard', Israel.

(4) Clearly opposition had built up against Jesus before he went to Jerusalem for his final Passover. His radical mission had already provoked various charges: of violating the Sabbath, working wonders through diabolic power, rejecting the purity regulations, acting as a false prophet, and expressing blasphemous pretensions about such matters as the forgiveness of sins. Then his protest in cleansing the Temple, if it did happen at the end of the ministry (Mark 11: 1–19 parr.) and not at the beginning (John 2: 13–25), was a final, unflinching challenge to the religious authorities in the city and to the power they exercised through the Temple. Let us examine that climactic challenge.

(5) John Donahue and Daniel Harrington observe that the prophetic actions of Jesus in entering Jerusalem (Mark 11: 1–11) and cleansing the Temple (Mark 11: 15–19) 'go a long way toward explaining why the Jewish and Roman leaders acted so quickly to arrest and execute Jesus'.[7] Jesus must have been aware of that danger. Let us see the details. According to John's Gospel, Jesus went up to Jerusalem at least three times during his ministry (2: 13; 5: 1; 12: 12). On the first occasion he cleansed the Temple and spoke of the Temple being destroyed and restored (John 2: 13–22). Since the cleansing is separately attested by the Synoptic tradition (Mark, followed by Matthew and Luke) and the Johannine tradition, its historical status appears to be established satisfactorily. The dating is another issue, and I am inclined to follow Mark by locating the cleansing

---

[7] Donahue and Harrington, *The Gospel of Mark*, 331. On the 'royal' entry of Jesus into Jerusalem and his cleansing of the Temple, see ibid., 320–6 (entry) and 326–33 (cleansing); Fitzmyer, *The Gospel According to Luke X–XXIV*, 1241–53 (entry) and 1261–8 (cleansing); Hagner, *Matthew 14–28*, 589–97 (entry) and 597–603 (cleansing); Luz, *Matthew 21–28*, 3–19 (entry and cleansing); J. Nolland, *Luke 18:35–24:53* (Dallas: Word Books, 1993), 919–29 (entry) and 933–8 (cleansing).

at the end of Jesus' ministry.[8] I will discuss the words about the destruction and rebuilding of the Temple in the next section of this chapter.

The Synoptic tradition records only one journey that Jesus made to keep the Passover in Jerusalem. As Mark, followed by Matthew and Luke, tells the story of the entry into Jerusalem, it was a royal gesture, a prelude to the passion of Jesus, a symbolic action oriented to what was coming in his death and resurrection. We can reasonably accept this episode as historical and as being understood by friends and foes in a messianic sense. They interpreted Jesus' action of riding into Jerusalem on a colt as claiming royal authority. Yet it remains difficult to establish what Jesus himself intended (stage one). Did he consciously associate himself with Zechariah 9: 9: 'your king comes to you, triumphant and riding on a donkey'? Or did the early Christian tradition adopt this and other OT verses to present what had happened at Jesus' entry into Jerusalem (Matt. 21: 5; John 12: 15)? It is hard to decide. It seems easier to take a position on Jesus' intentions in the cleansing of the Temple—the incident which became the reason why the authorities moved definitively to do away with him.[9]

Merchants had turned the Temple precincts into a place of business. Such commercialism, perhaps allied with dishonest practices in the sale of animals for sacrifice and in the exchange of money, worked against the purpose of the Temple, which was meant to be a place of worship and instruction for Jews and for the world (e.g. Isa. 2: 2–4; 66: 22–3). *The* place of prayer had become a place where business transactions were distracting people from the real purpose of the Temple. What did Jesus intend by driving out the money changers and those who were buying and selling in the Temple? As Mark (followed by Matthew and Luke) tells the story, Jesus did not aim at symbolizing any coming destruction of the Temple and the building of a new and perfect temple. His action in cleansing the Temple was not as such a portent of its destruction. It seems to have been inspired

---

[8] On this issue of dating, see Fitzmyer, *The Gospel According to Luke X–XXIV*, 1264–5.

[9] In John's Gospel, where the cleansing is located early in the story, it is the raising of Lazarus that motivates the authorities into having Jesus put to death (John 11: 45–53).

by a 'vision of a purified and renewed Temple' that would also 'welcome non-Jews'.[10]

Much turns here on what we maintain about a verse cited by Jesus in Mark: 'My house shall be called a house of prayer for all the nations. But you have made it a den of robbers' (Mark 11: 17). Did Jesus himself quote this text on the occasion of the cleansing of the Temple (stage one)? In that case he intended to do something for the spiritual welfare not only of Jews but also of Gentiles. Or did the verse enter the story of the episode later (stage two)? Jesus knew well the sacred scriptures and what they had to say about the defiling of the Temple (Isa. 56: 7; Jer. 7: 11), a promised purification of the Temple (Zech. 14: 20–1), and the messenger of the Lord who would come to the Temple and prepare for the day of the Lord's coming by first purifying the priesthood (Mal. 3: 1–4). It is plausible that Jesus could have quoted Isaiah 56: 7 to explain the meaning of his action.

One should not, however, take matters further by talking of this action as the purification expected of an anointed, 'messianic' agent of God. The OT texts that we have indicated do not speak of such an *anointed* figure who will bring about such a purification. Malachi simply promises a 'messenger' who will prepare for the day when God will appear to judge the wicked (Mal. 3: 4). To maintain that Jesus understood his action as a purification of the Temple that was long seen to be necessary and had been promised (if the Temple were to be truly 'a house of prayer for all the nations') is *not* the same as maintaining that Jesus understood his action to be that expected of 'the Messiah' or 'a Messiah'. In brief, the Temple action of Jesus fulfilled a promise but not a strictly messianic promise.[11]

To sum up. In cleansing the Temple Jesus did something that he knew to be dangerously provocative and could quickly bring about his execution. He may well have understood that his action could benefit both Jews and non-Jews by making the Temple a 'house of prayer' for everyone.

(6) When faced with questions about Jesus anticipating his violent death, many readers of the Gospels turn naturally to the three

---

[10] Donahue and Harrington, *The Gospel of Mark*, 328.

[11] As Fitzmyer rightly insists, Jesus does not purge the Temple as Messiah—either in the Synoptic tradition or in the Johannine tradition (*The Gospel According to Luke X–XXIV*, 1266–7).

predictions of the passion in Mark, which Matthew and Luke take over
and which associate 'the Son of man' with suffering, death, and a
vindication through resurrection. Let us see the texts:

The Son of man must suffer many things, and be rejected by the elders and
the chief priests and the scribes, and be killed, and after three days rise again.
(Mark 8: 31)

The Son of man will be delivered into the hands of men, and they will kill
him; and when he is killed, after three days he will rise again. (Mark 9: 31)

The Son of man will be delivered to the chief priests and the scribes, and they
will condemn him to death, and deliver him to the Gentiles, and they will
mock him, and spit upon him, and scourge him, and kill him, and after
three days he will rise again. (Mark 10: 33–4)[12]

Frequently these predictions have been flatly dismissed as 'prophecies
after the event', created by early Christians who wanted to show that
Jesus' death was a necessary part of the divine plan. To be sure, the
precise details from Jesus' passion, especially those in the third
prediction, clearly look like elements that emerged in the course of
the events and were added in the early Christian tradition. Nevertheless, we should distinguish between the essential content of the
predictions and their formulation. Even if they were to some extent
embellished during stage two (the post-Easter tradition), they need
not simply be later statements retrospectively attributed to what Jesus
said during his early ministry. Some of the content could well derive
from the earthly Jesus (stage one).[13] In particular, the second passion
prediction, the shortest and the vaguest of the three, seems likely to
be an authentic saying.

Two further items call for attention here. First, if the predictions
were no more than post-Easter statements about Jesus' death and
resurrection, one early and pervasive piece of interpretation is missing
in these predictions. It is *not* stated that 'the Son of man must suffer

[12] Unlike the sheer fact announced by the second and third prediction ('the Son of
man will be delivered'), the first prediction ('the Son of man must suffer') injects a
sense of divine involvement. These events, freely brought about by some Jewish
leaders, Judas, and Pilate, will also take place according to the will of God, something
that Jesus in fidelity to his mission freely accepts in the garden of Gethsemane (Mark
14: 36). Human responsibility and the divine plan do not mutually exclude each other.
[13] See J. A. Fitzmyer, *The Gospel According to Luke I–IX* (New York: Doubleday,
1981), 777–82; Nolland, *Luke 9:21–18:34*, 557–68.

and be killed *for us and for our sins* and then rise again'. That standard reflection from the early Church which St Paul endorses repeatedly does not turn up in any of these three passion predictions. Second, the first and, especially, the third prediction provide some details which correspond to the story of the passion of Christ as reported by Mark (and the other Evangelists). But these details do not include one enormously important detail: the death of Christ by crucifixion. It is simply said that he would be killed, without the manner of death being specified. This and the other 'omission' encourage the view that the passion predictions are *by no means* free inventions of early Christians which simply reflect the actual course of historical events and post-Easter beliefs. The community traditions (stage two) and the evangelist Mark (stage three) knew their limits in creating and attributing statements retrospectively to the earthly Jesus.

Let me pull matters together. We can conclude that (at least to the core group of his disciples) Jesus announced his coming death and affirmed that his Father would quickly or 'in a short time' (in that less precise, biblical sense of 'after three days'[14]) vindicate him through resurrection. We should be cautious about tracing any precise wording back to Jesus (stage one). But we have good reasons for concluding that he anticipated his violent death and hoped for his speedy, subsequent vindication. Such a conclusion says something about Jesus' view of what that death entailed for himself: a contrast between a human verdict on him and a divine verdict on him. A rejection on the human side would be reversed by a resurrection on the divine side. But what did he make of his impending death *for others*? What did Jesus expect that his fate would bring to others, even to the whole human race?

DYING FOR ALL

(1) The theme of God's kingdom can help us here. It would take a sceptic with nerves of steel to deny the centrality of this theme in the

---

[14] On 'after three days', see Nolland, *Luke 9:21–18:34*, 466–7.

preaching of Jesus.[15] From the outset he announced the divine rule to
be at hand. It would be false to separate this proclamation of the
kingdom from his acceptance of his own victimhood. Jesus saw
suffering and persecution as characterizing the coming of that kingdom. The message of the kingdom led more or less straight to the
mystery of the passion. That message entailed and culminated in the
suffering ordeal to come: a time of crisis and distress which was to
move towards the day of the Son of Man (Mark 13 parr.), the
restoration of Israel (Matt. 19: 28 par.), the banquet of the saved,
and the salvation of the nations (Matt. 8: 11 par.). Thus the arrest,
trial, and crucifixion of Jesus dramatized the very thing which totally
engaged Jesus, that rule of God which was to come through a time of
ordeal.

At the Last Supper Jesus linked his imminent death with the divine
kingdom: 'Amen, I say to you, I shall not drink again of the fruit of
the vine until that day when I drink it new in the kingdom of God'
(Mark 14: 25 par.).[16] It is widely agreed that this text has not been
shaped by the eucharistic liturgy of the early Church. It derives from
something Jesus himself said during his last meal with his friends.
Jesus' death is approaching; he will have no occasion again to have a
festive meal of any kind. But after his death, God will vindicate the
cause of Jesus by fully establishing the divine kingdom. Jesus will be
seated at the final banquet—obviously with others at his side—when
he 'drinks wine new'. He looks forward with hope to this final time of
eschatological feasting.

In this saying the death of Jesus is implicit, since what we call 'the
Last Supper' will be the last festive meal of his life. The resurrection as
such is not mentioned, but it is implied that God will rescue Jesus out
of death and let him enjoy the final banquet. The saying as such does
not attribute to Jesus any redemptive function in the final triumph of
the kingdom. It is not stated, or at least not stated explicitly, that he
will restore the fellowship with his disciples which will be broken by

[15] On Jesus and the kingdom of God see G. R. Beasley-Murray, *Jesus and the Kingdom of God* (Exeter: Paternoster, 1986); B. Chilton, *God in Strength: Jesus' Announcement of the Kingdom* (Sheffield: JSOT Press, 1987); Meier, *A Marginal Jew*, ii. 289–506.
[16] See Meier, *A Marginal Jew*, ii. 302–9, 366–71.

death—let alone that he will mediate to others their access to the final banquet.

In these and further ways the saying from Mark 14: 25, taken by itself, leaves much unsaid. Yet it turns up in Mark's Gospel as the *final kingdom saying* from Jesus, a saying about the kingdom which is connected with his approaching death. The saying should be interpreted in the light of what Jesus has already said. He has constantly preached the future reign of God, which will be *the* saving event for all human beings. By linking his approaching death with the coming kingdom, Jesus implicitly interprets his death as somehow salvific for all. Through his preaching he has promised salvation for human beings at large. Now he associates his death with that future salvation and communion at the final banquet in the coming kingdom of God. The kingdom saying from the Last Supper may be laconic. But it is charged with meaning through what Jesus has already said about the coming kingdom.

It is hardly surprising that Jesus made such a positive integration between the coming kingdom and his death. The message about the divine reign was inseparable from the person of Jesus. This essential connection between the message of Jesus and his person meant that the vindication of his person in and beyond death entailed the vindication of God's kingdom and vice versa—a vindication that entailed salvation for all humanity.

(2) Together with the kingdom saying from the Last Supper, we can usefully consider Jesus' saying about the 'replacement' of the Temple, something closely connected with the destruction of Jerusalem. Joseph Fitzmyer surveys the evidence and is satisfied that Jesus did say something about the fate of Jerusalem and the fate of its Temple.[17] Let us see the details.

John's Gospel links the episode of the cleansing of the Temple with some words of Jesus about the coming destruction of the Temple and its rebuilding. To those who demanded a 'sign' to legitimate what he had done in cleansing the Temple, Jesus replied: 'Destroy this temple, and in three days I will raise it up.' The evangelist comments: 'he was speaking of the temple of his body' (John 2: 13–22).

---

[17] Fitzmyer, *The Gospel According to Luke X–XXIV*, 1254–5.

In Mark's Gospel (followed by Matthew and Luke) the Temple action comes not at the beginning but at the end of Jesus' ministry. Moreover, in the versions of the cleansing provided by these three evangelists nothing is said about the destruction and replacement of the Temple. It is a little later in Mark's narrative that Jesus, when predicting the destruction of Jerusalem, begins by announcing the destruction of the magnificent Temple (Mark 13: 2). But nothing is said here about rebuilding or replacing it. At the trial of Jesus some report that they had heard Jesus say: 'I will destroy this temple [or perhaps "this sanctuary", the holiest part of the Temple rather than the whole complex] that is made with [human] hands and in three days I will build another, not made with hands' (Mark 14: 58). Where Mark speaks here of 'false' witnesses, Matthew avoids calling them 'false' and also has the witnesses testify that Jesus said: 'I am able to destroy the temple of God and to build it in three days' (Matt. 26: 60–1). Apparently Matthew regards their witness as true, and does not want 'to deny that Jesus had said what is reported by the witnesses'.[18] Matthew also differs from Mark by alleging a power or possibility ('I am able to destroy') rather than a clear intention ('I will destroy') and by not including the contrast between human agency ('made with hands') and divine agency ('not made with hands'). In Mark's passion narrative, the charge recurs when some of those present at the crucifixion taunt Jesus by saying: 'You who would destroy the temple and build it in three days, save yourself, and come down from the cross' (Mark 15: 29; par. in Matt. 27: 40). In his Gospel, Luke does not include any such saying about the Temple. But in his second work he represents Stephen being charged with prophesying against the Temple by claiming that 'Jesus of Nazareth will destroy' it, as if the prophesy were still unfulfilled some years after the crucifixion and resurrection (Acts 6: 13–14).

The convergent evidence from the Johannine and Synoptic traditions suggests that the Temple saying in some form went back to Jesus himself. Yet differences remain: in John the destruction of the Temple is seemingly attributed to the critics of Jesus, whereas in Mark and Matthew Jesus himself will be the agent of

---

[18] Hagner, *Matthew 14–28*, 798.

that destruction.[19] The saying apparently points to some radical break with the past. Jesus announces that the coming divine kingdom will involve refashioning God's people at the heart of their religious existence, the Temple. In life and in death, Jesus' mission is to replace the Temple and its cult with some new, better, and final temple ('not made with hands'). The expression used for a short period of time ('in three days') seemingly alludes to Christ's death and resurrection after three days. By associating the Temple saying with the risen body of Christ, John's Gospel may have unpacked something of Jesus' intended meaning (John 2: 19–22).

Mark apparently understands the destruction of the Temple to be symbolically initiated when the death of Jesus was immediately followed by 'the curtain of the Temple being torn in two, from top to bottom' (Mark 15: 38). The evangelist refers either to the curtain before the Holy of Holies or to the curtain leading into the 'Holy Place' where the Holy of Holies stood. Either way, through Christ's death on the cross, a new age has come; God has definitively opened the way between heaven and earth. All people can now enjoy unhindered access to the divine presence (see Heb. 10: 19–20). Any link between the rending of the curtain and the Temple saying is made, however, at stage three or possibly two (the evangelist Mark and the traditions on which he draws) rather than with Jesus himself at stage one.[20]

(3) The strongest evidence for Jesus' own understanding of his coming death, its saving import, and its 'beneficiaries' comes from the Last Supper.[21] Convergent evidence from Paul and the Gospels clearly establishes as historically certain the farewell meal Jesus celebrated with his core group of disciples. Biblical scholars widely agree

[19] Even if Mark wrote his Gospel earlier, Matthew wrote after AD 70, and knew that it was the Romans, not Jesus, who had visibly destroyed the Temple.

[20] On Matthew's interpretation of the rending of the curtain, see D. M. Gurtner, *The Torn Veil: Matthew's Exposition of the Death of Jesus* (Cambridge: Cambridge University Press, 2007).

[21] On the Last Supper, see Fitzmyer, *The Gospel According to Luke X–XXIV*, 1385–1406; Luz, *Matthew 21–28*, 364–85; Nolland, *Luke 18:35–24:53*, 1035–57; A. C. Thiselton, *The First Epistle to the Corinthians* (Grand Rapids, Mich.: Eerdmans, 2000), 848–91. See further H. J. Klauck, 'Sacrifice and Sacrificial Offerings (NT)', *ABD* v. 86–91; F. J. Matera, 'Christ, Death of', *ABD* i. 923–5; R. F. O'Toole, 'Last Supper', ABD iv. 234–41.

that the 'bread saying' derives from the historical Jesus. Many argue as well that the 'cup saying' is also traceable to the historical Jesus. The 'words of institution', if taken at face value, show Jesus defining his death as a sacrifice which will not only representatively atone for sins but also initiate a new and enduring covenant between God and human beings. But here we must reckon with the question: how far have the sources of Paul, Mark, and the other evangelists been shaped by liturgical usages in early Christian communities? In 1 Corinthians 11: 23–5 we read: 'The Lord Jesus on the night when he was betrayed took bread, and when he had given thanks, he broke it, and said: "This is my body [which is given] for you. Do this in remembrance of me." In the same way [he took] also the cup, after supper, saying: "This cup is the new covenant in my blood. Do this, as often as you drink it, in remembrance of me."' In Mark's version of the Last Supper, however, the instructions calling for a future repetition of the Eucharist ('Do this in remembrance of me', and 'Do this as often as you drink it, in remembrance of me') are missing. And—what is more significant for the issue under discussion—the qualification of 'my body' as being 'for you' is also missing. Yet, unlike the Pauline tradition, Mark describes the blood as being 'poured out for many'. His version runs as follows: 'He took bread, blessed and broke it, and gave it to them, and said: "Take, this is my body." And he took a cup, and when he had given thanks he gave it to them, and they all drank of it. And he said to them, "This is my blood of the covenant, which is poured out for many"' (14: 22–4).

Obviously there are differences between the Pauline tradition (to which, apart from adding, apropos of 'my blood', which 'is poured out for you', and not including, apropos of the cup, 'do this in remembrance of me', Luke 22: 19–20 approximates) and the Markan tradition (which is more or less followed by Matthew 26: 26–8, apart from the latter adding that the blood is shed 'for the forgiveness of sins'). Confronted with these differences, some writers back away from relying too much on the words of institution as accurate sources for settling the way Jesus understood his death and its impact. In some form the words of institution go back to Jesus. But in what precise form? Admittedly the breaking of the bread, identified as his body, and the pouring out of his blood imaged forth the sacrificial surrender of his life, the action of total self-giving that was about to take place in his violent death. Clearly those followers present at the Last Supper shared in his body that was being given up to death and in his blood that would be shed. They were invited to participate in Jesus' destiny and enjoy a new, permanent communion or covenant with him. Whether Jesus spoke of a 'new covenant' (Paul and Luke) or only of a 'covenant' (Mark and Matthew) that was being instituted through his 'blood', he inevitably evoked key OT passages (e.g. through a cultic link to Exod. 24: 3–8; and through an eschatological link to Jer. 31: 31–3) that illuminated his action and words. He was making a new covenant, sealed and ratified by the shedding of his blood.

But, beyond the group present at the Last Supper, whom did Jesus intend to be the beneficiaries of his death and the new covenant? The 'for you' of the Pauline and Lukan tradition indicated immediately his disciples who shared the common cup at the Last Supper. Of course, in that case he might well have intended the group who participated in the Last Supper to represent others, even many others. If Jesus explicitly called for the *future* repetition of the bread ritual ('do this in remembrance of me'—Paul and Luke) and of the cup ritual ('do this in remembrance of me'—Paul only), he clearly wanted to confer on an indefinite number of others the saving benefits of his life and impending death. Even if Jesus did not literally express the directive 'do this in remembrance of me', one can reasonably argue that this addition from the Pauline and Lukan churches rendered explicit his intentions. He wanted to establish for countless others his continuing place and presence in the meal fellowship that he had instituted with a small, core group of disciples.

Mark (followed by Matthew) has Jesus speaking of his blood poured out 'for many', an inclusive Semitic expression for a great multitude or countless number (= 'for all'). But in that case did Jesus mean not merely all Jews but also all Gentiles?

If we understand 'for you' and 'for many' as both pointing to an indefinitely large group, we are still left with the question: did Jesus intend the benefits of his violent death and the new covenant to be conferred on all those and only on all those who were sharing and would share in the ritual and the fellowship he was creating? Would the benefits of his sacrificial death 'for many' be passed on only to the new covenant community, the fellowship of those who would share in the saving power of Jesus' death through eating his 'broken body' and drinking from the common cup? Should we then draw from Jesus himself at the Last Supper a limiting 'principle': 'outside the Eucharist no salvation (extra eucharistiam nulla salus)'?

A short answer to those tempted to imagine Jesus limiting the saving impact of the new covenant comes from a theme developed in the last chapter: the meals he shared with all manner of people, not least with the disreputable. That table fellowship conveyed forgiveness to sinners and celebrated in advance the happiness of the heavenly banquet to come, a banquet to which all were invited. Jesus' practice throws light on his intentions at the Last Supper. It was intended to be 'the last supper' or climax of a whole series of meals that revealed his saving outreach to everyone.[22] Ultimately the pressure on us to establish precisely what Jesus said and intended at the Last Supper can be eased by recalling his characteristic attitudes. They illuminate the universal scope of his saving intentions.

CHARACTERISTIC ATTITUDES

In general, characteristic ways in which people act and speak can fill their death with meaning, even when they have no chance at the end to express their motivation and make an explicit declaration of intent. Archbishop Oscar Romero (1917–80), for instance, was abruptly shot dead when celebrating the Eucharist. He had no last-minute opportunity to blurt out some statement interpreting the death which confronted him. Nevertheless, all that he had been saying and doing during his three years as archbishop of San Salvador served to indicate his basic intentions and fill his martyrdom with significance.

In the case of Jesus, even if he did not explicitly designate himself as 'the Servant of the Lord', he consistently behaved as one utterly subject to his Father's will and completely available for the service of all those who needed mercy and healing. His words and actions brought divine pardon to those who, in various ways, felt a great

---

[22] See Meier, *A Marginal Jew*, ii. 1035–7.

need of redemption. He never drove away the lepers, taxation agents, sinful women, children, and all those anonymous crowds of people who clamoured for his love and attention. He valued every individual, and not simply the socially advantaged (e.g. Mark 10: 21 parr.), as unique and irreplaceable.

Now it would be strange to imagine that the threat of the passion abruptly destroyed Jesus' resolution to show himself the servant of others. Rather, a straight line led from his serving ministry to his suffering death. Even if the community (stage two) or Mark himself (stage three) added the words 'to give his life as a ransom for many', there was a basis in Jesus' ministry for the saying, 'the Son of Man came not to be served but to serve, and to give his life as a ransom for many' (Mark 10: 45). He who had shown himself the servant of all was ready to die for all—to release them from various forms of oppressive servitude. As many have insisted, the service of Jesus had been offered especially to the outcasts and the religious pariahs. Part of the reason why Jesus' ministry led to his crucifixion stemmed from the fact that he faithfully and scandalously served the lost, the godless, and the alienated of his society. The physician who came to call and cure the unrighteous eventually died in their company. His serving ministry to the reprobates ended when he obediently accepted a shameful death between two reprobates. His association with society's outcasts and failures led to his solidarity with them in death. In these terms the passion of Jesus became integrated into his mission as a final act of service. In death, as in life, he served and sacrificed himself for others. Luke 22: 27 ('I am among you as one who serves') is an authentic pointer to this basic pattern in Jesus' behaviour.

Before developing plausible ways in which Jesus might have linked his servanthood and suffering and done so 'for all', we should recall some further universal characteristics of his ministry. As we saw in the last chapter, he understood his fellow Jews to be the immediate beneficiaries of the divine salvation he communicated through his mission. He aimed at the reform of Israel and through the circle of 'the Twelve' wanted to reconstruct the twelve tribes. He said to that circle: 'Truly I tell you, at the regeneration of all things, when the Son of Man is seated on the throne of his glory, you who have followed me will yourselves also sit on twelve thrones and will judge the twelve tribes of Israel' (Matt. 19: 28; par.).[23] At the resurrection of the dead, the twelve tribes would be finally restored and be judged by the circle of 'the Twelve' gathered during his ministry around Jesus—an amazing promise for that core group. The promise stood in tension with (but did not contradict) the scene of the great judgement, which we examined in the previous chapter. That scene showed the Son of Man alone 'sitting' in judgement on 'his throne of glory' to judge 'all the nations' (Matt. 25: 31–4).

Israel was the context for the ministry of Jesus; yet, as we argued in the last chapter, that ministry had a universal dimension. His message of the kingdom reached beyond the frontiers of religious and racial separations. God's reign here and hereafter was for all human beings. The parables of Jesus show this universal horizon. Even in the Parable of the Tax-collector and the Pharisee, the only parable set in the most Jewish of settings, the Temple, this universality showed through. Jesus asserted that the full extent of God's generosity had hitherto been ignored: the divine pardon was offered to all.

By rejecting or at least relativizing dietary laws and merely external purity regulations (Mark 7: 14–23 par.), which established and preserved the boundaries between Jews and Gentiles, Jesus implied that these distinctions had no ultimate significance before God. What mattered was the internal state of the 'heart'—its purity or corruption.[24] Hence Jesus' vision of Israel's future entailed 'many coming from the east and the west to sit at table with Abraham, Isaac, and Jacob in the kingdom of heaven' (Matt. 8: 11 par.). The ministry of Jesus envisaged salvation for the nations. Having lived and preached such a universal vision, at the end Jesus, one can reasonably suppose, accepted in some sense that he would die for all people.

CONTEMPORARY IDEAS

Some contemporary ideas can also serve as pointers to the intentions of Jesus in the face of death. Various OT books endorse the notion that the righteous will suffer (e.g. Ps. 34: 19) and do so at the hands of

---

[23] See U. Luz, *Matthew 6–20* (Minneapolis: Fortress Press, 2001), 510–11, 517.

[24] Marcus, *Mark 1–8*, 446–7, 452–61.

the unrighteous (e.g. Wisd. 2: 10–20). Prophets could expect to be persecuted because of their faithfulness to God. Such notions surface in the beatitudes taught by Jesus (e.g. Matt. 5: 10–12).

The experiences of the Maccabean martyrs in the second century BC helped to give rise to a further development that was in the air at the time of Jesus. The suffering and violent death of righteous persons could bring healing and forgiveness to others and expiate their sins. The martyrdom of even one individual could representatively atone for the sins of a group (e.g. 2 Macc. 7: 37–8). Martin Hengel has marshalled evidence to show how earlier Greek and Roman literature, history, and customs supported the notion that someone could die 'for' his/her city or people and so atone for their sins. In fact the Jewish conviction to this effect may have been taken over from Greek sources.[25]

But my aim here is not to discuss questions of provenance but rather to recall a relevant belief found at the time of Jesus. Once the threat of violent death loomed up, it would have been somewhat strange if Jesus had never applied to himself that religious conviction of his contemporaries and had not done so through the universal horizon that characterized his ministry. Through his martyrdom he could vicariously set right for all people a moral order universally disturbed by sin.

Here I should add a parenthesis on the poem from Second Isaiah (52: 13–53: 12) about the Servant of the Lord, who—whether understood primarily in an individual or a collective sense—suffers for the sins of 'the many'.[26] Although this material dates from the sixth century BC and could obviously support reflections on vicarious atonement, the text is never *quoted* either by later works of the OT or

[25] M. Hengel, *The Cross and the Son of God* (London: SCM Press, 1986), 189–284; see N. T. Wright, *The Climax of the Covenant* (Edinburgh: T. & T. Clark, 1991), 60–1.
[26] See K. Baltzer, *Deutero-Isaiah* (Minneapolis: Fortress, 2001), 392–429; W. H. Bellinger and W. R. Farmer (eds.), *Jesus and the Suffering Servant: Isaiah 53 and Christian Origins* (Harrisburg, Pa.: Trinity Press International, 1998); R. Meynet, 'Le quatrième chant du serviteur', *Gregorianum* 80 (1999), 407–40; G. O'Collins, *Jesus Our Redeemer: A Christian Approach to Salvation* (Oxford: Oxford University Press, 2007), 148–52; C. Seitz, 'Reconciliation and the Plain Sense Witness of Scripture', in S. T. Davis, D. Kendall, and G. O'Collins (eds.), *The Redemption: An Interdisciplinary Symposium on Christ as Redeemer* (Oxford: Oxford University Press, 2004), 25–42.

by non-canonical books of the intertestamental period. Even where *allusions* to this poem about the Suffering Servant can be detected in subsequent texts (e.g. Zech. 12: 10), we do not find the notion of a death which representatively atones for others. Nevertheless, this fourth poem about the Servant helped to shape early Christian thinking and preaching. There are hints in Paul's letters (e.g. Rom. 4: 25), and 1 Peter was to develop the theme of Christ as the servant whose vicarious suffering brings healing and forgiveness. Eventually, the NT was to include eleven quotations from this poem and at least thirty-two allusions to it. Early Christians were to see Isaiah 53 as an elaborate prefiguration of Christ in his atoning suffering. In the late first century St Clement of Rome simply quoted the whole of this text when expounding the meaning of Jesus' death (*I Clement* 16). In his *Dialogue with Trypho* St Justin Martyr would quote Isaiah 53 in full (no. 13).

What conclusions does this parenthesis point to? We should be cautious about invoking the fourth poem on the Lord's Servant to establish contemporary ideas of vicarious atonement which Jesus could easily have applied to himself. As we have seen above, Palestinian Judaism of the first century AD included the belief that the death of a martyr could representatively atone for the sins of others. But, curiously enough, it is not clear that this belief drew on the song of the Suffering Servant. Certainly we have no unambiguous text from pre-Christian Judaism which speaks of the anointed Messiah's vicarious suffering in connection with Isaiah 53. That fact *by itself* does not, of course, rule out Jesus' sense of mission in the face of death being shaped by Suffering Servant imagery. Yet it was one thing for him to envisage his vicarious suffering as Messiah and quite another thing for him to have done so in terms of the Suffering Servant of Isaiah 53. We have no strong evidence that Jesus clearly made this association.[27]

Further, we should add that pre-Christian notions of representative expiation never envisaged vicarious atonement coming through a just person's death by *crucifixion*. Death on a cross, so far from being a possible form of atoning martyrdom 'for others', signified

---

[27] If we had such a clear self-reference, we could argue, or at least reasonably speculate, that Jesus expected the atoning suffering of the Servant (Isa. 53: 4–9), his own impending suffering, to bring as its redemptive result the confession of 'many nations', the Gentiles (Isa. 52: 13–15).

being cursed by God as one who violated the covenant (Deut. 21: 23; Gal. 3: 13).[28] Judaism was not prepared for the atoning meaning of the cross.

Finally, Paul's letters abundantly document the pre-Pauline tradition that Jesus' crucifixion was a death 'for us', which representatively atoned for the sins of human beings, Jews and Gentiles alike (e.g. 1 Thess. 5: 10; 1 Cor. 15: 3; Rom. 4: 25; 8: 32). As Hengel argues, we meet in these formulations from the earliest Christian tradition a conviction that ran clean counter to the predominant Jewish beliefs. At the time of Jesus the popular messianic hopes did not include a suffering Messiah. To proclaim a crucified Messiah was incredible, even blasphemous talk. Hence the early Christians defended something utterly offensive when they proclaimed that the crucifixion of someone who was executed precisely as a messianic pretender was in fact a sacrificial death which atoned representatively for the sins of all people.

How can we account for this understanding of Jesus' crucifixion as the vicarious atoning death of the Messiah that had universal impact by atoning for human sin? Certainly the disciples' encounters with the risen Jesus played their role in legitimating this interpretation. But it seems that could hardly have made such an outrageous claim unless the earthly Jesus had already in some way claimed to be Messiah and indicated that his coming death would have such an atoning value for all people. Unless before his death he had given some indication of making these claims, it does not seem plausible that the disciples alone developed the scandalous idea that his death on the cross had representatively atoned for the sins of all people.

CONCLUSION

This chapter has aimed at establishing that Jesus not only anticipated a violent death but also interpreted it in advance as somehow proving redemptive for Jews and Gentiles alike. Faced with death, Jesus

---

[28] See G. O'Collins, 'Crucifixion', *ABD* i. 1207–10; J. D. G. Dunn, *The Partings of the Ways* (London: SCM Press, 1991), 120, 122–3, 304 n. 29; id., *The Theology of Paul the Apostle* (Grand Rapids, Mich.: Eerdmans, 1998), 208–27; Hengel, *The Cross and the Son of God*, 93–185. On Jesus' crucifixion and other aspects of his passion, see R. E. Brown, *The Death of the Messiah*, 2 vols. (New York: Doubleday, 1994).

understood it as a representative and redemptive service for all others. The post-Easter interpretation of salvation was partly supported by the earthly Jesus' understanding of the mission that led to his death. We turn now to examine what in the post-Easter situation Christians believed about the scope of the salvation effected by the crucified and risen Jesus.

9

The Apostle to the Gentiles

When we chart the history of Judaism and Christianity, we reach a decisive watershed with the death and resurrection of Jesus, along with the coming of the Holy Spirit. New and multiple perspectives open up—both about the ongoing place of Israel in God's saving plans and about the situation of those very many Jews and Gentiles who have not (or have not yet) joined the emerging Church through faith in Christ and baptism in the name of the tripersonal God. Before presenting and evaluating St Paul's view of the religious meaning of this new situation, let me introduce a brief parenthesis on terminology.

In earlier chapters—and, especially, in the last two chapters—I have already used such terms as save/salvation, redeem/redemption, and expiation of sin. Coming out of a long history of usage in the Bible, Jewish and Christian liturgy, official teaching, theology, and 'ordinary' literature, this language normally communicates well but can provide some difficulties. Right from the start of my *Jesus Our Redeemer: A Christian Approach to Salvation*,[1] I spent pages clarifying the terminology of redemption. That book could help any readers who may puzzle over this terminology and the way I employ it. Let me now turn to the Apostle to the Gentiles (Gal. 1: 16; 2: 9) and what he has to say in his letters about the salvation of 'the others'. But first we should clarify the *universal* impact Paul claims for redeeming activity of the crucified and risen Jesus. The Apostle offers several perspectives on this claim.

---

[1] (Oxford: Oxford University Press, 2007), 1–18.

I

CHRIST THE UNIVERSAL RECONCILER

Paul declares twice that Christ died 'for all' (2 Cor. 5: 14–15), and does so shortly before his first classic passage on the universal *reconciling* activity of God: 'through Christ God reconciled us [all humanity] to himself and gave us [Paul] the ministry of reconciliation; that is, God was in Christ reconciling the world to himself' (2 Cor. 5: 18–19). The first 'us' denotes all human beings, Jews and Gentiles alike, whom God has reconciled to himself through Christ. God took the initiative to reconcile to himself the 'world', that is to say, all of sinful humanity and perhaps also (in the light of the 'new creation' in v. 17) the whole created universe.[2]

The second classic passage in which Paul writes of this reconciling action of God comes in Romans: 'while we were yet enemies, we were reconciled to God through the death of his Son' (Rom. 5: 10). The 'we' embraces both Jews and Gentiles. A few chapters later in the same letter Paul uses the same language of reconciliation to expound the universal impact of Christ's death and resurrection. With a view to the Gentiles embracing Christian faith and so drawing some more Jews to Christ, he writes of Christ effecting 'the reconciliation of the world' (Rom. 11: 15). Here 'world' denotes the human race, or at least the Gentiles, who make up the overwhelming majority of human beings. 'World' may also point beyond the reconciliation of humanity to a 'cosmic extension of that effect' in 'the whole universe'.[3] In these terms, the reconciliation with God brought by Christ would thus touch both humanity and the whole created world. One is encouraged to interpret cosmically 'the reconciliation of the world' by what Paul expounded three chapters earlier. Created nature, he

---

[2] See V. P. Furnish, *II Corinthians* (New York: Doubleday, 1984), 319; M. J. Harris, *The Second Epistle to the Corinthians* (Grand Rapids, Mich.: Eerdmans, 2005), 424–63; T. Stegman, *The Character of Jesus: The Linchpin of Paul's Argument in 2 Corinthians* (Rome: Pontificio Istituto Biblico, 2005), 181–3, 271–82; M. E. Thrall, *A Critical and Exegetical Commentary on the Second Epistle to the Corinthians*, i (Edinburgh: T. & T. Clark, 1994), 407–49.

[3] See J. A. Fitzmyer, *Romans* (New York: Doubleday, 1993), 612.

expects, will be liberated from decay and share with human beings in the final freedom and glory (Rom. 8: 18–25).

A letter which may not have been written directly by Paul is, however, clear about the cosmic dimension of the reconciliation brought by the crucified and risen Jesus: 'In him [Christ] all the fullness [of God] was pleased to dwell, and through him [God was pleased] to reconcile to himself all things, whether on earth or in the heavens, making peace by the blood of his cross' (Col. 1: 19–20). However we interpret the nuances of 'all the fullness', our question here concerns something else: only conscious and willing agents can, properly speaking, be at enmity and then reconciled with each other in a new, peaceful situation. 'All things' here includes such agents (whether Jews or Gentiles) but evidently refers to more than them. It makes better sense to think of this 'reconciliation' not as merely establishing friendly relations between personal agents (God and sinners),[4] but rather as Christ making all created things peacefully conform, at least in principle, to the wise plan of God.[5]

These two verses complete a hymn which depicts the utter supremacy and universal relevance of Christ not only in the order of redemption but also in that of creation. He is 'the firstborn over all creation', since every created thing has its origin 'through him', exists 'for him', and 'holds together in him' (Col. 1: 15–17). 'New creation' and the total created order define a further perspective in Paul's recognition of Christ's universal dominion and universal redemptive impact.

NEW CREATION AND NEW ADAM

Along with his fellow Christians, the Apostle knew that Jesus, through his death and resurrection (along with the outpouring of

[4] Even if the hymn in Col. 1: 15–20 does not refer explicitly to human sin, the verses that follow make it clear that the divine work of reconciliation includes those who were formerly 'enemies' of God (Col. 1: 21–2). This recalls Rom. 5: 10 and 2 Cor. 5: 18–19, which designate enemies and sinners as the beneficiaries of God's reconciling activity.

[5] On this hymn, see M. Barth and H. Blanke, *Colossians* (New York: Doubleday, 1994), 193–251, esp. 213–24.

the Holy Spirit) had brought them the *new creation* of graced life (2 Cor. 5: 17; Gal. 6: 15). The same 'power' or creative force of God deployed at the beginning in the making of the world was now revealed as the principle of the new creation or salvation offered to all (Rom. 1: 16). As agent of this new creation that was final salvation, Jesus must also be, so they recognized, the divine agent for the *original creation* of all things. What held true at the end must also be true at the beginning. Eschatological claims about Christ as agent of final salvation led quickly to 'protological' claims or claims about 'first things': namely, that he was also involved in the divine act of creation.

In 1 Corinthians Paul expanded the confession of monotheism expressed in the central Jewish prayer, the 'Shema' or 'Hear, O Israel' (Deut. 6: 4), so as to acknowledge a personal distinction within the godhead. The Apostle glossed 'God' with 'Father' and 'Lord' with 'Jesus Christ' to put Jesus as risen and exalted Lord alongside God the Father: 'For us there is one God, the Father, from whom are all things and for whom we exist, and one Lord, Jesus Christ, through whom are all things and through whom we exist' (1 Cor. 8: 6). Paul's redefining of Jewish monotheism involved acknowledging Christ as agent of the whole of creation, 'through whom are all things and through whom we exist'.[6] This belief parallels the vision of Christ as universal creator found in the hymn from Colossians 1 which we examined above. As the agent of the 'new creation' and of 'creation', Christ is intimately involved with all human beings and the whole created world.

Talk of creation readily evoked the story of our 'first parents'. To express the blessings of grace and eternal life that Christ had brought for all human beings, Paul introduced another corporate figure, the first Adam, who was pictured as triggering the whole story of human sin. The Apostle seems to have drawn on Jewish traditions and scriptures to develop in his own striking way the doctrine of the 'New' or 'Last' Adam to be found in 1 Corinthians and Romans. Joseph Fitzmyer gathers the evidence to show that 'the incorporation of all human beings in Adam' is an idea which 'seems to appear for

---

[6] See A. C. Thiselton, *The First Epistle to the Corinthians* (Grand Rapids, Mich.: Eerdmans, 2000), 635–8.

the first time in 1 Corinthians 15: 22'. He likewise offers evidence that allows him to qualify as 'novel teaching' Paul's argument in Romans 5 about the 'maleficent influence' that Adam's sin had 'on all human beings'.[7]

Paul's contribution here proved very successful in the life of Christianity. St Irenaeus (d. around 200) and other notable writers enriched Christian theology by reflecting on Jesus as the New/Second Adam. Liturgical texts (e.g. the *Exultet* or Easter Proclamation), poets (e.g. John Donne and John Milton), painters (e.g. Masaccio and Michelangelo), icons of Eastern Christianity, and enduring legends (see the *Legenda aurea* (*Golden Legend*) by Blessed James of Voragine or Varazze (d. 1298)) have linked the images of Adam and Christ to illustrate the universal scope of the redemption effected by the Second Adam. Just as all humanity was harmed by the sin of Adam and Eve, so the redemption brought by Christ, the Last Adam, has a radical impact on the entire human race and on the whole created cosmos.[8]

One should add here that when Paul introduced Adam and Christ as two corporate, universally influential figures and saw all human beings as bearing the image of both Adam and Christ (1 Cor. 15: 49), he did not leave Christ simply on the human level. As the 'second man from heaven' (1 Cor. 15: 47) and 'life-giving spirit' (1 Cor. 15: 45), the Last Adam went far beyond merely human standards and power. This language of being 'from heaven' and even more of being a/the 'life-giving spirit' lifts matters beyond the human level. It points to the risen Christ exercising a universal, divine role as the source of all life.[9]

In 1 Corinthians 15 Paul's exposition of Christ as the Last Adam occurred within a long passage on the significance and nature of the resurrection (1 Cor. 15: 12–55). It is through Christ, the 'first fruits' of those who have died (1 Cor. 15: 23) that resurrection will come for others. The resurrection of the dead was a theme to which Paul returned over the years. His first letter envisaged *Christians* being united with the risen Christ (1 Thess. 4: 13–5: 11). Nothing was said

---

[7] Fitzmyer, *Romans*, 136, 406, 412.

[8] See my *Jesus Our Redeemer: A Christian Approach to Salvation* (Oxford: Oxford University Press, 2007), 37–42, 107–8, 113.

[9] See Thiselton, *The First Epistle to the Corinthians*, 1224–9, 1281–90.

(or denied) about the resurrection of others. By the time the Apostle reached the height of his career and wrote Romans, he had come to recognize the full impact of the coming resurrection. Not only *all human beings* but also the *whole of created nature* is called to share in the freedom of a glorious resurrection.[10]

THE LORD OF THE UNIVERSE

The closing benediction of Paul's 1 Corinthians contains one of the oldest and briefest Christian prayers: 'Maranatha' (1 Cor. 16: 22). Transliterated into Greek from two Aramaic words, in this context 'Maranatha' probably means, 'Our Lord, come' rather than 'Our Lord has come'. In this way Paul prayed with other Christians that the risen and exalted Jesus would come to them in his post-Easter glory at the end of the age.

Applying the title 'Lord' to the crucified and risen Jesus began very early in Christianity. Our oldest Christian document, 1 Thessalonians, called him by that title 24 times, in particular with reference to his future coming as 'Lord' (e.g. 1 Thess. 4: 13–5: 3). Altogether in the letters that scholars very widely recognize as written by Paul, he applied the title of 'Lord' to Jesus around 230 times. Sometimes he did so in passages that seem to derive from a pre-Pauline tradition (e.g. Rom. 10: 9; 1 Cor. 12: 3; 2 Cor. 13: 13). The mark of a Christian was the confession of Jesus as divine Lord (Rom. 10: 9; 2 Cor. 4: 5; Phil. 2: 11).[11] Along with other early Christians, Paul worshipped and believed in Christ as the divine *Kyrios*.

Passages in the OT which call God *Kyrios* are referred to Christ. Thus Romans 10: 13 cites Joel 2: 32: 'Everyone who calls on the name of the Lord will be saved.' Philippians 2: 10–11 echoes Isaiah 45: 23–4, one of the classic OT passages celebrating YHWH, the one and only God of Israel and of the whole world. 'At the name of Jesus every knee

[10] See D. M. Stanley, *Christ's Resurrection in Pauline Soteriology* (Rome: Pontificio Istituto Biblico, 1961).

[11] See L. W. Hurtado, *Lord Jesus Christ: Devotion to Jesus in Earliest Christianity* (Grand Rapids, Mich.: Eerdmans, 2003), 20–1, 108–18, 178–84, 197–207.

should bend, in heaven, on earth, and under the earth, and every tongue should confess that Jesus Christ is Lord (*Kyrios*).' This divine title serves Paul in expressing his faith that the crucified and risen Jesus enjoys lordship over everyone and everything. Whether invoked as Lord or in terms of universal reconciliation, the new creation and the first creation, his function as Last Adam, and his being 'first fruits' of the resurrected life to come, the risen and exalted Jesus exercises an all-determining role, a universal divine sovereignty. As Paul's repeated opening salutation puts matters, 'grace and peace' (= integral salvation) comes and comes only from 'God our Father and the Lord Jesus Christ' (e.g. Rom. 1: 7).

Apropos of salvation, the Apostle typically thinks 'horizontally' or in terms of the ongoing history of humanity. The dying and rising of Christ, along with the gift of the Spirit, have ushered in the final age, which will climax when the end comes and 'God will be all in all' (1 Cor. 15: 28). With the rising of the crucified Jesus, the completion of all things has already begun; his resurrection, 'the first fruits of those who have died' (1 Cor. 15: 20), has made present the end of all history. As Gordon Fee reflects on Paul's view of salvation, 'God has set in motion the new creation, in which all things eventually will be made new.'[12] Paul's vision differs in 'direction' from the characteristic (but not exclusive) vision of John's Gospel. It is because the Word descended 'from above' or 'vertically' from his eternal communion with the Father and 'became flesh' (John 1: 14) that he should be acknowledged as '*the* Light' of all people, 'the Way, the Truth, and the Life' for everyone (John 1: 4; 9: 5; 14: 6). Occasionally Paul adopts a somewhat 'vertical' approach which associates the incarnation or coming down from heaven with the function of Jesus as universal Redeemer (e.g. Rom. 8: 3–4; Gal. 4: 4–7). But normally the Apostle thinks of a dynamic history,[13] a new and final age initiated with the resurrection of the crucified Jesus and the gift of the Holy Spirit, a history that will be consummated when 'the Lord Jesus Christ will transform our humble bodies and conform them to his glorious body' (Phil. 3: 20–1).

[12] 'Paul and the Metaphors of Salvation: Some Reflections on Pauline Soteriology', in S. T. Davis, D. Kendall, and G. O'Collins (eds.), *The Redemption: An Interdisciplinary Symposium on Christ as Redeemer* (Oxford: Oxford University Press, 2004), 43.

[13] This 'historical' dynamism is not absent in Paul's (few) statements about the incarnation: e.g. it was 'in the fullness of time' that God sent his Son (Gal. 4: 4).

Thus far this chapter has been concerned to sketch some major points in Paul's vision of Christ and the Spirit being all-determining for the salvation of every human being and, indeed, for the entire created world. The Apostle expresses this all-embracing function of Christ in terms of his being the agent of universal reconciliation, the initiator of the new and final creation, the New Adam who heads all humanity, and the divine Lord of the universe. What then does Paul say, specifically, about the Gentiles? Obviously he goes beyond the vision of OT prophets that the nations will be saved in the end time, through a final pilgrimage to Mount Zion (see Chapter 4 and Chapter 6 above). What does Paul profess about the salvation of the Gentiles in this present age?

II

REDEEMING THE GENTILES

Paul recalls how the earthly Jesus ministered to the Jews, and so proved the divine fidelity to 'the promises given to the patriarchs'. Yet the Apostle can also provide a chain of OT quotations to emphasize that the promised salvation now extends also to the Gentiles (Rom. 15: 8–12). In the post-Easter situation, Paul's own apostleship aims at 'bringing about the obedience of faith among *all* the nations' (Rom. 1: 5). Paul wants to proclaim the good news to as many Gentiles as possible and as soon as possible. He sees his ministry as playing an essential part in completing God's plan for the salvation of the world. A few verses later, however, he tells the Christians of Rome of his (more modest) hope to 'reap *some* harvest among you as I have among the rest of the Gentiles' (Rom. 1: 13). At the end of the same letter Paul summarizes for the Romans what he has already done as 'a minister of Christ Jesus to the Gentiles', and reports his plans to take the good news of Christ to new territories (Rom. 15: 14–29). The Apostle seriously expects this mission to be achieved within his own lifetime.

Before expounding the divine act of redemption in Jesus Christ, Paul sets out how 'all', Jews and Gentiles alike, 'have sinned' (Rom. 3:

23). In vivid language the Apostle pictures the moral degradation to be found among Gentiles. As Wisdom 14 had done (see Chapter 5 above), Paul spells out in detail the evil results of fashioning and worshipping idols (Rom. 1: 18–32). In other letters the Apostle has similar lists of vices that characterize the lives of some or even many Gentiles (e.g. 1 Cor. 6: 9–11). Yet moral failure is universal. Many Jews, even though they are blessed by the written law of God, fall short of even ordinary morality (Rom. 2: 17–24). As Paul concludes, 'all, both Jews and Gentiles are under the power of sin' (Rom. 3: 9). To counter the way sin universally ravages the entire human race, the whole race needs the saving work of Jesus Christ.

God has acted powerfully to save both Jews and Gentiles—in that order: 'the power of God' is 'for the salvation of everyone who has faith, to the Jew first and also to the Greek' (Rom. 1: 16). In the story of salvation God treats Jews and Gentiles in that order, yet justifies them on the same basis, namely through faith. Paul asks dramatically: 'is God the God of Jews only? Is he not the God of Gentiles also? Yes, of Gentiles also' (Rom. 3: 29–30).

Paul will go on to argue that the true descendants of Abraham are all those who have faith in Christ, whether Jews or Gentiles (Rom. 4: 13–25; see Gal. 3: 6–29). In the chapters that follow (Rom. 5: 1–8: 39), the Apostle is not bent on distinguishing between Jews and Gentiles. The same conditions apply to everyone. The 'we' and 'us' persistently includes all human beings, or at least all Christians, no matter whether they have a Jewish or Gentile background.

Those chapters, as well as the earlier ones, leave us with a painful question about the Gentiles. As we have just seen, faith is the condition of salvation. God's righteousness comes through 'faith in Jesus Christ'; 'redemption is effective through faith' (Rom. 3: 22, 25).[14] Paul talks for everyone when he declares: 'We are justified by faith' (Rom. 5: 1). What then of all those Gentiles who have never had a chance of accepting with faith the good news, either because they have never heard the gospel or because it was not effectively presented to them? Either as groups or as individuals, they were never in

---

[14] Some scholars interpret the 'faith of Jesus Christ' as a subjective genitive, the faith or faithfulness exercised by Christ, rather than as an objective genitive, the faith of those who believe in Christ. We will return below to this possibility.

the position to join the community of Christian faith. Paul ends his letter to the Romans by boldly stating that the good news of Jesus Christ has been 'made known to *all* the Gentiles' in order to 'bring about the obedience of faith [or the obedience which is faith]' (Rom. 16: 25–6). In its opening chapter Colossians (coming either directly from Paul or from one of his 'disciples') affirms that the gospel 'has been proclaimed to every creature under heaven' (Col. 1: 23).[15] One might say, yes, this has been done *in principle* and the Apostle's hope is universal. But, at the time when Paul writes, has the good news already been proclaimed *in fact* to 'all the Gentiles' and to 'every creature under heaven'?

For a modern reader at least, what Paul wrote repeatedly raises this question about the non-evangelized Gentiles. He eloquently expressed the divine plan of salvation: 'those whom he [God] foreknew he also predestined to be conformed to the image of his Son, in order that he might be the firstborn among many brothers. And those whom he predestined he also called; and those whom he called he also justified; and those whom he justified he also glorified' (Rom. 8: 29–30). One can and should concur with Paul: people become Christians through God's initiative. But why has this initiative not been extended to all others, through a call that leads to their being justified and glorified?

A little later in Romans, dealing with the failure of many Jews to believe in Christ, Paul enunciated the general principle: faith comes through hearing the proclamation of those who bring the good news. He drew on Isaiah 52: 7 and Psalm 19 to insist that the evangelists, sent with the authority of Christ, had already proclaimed good news about him everywhere: 'their voice has gone out to all the earth, and their words to the end of the world' (Rom. 10: 14–18). Once again one can or must say: in principle, yes. But one must also ask: in Paul's day and even (or especially) now, has this proclamation in practice gone out everywhere? Since faith comes from the act of hearing and/ or from what is heard, how does everyone have the possibility of believing, if they have never had the chance to 'hear'?

---

[15] The relevant participle, which is in the aorist, could be translated as 'is proclaimed', and so would designate a present state or activity: the Gospel is being proclaimed everywhere. See Barth and Blanke, *Colossians*, 224.

The same issue had already come up in Paul's first letter. In expressing thanksgiving for the way the Thessalonians had persevered, he wrote: 'we know that he [God] has chosen you, because our message of the gospel came to you not in word only, but also in power and in the Holy Spirit' (1 Thess. 1: 4–5). The saving power of the Holy Spirit worked to change the hearts and lives of those who heard the Apostle. But what of all those in the first century and later times to whom the message of the gospel never came? They never heard the 'word' that the power of the Spirit could make fruitful in Christian lives of faith, hope, and love.

Paul struggles with a different issue. He agonizes over the failure of many Israelites to believe in Jesus Christ (Rom. 9–11). He argues that God's promise to Israel has not failed, that any apparent rejection of Israel by God is not final, that the election of Israel is irrevocable, and that resistance to the gospel on the part of many Israelites has the providential effect of allowing the Gentiles to hear and receive the gospel. The Gentiles who believe in Christ are like branches grafted into an olive tree, which is and remains Israel. But what of the Gentiles who, for one reason or another, 'fail' to come to faith in Jesus Christ? Paul does not explicitly pose, let alone answer this question.

But some passages in his letters offer possible lines of response, when they are reread in the context of the twenty-first century and its questions: for instance, Romans 2: 14–16 and Galatians 4: 1–7. Such rereadings will go beyond what Paul evidently wished to communicate in his first-century, Mediterranean context at the start of Christian history. But, without going against or violating the Apostle's original meaning, our new context and questions can trigger some valid and illuminating rereadings. There is a plus-value in Paul's texts that, I hope to show, can guide Christians today in understanding the role of the Holy Spirit in the situation of 'other believers' and 'others' in general.

THE HOLY SPIRIT AND THE NON-EVANGELIZED

(1) As the ultimate basis for divine judgement, Paul proposes the law of Moses for Jews and the rule of conscience for the Gentiles (Rom. 2:

12–29). Despite his list of terrible sins that Gentiles commit, the Apostle recognizes that there are also morally sensitive and responsible Gentiles: 'When Gentiles, who do not have the law, do by nature what the law requires, these, while not having the law, are a law for themselves' (Rom. 2: 14). In the translation of the New Jerusalem Bible, these Gentiles 'through their innate sense behave as the law commands'. James Dunn observes that Paul does not 'envisage some Gentiles as *always* doing what the law requires, but simply the fact that there are Gentiles who for some of the time at least live as the law lays down'.[16] Their honourable and praiseworthy conduct prompts Paul to draw the conclusion: 'they give proof that what the law requires is written on their hearts, to which their own conscience also bears witness' (Rom. 2: 15). Their conscience, or moral sensibility, lets them know what is right or wrong. Hence the Apostle expects that such Gentiles will not be condemned in God's final judgement. They have lived responsibly and avoided actions that went against their conscience (Rom. 2: 15–16). The obedience of the heart of these honourable Gentiles, who have not lived as either Jews or Christians, will be seen to have existed and flourished beyond ethnic and religious boundaries. They will be justified by 'the law' which has been 'written on their hearts'—with 'heart' understood biblically as the personal centre that receives knowledge and revelation and is the seat of the emotions and the will.

Paul spells out later in the same letter the content of the law. It is love that 'fulfils' the law. One 'word', 'love your neighbour as yourself', sums up the commandments of the law: 'You shall not commit adultery. You shall not murder. You shall not steal; you shall not covet' and the further commandments (Rom. 13: 8–10). When Paul recalls the Ten Commandments and draws them together into the

[16] *Romans 1–8* (Dallas: Word Books, 1988), 98. Dunn rightly remarks that Paul does not attribute this 'doing the law' to the 'unaided efforts' of these Gentiles. He explains: ' "Doing the things of the law", even when the law itself is unknown, is possible only where "what is known/knowable of God" (Rom. 1: 19, 21) is the basis of conduct . . . in Paul's mind there is an immediate connection between knowing God and doing what God wants' (ibid., 98–9). One should add, however, that, for Paul, doing what God wants *also* essentially requires being helped by God in the struggle against the evil power of sin (Rom. 7: 14–8: 4). On Rom. 2: 14–16, see also Fitzmyer, *Romans*, 128–9, 305–12.

central law of love, he fills out what the law written on the hearts of the Gentiles entails. He also stands in clear continuity with Jesus, who had combined two classic OT texts on love of God and love of neighbour to highlight the centrality and simplicity of the 'love command'. Jesus went on to propose that the standard of final judgement for *all people* would be loving deeds of mercy that they have exercised (or failed to exercise) towards anybody in desperate need (see Chapter 7 above). The teaching of Jesus, no less than the ethical exhortations of Paul, unpacks what the latter left cryptically concise about Gentiles winning divine approval when they conscientiously perform what the law 'written on their hearts' summons them to.

Besides reading Romans 2: 14–16 in the light of a later passage in Romans and of Jesus' own teaching on deeds of love, we should be alerted to some key OT texts by the language about the law 'written on their hearts'. These words echo some passages from Jeremiah and Ezekiel. Opposing an increasingly limited view of the Sinai covenant, Jeremiah announced God's promise to make a new covenant inscribed on the hearts of his people: 'this is the covenant I will make with the house of Israel... I will put my law within them, and I will write it on their hearts' (Jer. 31: 33). Here Jeremiah promised 'an inward knowledge of God's will, written in the heart, which will obtain when the new covenant is established'.[17] Without speaking of a new covenant, a divine oracle in Ezekiel promises the gift of God's 'spirit' and of hearts of 'flesh' (responsive hearts) to replace hearts of 'stone' (insensitive hearts): 'I will give them a new heart and put a new spirit within them. I will remove the heart of stone from their flesh and give them a heart of flesh, so that they may follow my statutes and keep my ordinances and obey them' (Ezek. 11: 19–20). This promise of God's spirit and of new, morally sensitive hearts (which will make Israel observe the divine law) recurs in a later chapter of Ezekiel: 'A new heart I will give you, and a new spirit I will put within you, and I will remove from your body the heart of stone and give you a heart of flesh. I will put my spirit within you, and make you follow my statutes and be careful to observe my ordinances' (Ezek. 36: 26–7).

---

[17] Thrall, *The Second Epistle to the Corinthians*, i. 222.

Whether or not he consciously intended to do so, the language of
Paul in Romans 2 extends these prophetic promises to Gentiles. He
speaks, as we saw above, of the divine law and what it requires being
written in their hearts and enabling them to know, instinctively and
without being taught, what they should do. With the law written on
their hearts, their situation does not seem radically different from the
Israelites who were to have the law 'written on their hearts' and
receive 'a new heart' and a 'a new spirit', so that they can observe
the divine ordinances. Even if Paul does not follow Ezekiel in con-
trasting an old, 'stony' heart to be replaced by a heart of flesh, he
echoes the language of Ezekiel (and Jeremiah). Should we recognize
the Holy Spirit touching the hearts and lives of all those 'outsiders'
who show themselves ready to follow the essence of God's law, love
towards God and one's neighbour? Or has Christ 'written on their
hearts' what the law essentially requires?

The metaphor of writing implies a writer. This is not to extend
falsely the metaphor in question. The passage we cited from Jeremiah
and one we will cite from Paul both include a writer in their meta-
phorical talk of 'writing'. Jeremiah envisages YHWH not only as the
present 'Speaker' but also as the future 'Writer' on human hearts, just
as Ezekiel envisages God as the 'Implanter' of new, responsive hearts
of flesh. In Romans 2, Paul presumably has in mind a divine 'Writer'
as the one who writes on the hearts of Gentiles; the writing does not
involve any human agent. But the Apostle remains discreetly silent
about the precise identity of this divine 'Writer'.

Elsewhere and in another context, the Apostle identifies the 'Writer'.
Addressing the Christians of Corinth, Paul states his apostolic credentials: 'you yourselves are our letter, written on our [or your] hearts, to
be known and read by all, and you show that you are a letter of [=
about] Christ, prepared by us, written not with ink but with the Spirit
of the living God, not on tablets of stone but on tablets of human
hearts' (2 Cor. 3: 2–3).[18] The operation of the Holy Spirit has rooted
the presence of Christ deeply in the existence of Paul's readers. He
imagines their life as a letter about Christ which has come through the
apostolic ministry of Paul, and which has been inscribed on their
hearts by the Holy Spirit through the ministry of Paul himself. Here

----

[18] Furnish, *II Corinthians*, 181–3, 192–6.

the Apostle draws a contrast not between 'stony' or insensitive hearts and receptive hearts 'of flesh' but between the tablets of stone on which God wrote the covenant with Moses (Exod. 24: 12) and the responsive, living 'tablets' of the new covenant, the human hearts on which the Spirit writes.[19] What the Spirit writes on the hearts of Paul's readers is the image of Christ; they are 'all being transformed into the image' of the glorious Christ (2 Cor. 3: 18; see Rom. 8: 29).

In his Letter to the Romans Paul vividly presents the activity of the Holy Spirit in the life of Christians, whether Jew or Gentile in origin. 'The love of God', he writes, 'has been poured into our hearts through the Holy Spirit who has been given to us' (5: 5). The Spirit 'leads' Christians (8: 14), 'helps' them in their weakness (8: 26), and 'intercedes' for them (8: 27). Paul calls Christian life 'walking according to the Spirit' (8: 4). And although he never uses such language about the morally responsible Gentiles he envisages in Romans 2, yet he never explicitly denies the activity of the Spirit in their hearts and lives. Clearly God is involved in the law being written on their hearts. It is open to us to go beyond Paul's explicit statements and recognize the Holy Spirit at work with such Gentiles: writing the law on the hearts of these Gentiles, supporting them in the 'witness of their conscience', and empowering them to put into practice the essential requirements of the law.

Even if he never made such an application, the contrast Paul draws between 'life in the flesh and life in the Spirit' (Rom. 8: 5–11) surely applies to the case of honourable Gentiles. The Apostle states that 'the mind that is set on the flesh is hostile to God; it does not submit to God's law—indeed it cannot, and those who are in the flesh cannot please God' (Rom. 8: 7–8). If and when honourable Gentiles 'submit to the law' in the sense of doing what the law requires, they must be living 'according to the Spirit'. By definition they are not living according to the flesh, so as to be dominated by selfish passions and incapable of submitting to God's law. The classic contrast Paul draws in Romans 8 encourages us to interpret what he writes about honourable Gentiles in chapter 2 and understand their conduct to be living 'according to the Spirit'.

---

[19] Paul switches images here. We write with ink on parchment or paper, but carve messages on stone tablets.

(2) We come next to Galatians 4: 1–7 and what it can yield about the situation of unbaptized Gentiles. In the course of his dense Letter to the Galatians, Paul expounds the implications of what it means to be 'baptized into Christ'. Baptism brings a new equality that transcends ethnic, religious, social, and gender barriers: 'There is no longer Jew or Greek, there is no longer slave or free, there is no longer male and female; for all of you are one in Christ Jesus' (Gal. 3: 28).

The reference to 'slave or free' leads Paul to reflect on the situation of universal enslavement that prevailed before God acted to change radically the human situation (Gal. 4: 1–7).[20] Cosmic powers controlling the universe (for Gentiles) and the Mosaic Law (for Jews) functioned similarly to 'enslave' all human beings. Before the sending of the Son of God, they were 'under the power of' the cosmic elements (Gentiles)[21] and the Law (Jews). When God's Son was 'sent' and became a human being ('born of a woman'), the purpose of his being sent was to deliver the whole human race from slavery and take them all, through adoption, into the new family of God. The mission of the Holy Spirit was inseparably synchronized with the sending of the Son: 'because you are sons, God has sent the Spirit of his Son into our hearts, crying, "Abba! Father!"' (v. 6).[22] The 'our' of the Spirit sent 'into our hearts' (v. 6) matches the 'we' of 'so that we might receive adoption as sons' (v. 5); Paul (a Jew) and the Galatians (Gentiles) are all one in Christ and through the Spirit.

But where does the sending of the Son and the Spirit leave all those Gentiles (and Jews) who have never heard (and accepted) the gospel Paul preaches and have not entered through baptism into the new family of God? The Apostle does not address their situation as such. Presumably he understands them to share in the universal enslavement. But what then of the salvation of these non-evangelized and non-baptized?

---

[20] On these verses see J. L. Martyn, *Galatians* (New York: Doubleday, 1998), 384–408.

[21] 'The elements of the world' seem to denote what were understood to be the basic components of the universe (earth, air, fire, and water), which Gentiles linked to the gods they worshipped.

[22] 'Sons' is to be understood inclusively, in the light of Gal. 3: 28: 'there is no longer male and female; for all of you are one in Christ Jesus'.

The double mission 'from on high' that shapes this passage from Galatians yields a possible answer. Paul uses the same verb ('exapostellô') for the sending of the Son and the Spirit. God's action took the form of two distinct, but inseparable, missions. The former 'sending' was conspicuously visible—from the birth of Jesus (v. 4) through to his crucifixion, an event that is repeatedly recalled in the Letter to the Galatians. But the Spirit was not 'born of a woman' to live, preach, and die very publicly. Being 'sent into our hearts' denotes something intimate that concerns the inmost self of human beings, even if the presence of the Spirit prompts Christian believers into crying 'Abba! Father!' The mission of the Spirit, for all its visible results, is not as directly 'seeable' or manifestly identifiable as the mission of the Son.

Paul's language about the mission of the Holy Spirit opens up the possibility of acknowledging a wider, even universal impact of the Spirit on human hearts. The Apostle mentions the enslavement that afflicts all human beings (v. 3) before recalling the sending of the Spirit (v. 6). Since the enslavement is universal in fact, one could expect the sending of the Spirit to prove also universal in fact and not merely universal in principle (or qualified by the condition of accepting faith in Christ and receiving baptism).

Joining here some scholars who interpret the repeated Pauline expression 'faith of Jesus Christ' (e.g. Rom. 3: 22) as a subjective genitive (the faithfulness exercised by Jesus Christ) would help our argument about the universality of the Spirit's mission.[23] The faithfulness shown by Jesus in his life and death affects in fact all human beings, including those who never hear of him and thus have no chance of accepting *faith in him.* Through the mission of the Spirit, the faithfulness of Jesus is universally effective and touches all men and women. They too are empowered to live 'according to the Spirit' (Rom. 8: 5–11) and show moral responsibility in their behaviour (Rom. 2: 14–16)—in short, to act like Jesus with faithfulness towards the divine will.

The OT 'prefiguring' of the Holy Spirit can encourage this universal 'application' of what Paul proposes about the sending of the Spirit. According to the OT, the 'spirit' of God creates and sustains in existence all things (e.g. Ps. 104: 29–30; Job 34: 14–15).

---

[23] See e.g. Stegman, *The Character of Jesus*, 98–110, 146–68.

Mysteriously incalculable, the divine 'spirit' will transform Israel into a true and faithful people of God (Ezek. 36: 26–7), and can refashion creatively the lives of repentant sinners (Ps. 51: 10–11). Undoubtedly, the OT pays more attention to the impact of the 'spirit' of God on Israel as a whole and on individuals who belong to the people of God. Nevertheless, the creative power of the 'spirit' is not limited to the chosen people but can accomplish the divine will religiously and morally among 'outsiders' and, indeed, on the whole universe. In Chapter 3 above we saw a spectacular example of this, when 'the spirit of God came upon Balaam' (Num. 24: 2) and this non-Israelite diviner pronounced oracles concerning Israel, David, and Christ himself.

In short, what Paul remarks about the sending of the Holy Spirit into the 'hearts' of Christian believers can be legitimately understood about some kind of sending of the Spirit into the hearts of those not yet evangelized and baptized. We could move beyond Romans 2 and Galatians 4, and also press the application to non-evangelized Gentiles of what Paul writes about the life-giving Spirit of God in Romans 8: 1–27. To be sure, some of what the Apostle develops there about the Holy Spirit as the vital principle of the new order created through Christ's death and resurrection specifically concerns Christian believers: for instance, the passage about their adoption into God's family in which they are 'led' by the Spirit (vv. 12–17). Yet this adoption, 'the first fruits of the Spirit', embodies what the Spirit is doing for the whole of creation—for everything and everybody (vv. 18–25). The life-giving and life-enhancing power of the Spirit touches all human beings, Christians, Jews, and Gentiles alike. They are all being brought to the final fulfilment of the entire universe.

CHRIST AND THE NON-EVANGELIZED

What I have just argued for about the universal presence and impact of the Holy Spirit in the lives of the non-baptized finds its matching counterpart in what Paul says about Christ. Here the task is considerably easier, given the all-embracing language we cited from Paul in the first half of this chapter. Major themes from that first part can be readily focused on the powerful presence of Christ in the existence of all human beings, baptized or otherwise.

(1) The involvement of Christ in the reconciliation set out by Paul in 2 Corinthians 5 and Romans 5 (plus Rom. 11: 15) certainly embraces all humanity and may even enjoy also a cosmic dimension. In another letter the scope of reconciliation envisaged 'all things, whether on earth or in the heavens' (Col. 1: 20). Clearly this reconciliation of human beings through Christ affected and affects all those millions not yet evangelized. The powerful presence of Christ as universal 'Reconciler' touches all human beings, whether or not they come to accept baptism.

(2) The Christian redefining of monotheism meant recognizing Christ as agent of all creation: 'For us there is one God, the Father, from whom are all things and for whom we exist, and one Lord, Jesus Christ, through whom are all things and through whom we exist' (1 Cor. 8: 6). Presumably the 'we' of 'we exist', like the 'for us', points to Paul and his fellow Christians. But 'through whom are all things' comes across as all-embracing: everything and everyone exist through the power of Christ. As one who creates all and keeps all in existence, he is intimately involved in the existence of all human beings. Even though Paul does not draw here such a conclusion, his statement implies the sovereign rule and profound presence of Christ in the life of every man and every woman, including the non-evangelized.

A little later in 1 Corinthians Paul proposes some principles on the question of eating meat that may have come from an offering to an idol. He advises Christians: 'Eat whatever is sold in the meat market without raising any question on the ground of conscience.' In support of his position, Paul quotes at once language drawn from several psalms (24: 1; 50: 12; 89: 11): 'the earth and its fullness are the Lord's' (1 Cor. 10: 25–6). Since Paul has just spoken of Christ three times as 'the Lord' (1 Cor. 10: 21–2), he clearly seems to be attributing this language of the psalms to Christ and calling him 'the Lord', who has made the whole earth and to whom everything that exists belongs. Christ's divine sovereignty over all things underpins the decision for Christian freedom. Christ holds sway over everyone and everything, even over meat that may or may not have come on the market by passing through a pagan temple. Thus, in the course of resolving a particular issue about food to be eaten by Christians, Paul appeals to the universal power and presence of Christ in the existence of the whole created world and its inhabitants.

(3) Besides being the 'one Lord' of creation, Christ is the Last Adam, the new head of redeemed humanity, who has ushered in a new order for everyone. As we saw from what Paul writes in 1 Corinthians 15 and Romans 5, the influence of the Last Adam extends to all human beings: 'the grace of one man, Jesus Christ, has abounded for the many [= all]'. Christ's perfect obedience and faithfulness have led to 'justification and life for all' (Rom. 5: 15, 18). The universal impact of the Last Adam includes the promise of resurrection for all: 'as all die in Adam, so all will be made alive in Christ' (1 Cor. 15: 22).

Thus Paul pictures the Last Adam as a corporate figure whose benefits are all-encompassing, both here and hereafter. Even if the Apostle does not draw this explicit conclusion, his image of the Last Adam involves all people, including the non-baptized, as being intimately connected with Christ. He is the one who brings them all grace, justification, and life.

One could press further the universal relevance of Paul's New/Last Adam teaching by stressing how Jesus in his obedience perfectly embodied human existence as intended by God's original plan (e.g. Rom. 5: 19; Phil. 2: 8). This obedience was manifested in Jesus' self-giving love for others (2 Cor. 5: 14–15; Gal. 2: 20; Eph. 5: 2). Wherever and whenever Gentiles manifest something of this mode of existence, they give evidence of the New Adam's powerful presence—a presence, one should add, made effective through the Holy Spirit.

(4) Paul also presents Christ as the risen 'Lord' who exercises a divine sovereignty over all. A hymn expresses the Apostle's faith that the crucified and exalted Jesus enjoys lordship over everyone and everything: 'At the name of Jesus every knee should bend, in heaven, on earth, and under the earth, and every tongue confess that Jesus Christ is Lord' (Phil. 2: 10–11). The universal sovereignty could not be clearer. This sovereignty obviously extends to everybody, including those very many Jews and Gentiles who have not (or have not yet) joined the emerging Church through faith and baptism.

In conclusion, what Paul had to say about Jesus as universal 'Reconciler', agent of creation, New Adam, and exalted Lord clearly proposed his universal sovereignty, power, and presence. Even though he never formally posed the question, Paul wrote in ways that implied the intimate activity of Christ in the lives of all those who had not heard and accepted the gospel.

Examining Romans 2: 14–16 (in the light of 2 Cor. 3: 2–3) and Galatians 4: 1–7, I found significant ways of extending Paul's teaching to include the presence and activity of the Holy Spirit also in the lives of non-Christians. One might, of course, take a short cut here and simply press the case for this presence and activity on the grounds of the universal activity of Christ. The operations of Christ and the Holy Spirit are distinguishable but not separable—a point nicely illustrated by what we found Paul teaching in 2 Corinthians 3: 2–3 and Galatians 4: 1–7. Where Christ is, there is the Spirit also. Hence if the operations of Christ extend universally and touch intimately the lives of all, that must be true also of the Holy Spirit. Since all human beings are in some way 'in Christ', the Holy Spirit must also in some sense be 'in them'. This association between Christ and the Spirit emerges clearly in the work of Luke–Acts, to which we now turn.

10

Luke on Jesus and Salvation

Right from the start of his Gospel, Luke articulates the key theme of 'salvation' and the universal scope of the saving work of God. Two majestic prayers enunciate this theme: the 'Benedictus' glorifies God for 'salvation from our enemies and from the hand of all who hate us' (1: 71), and the 'Magnificat' praises 'God my Saviour' (1: 47). When Jesus is born, an angel of the Lord announces to the shepherds 'good news of great joy': 'to you is born this day in the city of David a Saviour' (2: 10–11). A third wonderful prayer, the 'Nunc Dimittis' of Simeon, indicates Luke's purpose in writing his two works. The old man expresses his thanks to God: 'my eyes have seen your salvation (sôtêrion), which you have prepared in the presence of all peoples, a light for revelation to the Gentiles and for glory to your people Israel' (Luke 2: 30–2). The climax of revelation and salvation has come for Israel and for all the nations.

These words from Simeon that form the climax of the birth narrative lead on to the ministry of John the Baptist, which signals the coming of God's salvation. To make this clear Luke quotes Isaiah 40: 5: 'All flesh will see the salvation (sôtêrion) of God' (Luke 3: 6). Through Jesus, this promise has been fulfilled: salvation has appeared for Jews and Gentiles. Part of this quotation from Isaiah reappears at the very end of Acts (28: 28), and serves to hold together through an 'inclusion' Luke's Gospel and Acts.[1]

In the OT, God is called the 'Saviour' (e.g. Isa. 45: 15, 21), who brings 'salvation' (e.g. Isa. 49: 6) and who raises up 'saviours' to deliver Israel (e.g. Judg. 3: 9, 15; 6: 36). Unlike the OT which extends

---

[1] This inclusion is strengthened by the way in which the theme of 'light' to both Jews and Gentiles turns up again close to the end of Acts (26: 17–18, 23).

the title to merely human figures, the NT limits it to God (the Father), called 'Saviour' eight times, and to Christ, called 'Saviour' sixteen times. Where Mark and Matthew never call Jesus 'Saviour' and John does so only once (John 4: 42), Luke does so three times (Luke 2: 11; Acts 5: 31; 13: 23). Luke also shows a liking for the verb 'to save (sôzein)'; he uses it thirty times in Luke–Acts.[2]

After recalling these headlines of theme and language, this chapter takes up two central questions. How centralized in Jesus, according to Luke, is the salvation of human beings? What would Luke imply about the situation of those who have not (or have not yet) heard the good news of Jesus and responded to him in faith? When raising the second question, I agree with Joseph Fitzmyer that Luke 'does not envisage the modern problem of salvation for human beings who have never heard of Christ or who are devotees of other religions, like Hinduism [or] Buddhism'.[3] Nevertheless, what Luke presents about such figures as an Ethiopian eunuch, Cornelius the centurion, and Paul's audiences in Lystra and Athens can yield some pointers towards answering the second question.

JESUS THE ONLY NAME

In his Gospel and Acts, the central message of Luke is that human beings are saved only through the crucified and resurrected Christ. Jesus is the sole agent of final salvation, and this salvation is available for all human beings. Luke's two-part work on Christian origins climaxes with the claim: 'There is the salvation through no one else [than Jesus]; for there is no other name under heaven given among human beings by which we must be saved' (Acts 4: 12).[4] This claim from a speech by St Peter fits into a whole pattern of speeches in Acts[5]

---

[2] For further details of scriptural usage, see G. O'Collins, 'Salvation', *ABD* v. 907–14.

[3] J. A. Fitzmyer, *The Acts of the Apostles* (New York: Doubleday, 1998), 302. See also M. Dumais, 'Le salut universel par le Christ selon les Acts des Apôtres', *Studien zum Neuen Testament und seiner Umwelt* 18 (1993), 113–31.

[4] See Fitzmyer, *The Acts of the Apostles*, 297, 301–2.

[5] While the substantial historical reliability of many of the narratives in Acts can be solidly defended (ibid., 124–8), the speeches and missionary discourses (which make up nearly one-third of the whole book) appear to be Lukan compositions, albeit

and introduces some of the most recurrent themes: the *universal* significance of his message (for all 'human beings' 'under heaven') and the *name* of Jesus. In Acts, the apostles and others baptize 'in the name of Jesus', preach and teach in his name, and work miracles in his name. The 'name' is to be identified as Jesus himself; it re-presents Jesus really and effectively. When people put their faith in his 'name', they put their faith in Jesus himself and find salvation in him.[6] As regards 'salvation (sôtêria)', Luke uses the word ten times in his Gospel and Acts. It is never found in Mark and Matthew and only once in John (4: 22). It is only here in Acts 4: 12 that Luke attaches the definite article to 'salvation' ('hê sôtêria, the salvation'). In short, the language of this verse suggests that it offers us Luke's primary message in miniature.[7]

This message is to be proclaimed everywhere, starting from Jerusalem and reaching 'the ends of the earth' (Acts 1: 8). Luke gathers into his scene in Jerusalem on the day of Pentecost 'the whole house of Israel' (Acts 2: 36)—not only local Jews but also those diaspora Jews who have come from 'every nation under heaven' (Acts 2: 5–11). The latter group of Jews represent their homelands and the Gentile inhabitants of those lands. Their presence in Jerusalem symbolizes that the Gospel is to be addressed both to all Israel, scattered throughout the world, and to the Gentiles in the nations from which these Jews come. Thus it is a message also for 'all those far away' (Acts 2: 39) and, indeed, for 'all the families of the earth' (Acts 3: 25). The mission will cross ethnic and religious boundaries. After scenes of evangelization in different locations, the

passages in which Luke draws on some historical details and may give the general sense of what was actually said (ibid., 103–13). The speeches and discourses cannot be taken to be verbatim reports; they show repeatedly Luke's style and formulations.

[6] To indicate that 'calling upon the *name* of the Lord' brings salvation, Acts 2: 21 has quoted Joel 2: 32. This prophetic text originally referred to calling on the name of YHWH, to whom in the OT prayers and sacrifices were offered (e.g. Gen. 4: 26; 13: 4). Now in Acts and elsewhere in the NT (Rom. 10: 9–13), 'calling on the name of the Lord' is applied to invoking and venerating Jesus in early Christian worship. Acts 4: 12 implies such cultic veneration of Jesus: salvation comes through calling on the name of the Lord Jesus. See L. W. Hurtado, *Lord Jesus Christ: Devotion to Jesus in Earliest Christianity* (Grand Rapids, Mich.: Eerdmans, 2003), 179–85.

[7] This conclusion emerges from the *whole* context of Luke's Gospel and Acts. In the *immediate* context of Acts 4: 12, Peter is talking only to fellow Jews ('we' in that sense) and not to those who adhere to other faiths.

Book of Acts ends when St Paul arrives in Rome and announces there the gospel 'with all boldness and without hindrance' (Acts 28: 31).

Luke's narrative unfolds geographically, as various apostles and others accepted the mission to evangelize the world and took the Christian message into Asia and around the Mediterranean world. At first located in Jerusalem, the Church became a universal society. This is hinted at by the gift of tongues which enabled the twelve apostles to speak to people of all nations (Acts 2: 6–11). They would proclaim their new message to Israel and, eventually, to all the world. Right from the day of Pentecost the Holy Spirit not only proved central in the blessings of salvation but also worked to guide this missionary outreach (e.g. Acts 8: 29; 10: 19). When controversy arose about the conditions for admitting Gentiles into the Church, the community in Jerusalem, led by the apostles and elders, decided under the guidance of the Holy Spirit (Acts 15: 28) not to impose on such converts circumcision and other items in the Mosaic law. They were merely asked to abstain from 'fornication' (meaning here 'illicit marital unions') and meat that had been sacrificed to idols (Acts 15: 20, 29). Although this was not stated, such 'fornication' and food offered to idols were understood to have been forbidden to the descendants of Noah, and so remain obligations to be observed by righteous people of all nations.[8]

While highlighting the activity of the Holy Spirit in founding and developing the Church and in inspiring prophetic utterances and actions at crucial moments (e.g. Acts 4: 8), Luke does not imply that the ascension had removed the risen Jesus from the scene, as if he had gone away on a kind of extended 'sabbatical leave' that would last until his final coming (Acts 1: 9–11). Both Jesus and the Holy Spirit remain very much present to the expanding Christian Church. Luke moves easily from cases of guidance by the Holy Spirit (e.g. Acts 8: 29, 39; 13: 2–4; 16: 6) to cases of guidance by the exalted Christ (e.g. Acts 9: 10–16; 18: 9–10; 22: 17–21). Paul, whose missionary journeys dominate the second half of Acts, experiences the encouragement of Jesus (Acts 23: 11)—right through to the episodes that will bring him

---

[8] Fitzmyer rejects (but not convincingly) such a background in the Noachic regulations, and proposes finding a background in part of the Holiness Code (Lev. 17–18); see his *Acts of the Apostles*, 556–8.

ultimately to Rome. The final moments in the martyrdom of Stephen express vividly the inseparable operations of the risen Lord and the Spirit whom Jesus has sent from the Father (Acts 2: 33). Just before he is stoned to death, Stephen was 'filled with the Holy Spirit, gazed into heaven, and saw the glory of God and Jesus standing at the right hand of God' (Acts 7: 55).

Luke tells the story of the proclamation of the name of Jesus in a way that corresponds to Paul's order of responsibility: to the Jews first, and then to the Gentiles (Rom. 1: 16). On the day of Pentecost the audience were Jews. In Jerusalem many Jews accepted Jesus as God's Messiah and joined the community of his followers, but many did not. The Sanhedrin had the twelve apostles flogged (Acts 5: 40). Charged with prophesying against the Temple, Stephen was stoned to death (Acts 6: 8–8: 1). From Jerusalem the message about Jesus moved out to Samaria, the coast of Palestine, Damascus, and Antioch in Syria, the third largest city (after Rome and Alexandria) in the Roman Empire.

During his first missionary work in inner Asia Minor, Paul and his companions came to Pisidian Antioch. On successive sabbath days Paul preached the Gospel in the Jewish synagogue. After being spurned and driven away, Paul and his entourage took the message of Jesus to the Gentiles (Acts 13: 13–52). On his second missionary journey, the Apostle followed the same order in Thessalonica and Corinth: first, they proclaimed the good news to the Jews and then, when rebuffed, to the Gentiles (Acts 17: 1–15; 18: 1–17). Finally, when he arrived in Rome, Paul called together the local Jewish leaders. When rejected by many of them, he turned to the Gentiles (Acts 28: 17–28). Thus Luke punctuates the missionary journeys of Paul with three important scenes, in which the Apostle successively discharged his duty of proclaiming Jesus to Jewish audiences before solemnly turning to take his message to the Gentiles: in Pisidian Antioch (inner Asia Minor), Corinth, and Rome. Loyal to Israel, Paul persisted in his mission to the Jews, even though he met much rejection right through to the last major scene in Acts.

At the end of Matthew's Gospel, the risen Christ gives his followers a mission to the whole world: 'Go and make disciples of all nations, baptizing them in the name of the Father, and of the Son, and of the Holy Spirit, and teaching them to obey everything that I have commanded you. And remember, I am with you always, even to the end of the age' (Matt. 28: 19–20). The last chapter of Luke's Gospel ends with a similar commission: 'repentance and forgiveness of sins is to be proclaimed in his [Christ's] name to all nations' (Luke 24: 47). Matthew does not go on to write anything further after the closing commission. The conclusion to his Gospel might encourage readers, if they have forgotten earlier warnings (e.g. 10: 16–23; 24: 9–14), to imagine that the mission unfolded without much difficulty and danger. Luke, however, makes it clear in Acts that the mission to the world, along with its successes, also met with resistance and rejection. Conflict with unbelieving Jews and others will prove prominent in Acts, right through to the last chapter. Luke, along with the letters of St Paul, illustrates the pain, distress and experience of opposition involved in taking to the world the message of salvation through the crucified and risen Christ. From the arrest of Peter and John (Acts 4: 1–22), a series of arrests and releases punctuates the narrative of Acts. Imprisonment symbolizes various human efforts to block the spread of the gospel, but in one way or another all these efforts fail.

To sum up: Luke presents Jesus as the one Saviour for all people and the Christian community as the place where, through repentance and baptism in the name of Jesus, sins are forgiven and the Holy Spirit is communicated. The blessings of the messianic age are available for all who repent and call upon the name of Jesus (Acts 2: 21, 38–40). What then does Luke think, or at least imply, about those who continue to worship and live in other ways?

THE SITUATION OF OTHERS

To describe the new situation initiated by Pentecost, Luke cites some words from the prophet Joel about God declaring, 'I will pour out my Spirit upon all flesh' (Joel 2: 28). Joel understood 'all flesh' to refer primarily to the people of Judah (Joel 3: 2, 17, 19–21). For Luke, however, the gift of the Holy Spirit to all human beings characterizes the final age. The Spirit is not merely poured out on the day of Pentecost but remains a divine promise to be realized progressively through the whole of Acts. By means of the mission to the world, the Spirit is spread to new groups: in Samaria (Acts 8: 15–17), Caesarea (Acts 10: 45–6), and Ephesus (Acts 19: 1–7). Luke shows how the gift of the Spirit is now open to Gentiles.

But is sharing in the Spirit (and in Christ) limited to those Jews and Gentiles who repent of their sins and accept baptism in the name of Jesus (Acts 2: 38–9)? What of those who have not (or have not yet) heard the gospel and accepted faith in Christ? Our answer can take shape around three episodes in Acts, which involve, respectively, an Ethiopian eunuch, a Roman centurion, and an audience who hear Paul in Athens. Without doing violence to what Luke wishes to communicate, we can find a plus-value in his text which illuminates the situation of 'outsiders'.

(1) The story in Acts 8: 26–40 of the Ethiopian eunuch, an official from the court of the Candace or Queen of Ethiopia, has been called a 'stepping stone' *between* the conversion of the Samaritans and that of the Gentiles.[9] But it concerns someone who is most probably a Gentile (not a Jewish proselyte or convert), and is more like 'a leap to the extreme. Ethiopia was on the edge of the known world. This scene anticipates the power of the gospel to reach the end of the earth.'[10] In the narrative of Acts the encounter between the Ethiopian and Philip remains 'private'—an encounter on a road through the desert, which the church in Jerusalem does not seem to have heard about, let alone discussed. But it strikingly exemplifies the coming outreach of the good news, even to the remote limits of the world. Even if Acts cannot report that Christian evangelists reached the end of the earth, the Ethiopian stands for those who accept baptism at the very limits of the known world.

In meeting the eunuch on his mission to preach the word, Philip is prompted by the Holy Spirit (Acts 8: 26, 29). He acts with insight into the scriptures and with an authority that allows him to accept

---

[9] E. Haenchen, *The Acts of the Apostles* (Philadelphia: Westminster Press, 1971), 314. On the whole episode see R. C. Tannehill, *The Narrative Unity of Luke–Acts*, ii (Minneapolis: Fortress, 1990), 107–12.

[10] Tannehill, *The Narrative Unity of Luke–Acts*, ii. 107. Fitzmyer, however, understands the Ethiopian to be a Jew, or possibly a Jewish proselyte, but recognizes 'the difficulty' created by this interpretation (*The Acts of the Apostles*, 410).

the eunuch's request to be baptized after a very brief preparation. As an African and a eunuch, the Ethiopian is doubly an outsider. Luke may well have had in mind a passage in Second Isaiah which expresses God's loving concern with two excluded classes: eunuchs and foreigners (Isa. 56: 3–8). The Ethiopian may have been one of those whom Luke calls 'God-fearers' (e.g. Acts 10: 2, 22). He has travelled a long distance to worship in Jerusalem, even if he would have remained marginalized by the prohibition against passing beyond the outer court of the Temple. When Philip joins him, he is on the way home from Jerusalem and, significantly, is reading a passage from the Song of the Suffering Servant (Isa. 53: 7–8).

What interests me in the context of this book is the situation of the Ethiopian *before* he asked for baptism. He worshipped the one, true God of Israel, read the scriptures prayerfully, and, in particular, was moved by the Suffering Servant. Second Isaiah's mysterious prefiguring of Jesus in his suffering puzzled and affected the eunuch, a marginalized outsider. Philip then took up this text to proclaim to him 'the good news about Jesus' (Acts 8: 39). The Ethiopian represents those who are touched by suffering, and in prayer seek for the meaning of what they and others suffer. In Luke's narrative, while the Holy Spirit works in the life and choices of Philip, the suffering Christ is mysteriously challenging someone who is not yet a baptized Christian. The Ethiopian eunuch seems emblematic of those who seek (and sometimes find) Christ in their struggle with the mystery of suffering.[11]

(2) Interestingly it is the Holy Spirit who figures more prominently in the second episode, which involves repeated divine messages and actions (Acts 10: 1–11: 18)[12] and concerns the conversion to Christian faith of Cornelius, a Roman centurion, who with his household and friends represents the Gentile world. Luke presents him as follows: 'He was a devout man who feared God with all his

---

[11] See M. Parsons, 'Isaiah 53 and Acts 8', in W. H. Bellinger and W. R. Farmer, *Jesus and the Suffering Servant: Isaiah 53 and Christian Origins* (Harrisburg, Pa.: Trinity Press International, 1998), 104–19.

[12] On this whole section see Fitzmyer, *The Acts of the Apostles*, 446–73; R.W. Wall, *The Acts of the Apostles*, in *The New Interpreter's Bible*, x (Nashville: Abingdon, 2002), 162–72.

household; he gave alms generously to the (Jewish) people and prayed constantly to God' (Acts 10: 1–2).

One day, when he is praying at home in Caesarea Maritima, Cornelius has a vision and receives a divine message to send for Simon Peter. Cornelius obeys and despatches three messengers to invite Peter to leave Joppa and visit him (Acts 10: 3–8). The following day, when the messengers are approaching Joppa, Peter himself has a vision which declares all food to be clean and then is told by the Holy Spirit to welcome the messengers from Cornelius (Acts 10: 9–23). As Joseph Fitzmyer comments, 'God's Spirit first uses the symbolism of clean and unclean food to teach Peter a proper understanding of Gentiles in the divine plan of salvation. As no food that God has provided for his created people can be called unclean, so no human being can be considered unclean, i.e., unworthy of a share in that plan.'[13] The abolition of the dietary regulations for those of Gentile background means abolishing the deeper distinction between Jews and (unclean) non-Jews.

The next day Peter and the messengers leave for Caesarea and meet Cornelius, who has gathered 'his relatives and close friends'. After Cornelius has recounted his vision to Peter, Peter remarks significantly that he now clearly understands that 'God shows no partiality. But in every nation anyone who fears him and does what is right is acceptable to him.' Peter then summarizes the good news about Jesus. Thereupon, in a public way that repeats Pentecost the Holy Spirit falls upon Cornelius and his party. Jewish Christians who have come with Peter recognize that this manifestation corresponds to their own experience of the Spirit and that unbaptized Gentiles can share their experience of God. The spectacular outpouring of the Spirit persuades Peter that these Gentiles must be baptized without delay (Acts 10: 23–48).

When conservative Jewish Christians in Jerusalem object to Peter's association with Cornelius and other Gentiles, Peter defends his conduct. He becomes an advocate of the Gentiles (Acts 11: 5–17). Subsequently he does so, in a more theological way, at the 'Council of Jerusalem' (Acts 15: 7–11). Peter officially inaugurates the mission

---

[13] Fitzmyer, *The Acts of the Apostles*, 454.

to the Gentiles. They become part of God's people without undertaking the obligation to obey the prescriptions of the Mosaic law.

At least seven important themes emerge from the story of Cornelius. First, while he is still an unbaptized Gentile, his piety is exemplary. He leads his household by his life of constant prayer and generous almsgiving. Second, he is favoured with a vision in which an angel of God brings him a message that changes his own life and that of innumerable others.[14] To describe the angelic vision, Luke uses language that recalls the coming of a divine messenger to Mary (Luke 1: 26–38) and to Ananias (Acts 9: 10–17). Third, Luke retells (at greater or lesser length and with minor variations) the story of Cornelius' vision three times: the messengers of Cornelius do so (Acts 10: 22); Cornelius himself does so (Acts 10: 30–2); and Peter does so to the Christian community in Jerusalem (Acts 11: 13–14). By reporting repeatedly this vision of someone who is neither Jewish nor Christian, Luke emphasizes its importance and shows his readers that the religious experience of such 'outsiders' may bring them into remarkably close intimacy with God.

Fourth, through meeting Cornelius, Peter must face the question: How is he to respond to a Gentile with whom he would normally not associate but who devoutly worships God and receives an angelic message? How is he to make room for 'unclean' people, those with whom contact would cause defilement (Acts 10: 28)? It takes a vision and a subsequent prompting from the Holy Spirit to lead Peter into a relationship with 'outsiders'. He learns a major lesson: he may not declare such 'outsiders' unclean and unacceptable to God. Peter offers overnight hospitality to the Gentile messengers and presumably dines with them (Acts 10: 23). He then stays some days with Cornelius and, obviously, shares meals with him (Acts 10: 48; 11: 3). God has helped Peter to remove the religious and social barriers that previously kept him from such people. He learns to be like Jesus himself, who was reviled for eating with the wrong kind of people and lodging with them (Luke 5: 30; 15: 2; 19: 7).

---

[14] Through Peter and the subsequent 'Council of Jerusalem', Cornelius, his family, and his friends became the classic precedent for admitting Gentiles to baptism and Christian life, without imposing on them the Mosaic law about such matters as circumcision and food.

Fifth, any human beings, no matter who they are, provided they 'fear God and do what is right, are acceptable to God'. They can receive life-changing visions and enjoy the powerful presence of the Holy Spirit. Sixth, his own vision and the subsequent prompting of the Holy Spirit lead Peter into a relationship with someone of a different culture and faith. He must be open and ready to acknowledge powerful experiences of God enjoyed by outsiders. Seventh, if Cornelius is to discern the divine will and be led eventually to baptism, he must share his religious experience with other persons. Likewise, Peter will discern the divine will through appreciating what an 'outsider' has experienced and why he and his entourage are standing 'in the presence of God to listen to all that the Lord' commands Peter to say (Acts 10: 33).

Luke has a generous view of the religious life that 'outsiders' can live. They can even be favoured with divine visions and the manifest presence of the Holy Spirit. Furthermore, their religious experience may have something very significant to teach not only Christians in general but also the leaders of the Church. Anyone who treasures the authority of the NT scriptures dares not take a less generous view of the religious experience of 'outsiders' and their possibilities. Jesus is not merely Lord of the Jewish people (Luke 2: 11), but 'Lord of all' people (Acts 10: 36). If his authority applies to all (Acts 10: 42), his benefits are open to all (Acts 10: 43).

(3) Before examining a longer speech by Paul in Athens (Acts 17: 16–34), we need to take up a much shorter speech by Paul and Barnabas in Lystra (Acts 14: 15–17). This brief speech also touches the situation of Gentiles—in particular, those who (unlike the Ethiopian eunuch and Cornelius) do not share the faith of Judaism in one God and accept the Jewish scriptures.[15] Paul and Barnabas highlight the fruitfulness of nature which witnesses to the goodness towards all exercised by the Creator of the universe: 'he [God] has

[15] The centurion of Caesarea shares Jewish faith in one God, and apparently follows the Jewish hours for prayer. When introduced to the reader, he is praying 'about 3 o'clock' (Acts 10: 2). That he also accepts the Jewish scriptures should be presumed from his status as 'God-fearer'. Such 'God-fearers' (see Acts 13: 16, 26), while not submitting to circumcision and not observing the Torah in is entirety, agreed with the ethical monotheism of Jews and attended synagogue services and hence were familiar with the Jewish scriptures.

not left himself without a witness in doing good, giving you rains from heaven and fruitful seasons, and filling you with food and your hearts with joy' (Acts 14: 17). God has been the source of such blessings, which the Gentiles of Lystra have constantly received. All alike, Christians, Jews, and Gentiles, have been the beneficiaries of the generous benevolence that God reveals through nature. The fruitful constancy of the rains and the seasons recalls the covenant which God made through Noah with all peoples (Chapter 1 above). Here and there this theme surfaces when the psalms praise the providential care God shows to all his creatures: 'The eyes of all look to you, and you give them their food in due season. You open your hand, satisfying the desire of every living thing' (Ps. 145: 15–16).[16]

Paul and Barnabas firmly announce a radical change in the religious situation of the Gentiles whom they are addressing. They do not condemn them for their religious practices: 'in past generations he [God] permitted all the nations to follow their own ways' (Acts 14: 16). But what God tolerated has now come to an end. When Paul cures a crippled man, the people of Lystra shout out: 'the gods have come to us in human form'. They call Paul 'Hermes' ('because he was the chief speaker') and Barnabas 'Zeus', and, with the help of a priest from the temple of Zeus, want to offer sacrifice to them as if they were gods. Paul and Barnabas call on them to stop: 'Friends, why are you doing this? We are mortals just like you.' Then they proclaim their apostolic message, 'We bring you good news, that you should turn from these worthless things to the living God, who made the heaven, the earth, the sea, and all that is in them' (Acts 14: 15). The age of polytheism and the worship of idols ('worthless things') is past. The people of Lystra should turn to worship and follow the one, living God, who has created everything and provides all that is good for human life.

The brief episode and speech in Lystra faces for the first time in Acts the situation of those who believe in many gods and worship idols. Nothing is said about Jesus in the brief speech made by Paul and Barnabas. They are content to appeal to the 'book of nature' and its witness to the universal benevolence of the one, true God. The

---

[16] See also Ps. 146: 6; 147: 8–9; Jer. 5: 24.

story of what happens in Lystra is a brief prelude to what will be said in Athens. Yet the appeal to the constant fruitfulness of nature that reveals God's providential care for everyone remains important. The testimony of nature to the divine benevolence can be heard and accepted by all people everywhere.

When Paul speaks in Athens—either on the hill of the Areopagus or to the council of the Areopagus—his discourse appeals in a masterly way to the common ground he shares with his audience.[17] Thus he can make his message about Jesus effective in a wider world. The Apostle has already been preaching in the marketplace (the 'agora') the good news of Jesus and the resurrection, but some of his hearers have grossly misunderstood his message. They think that he is proclaiming two 'foreign divinities' ('Jesus' and his consort 'Anastasis (Resurrection)'). He must deliver his message in a fresh way that will communicate in the cultural and religious setting in which he now finds himself. The discourse of Paul is a model of missionary tact, but it also yields some suggestive pointers for the theme of this book: the religious situation of those who have not yet heard or not yet accepted the gospel. Let us see, first, the details of Paul's approach and how he introduces his message.

The basic cultural value familiar to Paul's audience concerns knowledge. They asked him: 'May we *know* what this new teaching is that you are proposing? It sounds rather strange to us, so we would like to *know* what it means' (Acts 17: 19–20; italics mine). Paul takes up the value of knowledge in his reply: 'Athenians, I see how extremely religious you are in every way. For as I went through the city and looked carefully at the objects of your worship, I found among them an altar with the inscription "To a God *Unknown*"' (Acts 17: 22–3; italics mine). The Apostle took this as a sign of their worshipping, yet without their really knowing, the one, true God. At the end Paul returns to the theme of knowledge and its absence, ignorance: 'God has overlooked the times of human *ignorance*.' 'All people everywhere' can know the divine command to repent and prepare themselves for the day of judgement (Acts 17: 30–1). A wonderful inclusion moves from the Athenians' worship of 'a God Unknown' to

---

[17] On Acts 17: 16–34 see Fitzmyer, *The Acts of the Apostles*, 599–617; Wall, *The Acts of the Apostles*, 241–50.

the end of the times of 'ignorance' for 'all people everywhere'. Paul has engaged a fundamental value of his audience, their desire for knowledge.

What all people can know is a relationship that transcends every racial and ethnic difference, the fundamental relationship of creatures to the Creator. God has 'made the world and everything in it'. In particular, 'from one ancestor [Adam, to whom Luke 3: 38 traces the human ancestry of Jesus] he [God] made all nations to inhabit the whole earth'. God is not merely close to every nation but also to every individual: 'in him we live and move and have our being'. Everyone is called to repent and prepare for the 'day on which he [God] will have the world judged in righteousness' (Acts 17: 24, 28, 30–1). Thus all human beings share the same basic relationship to God the Creator and final Judge. Together they make up God's 'offspring' (Acts 17: 28–9) or family. They are all God's people and God's children. Paul finds the basis for God's call to the whole of humanity not in the special history of the Jewish people (which climaxes with Christ) but in the created status that is shared by all human beings.

The Apostle highlights three serious misunderstandings of God: he 'does not live in shrines made by human hands'; he is not 'served by human hands' as though he needed meat or other offerings; he cannot be represented by gold, silver, or stone images 'formed by the art and imagination' of human beings (Acts 17: 24, 25, 29). God does not require or depend upon temples, rites, and beautiful images. God utterly transcends the needs that human beings experience. Yet the divine transcendence does not mean that God is distant or simply absent: 'he is not far from each of us. For in him we live and move and have our being' (Acts 17: 27–8). God 'gives to all human beings life and breath and all things … he allots the times of their existence and the boundaries of the places where they would live' (Acts 17: 25–6). The relationship between God and human beings is not symmetrical. In a sovereign way God creates, gives life, and provides for human needs. Human beings do not give life to God and provide for the divine needs.

Human beings are created by God and preserved in existence by God, 'so that they would grope' and 'search for God' (Acts 17: 26–7). Their life comes from God and exists in God. Hence their search for God is part of a radical relationship to God, which determines their total existence. The image of living, moving, and having one's being *in God* has its closest analogue for human beings during the first nine months of their existence. They live, move, and have their being within their mother, on whom they radically depend for life, sustenance, and growth. She is their total, all-determining environment. I do not allege that Luke understands in a 'maternal' way the notion, expressed in a frequent pattern of Greek language, about God being the One in whom we live, move, and have our being.[18] But the text is obviously open to be applied to the situation of human life in the maternal womb. God is constantly present as the all-determining One, even (or especially?) when human beings search and blindly grope for him.

In the strategy of his speech, Paul shows himself very tactful and focuses on what the situation in front of him provides. The reader has been told that he 'was deeply distressed to see that the city [Athens] was full of idols' (Acts 17: 16). But when Paul recalls his tour of the places and objects of worship, he does not express that feeling. Rather he congratulates the Athenians on being 'extremely religious in every way', and finds a specific point of contact through an altar with the inscription 'to a God Unknown'. That inscription, he suggests, testifies to the implicit awareness the Athenians already had of the God whom Paul now wishes to proclaim (Acts 17: 22–3). The Apostle is not going to introduce a 'foreign' or alien deity, who hitherto had nothing to do with the people of Athens (Acts 17: 18). Rather he will speak of the God already implicitly worshipped by them, even if hitherto not explicitly known. Paul presses on to find common ground with Greek poets and philosophers. He draws from 'your own poets'—specifically, a remark about God ('for we too are his offspring') that comes from the opening lines of a poem by Aratus.[19] From their point of view, some of the philosophers (Acts 17: 18) could agree with the misunderstandings of God that Paul lists (see above). The Apostle calls on the Athenians to break decisively

[18] Fitzmyer rightly dismisses theories that this 'Lucan tricolon' was drawn from Greek philosophical writing or was 'modelled on words' of the poet Epimenides. It is simply 'an old and frequent pattern in the Greek language' (*The Acts of the Apostles*, 610).

[19] Since Aratus was a Stoic, quoting him is a courteous gesture to the Stoic philosophers in Paul's audience.

with their religious past. The new time requires all people to repent and prepare for the world's judgement that will come through 'a man [Jesus] whom he [God] has appointed' and authorized 'by raising him from the dead' (Acts 17: 30–1). Thus at the end of a tactful speech that respects the Graeco-Roman culture of his audience, Paul makes his own faith clear: he views world history and its finale from only one perspective, that of the crucified and resurrected Jesus.

Clearly idolatry is a serious problem for Paul. Yet even here his approach is gentle: 'we ought not to think that the deity is like a statue of gold, or silver, or stone, a work of human art and imagination' (Acts 17: 20). The 'we ought not' puts things delicately. There is no 'I' denouncing what 'you' do. It is almost as if Paul himself felt inclined to make idols, but held back, realizing that this was something 'we should not do'.

In Paul's discourse, Luke presents a tactful masterpiece which enjoys some fruit. When Paul concluded, 'some joined him and became believers, including Dionysius the Areopagite, a woman called Damaris, and others with them' (Acts 17: 33). The skilful and respectful strategy of the speech provides a lasting model of how Christians should evangelize those who have had no contact with Jewish monotheism and scriptures. Does the speech yield any pointers for Christian thinking about the religious situation of those who have not yet been evangelized?

IMPLICATIONS FROM THE AREOPAGUS

Paul's sermon in Athens depicts the major Christian missionary in the second half of Acts seriously confronting and being confronted by the Graeco-Roman culture for the first time. In preaching to the Gentiles of the city, he faces pagan idolatry, Greek philosophy, and Athenian intellectual curiosity. And yet, as Joseph Fitzmyer helpfully points out, such 'speeches are addressed to the readers of Acts rather than to the individual audiences named in the narratives'.[20] Through the figure of Paul, Luke is preaching to his readers. Since that

[20] Fitzmyer, *The Acts of the Apostles*, 106.

includes readers nearly two thousand years later, one can feel even more justified in applying his texts to the question of the salvation of those human beings who have either never heard of Christ or have not (yet) accepted the message about him. To be sure, Luke does not raise this question. But the texts he directs to his readers provide some hints and suggestions for those who raise the question.

(1) First of all, what Luke writes inculcates a respectful appreciation for the cultures and religions of 'others'. The relatively brief sermon in Athens shows such respect for the Greek poets and philosophers. Paul quotes a line from Aratus, who was both a poet and a (Stoic) philosopher. At least some of the philosophers in the audience that Luke portrays would be in substantial agreement with the belief that God has 'made the world and everything in it' (Acts 17: 24). Instead of launching at once into a denunciation of idol worship, Paul congratulates the Athenians on being 'extremely religious in every way'. In particular, he thoughtfully appreciates what is implied by an altar with the inscription 'to a God Unknown' (Acts 17: 22–3). In other words, Luke pictures Paul as looking for what is true, valuable, and worthwhile in the culture and religion of these 'others'.

This attitude of positive appreciation is well based. God shows providential benevolence towards all human beings and supplies what is good for their life. Christian readers of the speech in Lystra cannot ignore the testimony of nature to the divine concern for all people everywhere (Acts 14: 17). Since God acts with such positive goodness towards everyone, a Christian should share something of that generous attitude when he or she reflects on the religious status of the 'others'. In fact, they are not truly 'others'. All human beings are God's 'offspring' (Acts 17: 28–9) and make up the one family of God.

(2) This brings us to a second guideline to be drawn from the Areopagus meeting. Luke recognizes a most significant factor in the common ground shared by Paul and those whom he addresses: their basic orientation to God. The whole of humanity is united in its origin from one and the same Creator, who 'made the world and everything in it'. All created existence comes from God, who 'made all nations to inhabit the whole earth, and allotted the times of their existence and the boundaries of the places where they should live' (Acts 17: 24, 26). All human beings, both collectively and individually, are near to the creator God: in him they 'live and move and have

[their] being'. Their lives are always enveloped by God, on whom they are utterly dependent—physically, spiritually, and intellectually. God sustains them constantly in the ultimate purpose of their human existence, that of groping and searching for God. When Christians reflect on and approach 'others', they should never forget how all human beings share alike the same radical closeness and orientation to God. To apply the maternal image suggested above, all human beings meet each other as those who share the same womb of God and who will look upon the face of God, when born to eternal life.

(3) Third, the way in which Paul engages the Athenians' desire for *knowledge* hints at a feature of human orientation to God that has been appreciated and expressed in various ways by great Christian thinkers, ancient and modern.[21] Karl Rahner (1904–84) understood the human spirit to be dynamically open to the fullness of being. Our mind is born with a primordial desire to know the Infinite One.[22] We might adapt what St Augustine of Hippo (354–430) wrote at the start of his *Confessions* and say: 'our minds were made for you, O Lord, and will not rest until they rest in you, O Lord'. Whether they clearly realize this or not, all people share the same deep hunger to know (and love) God. Whenever we meet each other, we meet people with a radical hunger in their minds and hearts—a deep hunger for God.

(4) Finally, there are many ways in which God continues to be misunderstood. Such misunderstandings of God are found everywhere and are not limited to the three that Luke pictures Paul as highlighting in Athens. But whatever the situation, God is no 'stranger'. As Luke appreciates, Paul does not aim to introduce into the cultural and religious context of Athens a 'foreign' or alien deity. Even if hitherto not explicitly known, the 'God Unknown' has

[21] The list would include Plotinus (*c.*205–70), St Augustine of Hippo (354–430), Dionysius the Pseudo-Areopagite (*c.*500), St Bonaventure (*c.*1217–74), St Thomas Aquinas (*c.*1225–74), Joseph Maréchal (1878–1944), and Bernard Lonergan (1904–84). Long before Christianity began, such philosophers as Plato (d. 347 BC) and Aristotle (d. 322 BC) grasped something of the dynamic human drive towards the infinite One.

[22] See e.g. K. Rahner, *Foundations of Christian Faith* (New York: Seabury Press, 1978), 31–5, 51–5; id., *Hearers of the Word* (New York: Herder and Herder, 1969), *passim.*

already been present among the Athenians. Paul gives a face and a name to the divine Anonymous One: it is the man Jesus whom God has raised from the dead and authorized to be the divine judge of everyone at the end of world history.

CONCLUSION

This chapter, by gleaning from Luke and Acts some themes on Jesus and the salvation of all, completes the first, biblical part of this book. We have retrieved much scriptural data, which seems, in one way or another, to illuminate the existence of those who enjoy no real possibility of embracing faith in Christ. There is considerably more to draw from the four Gospels and Paul, not to mention turning to the Letter to the Hebrews and the Book of Revelation or going back to further books in the OT. During this first part of the book, I have offered here and there some theological evaluation of biblical data. This will be done more thoroughly and systematically in the second part, which will also, where appropriate, introduce some further biblical testimony.

By definition Christians should not challenge the appeal to the NT scriptures. But what of the OT scriptures? May they be used in the coming chapters to clarify the condition of those who have or have not yet had the chance of responding to the message of Christ? Surely his life, death, and resurrection, with the coming of the Holy Spirit, have so altered the whole situation that any OT understanding of the status of 'others' no longer applies?

Yet it would seem a false step to eliminate en bloc the relevance of the OT to our issue. After all, the OT remains an essential guide to Christian moral behaviour (e.g. the Ten Commandments); in the Psalms it provides *the* Christian book of prayer. It remains essential if one is to grasp such central doctrines as the nature of faith; Paul (Rom. 4: 13–25) and Hebrews (11: 8–12) hold up the figures of Abraham and Sarah when expounding their understanding of faith. Apropos of those who are not (or are not yet) Christian, scholars have sought enlightenment by appealing to such episodes as God's covenant with Noah and such figures as Melchizedek and the Queen of Sheba. But much more should be said, even if guidelines for our question drawn from the OT need to be discerned carefully.[23]

In attempting to see how the Bible sheds light on the status of 'others', let us begin with issues that are more central and seem less controversial.

[23] See Pontifical Biblical Commission, *The Jewish People and Their Sacred Scriptures in the Christian Bible* (Vatican City: Libreria Editrice Vaticana, 2001).

11

Jesus, the Church, and Israel

We begin with the big picture. What do the NT scriptures propose about the role of Jesus for human salvation, about the function of the Church in communicating salvation, and about the enduring place of Israel in the divine plan of salvation?

JESUS THE UNIVERSAL SAVIOUR

The testimony from the NT cited in the previous four chapters leads to a clear conclusion. The original followers of Jesus held him to be *the* unique, universal Saviour: that is to say, the only one of his kind in being the Saviour of all men and women in all times and places. They did not accept and proclaim him as merely one saviour figure among others, a saviour who differed perhaps in degree from other saviour figures but was not unique in that role. For them, he was the only one of his kind in saving all people *from* sin, death, and other evils and saving them *for* life with God, here and hereafter. Let us recall and summarize the details.

(1) Chapter 7 drew together the evidence to establish that, while Jesus directed his mission primarily towards his fellow Jews, he also extended ministry to others. He responded to the needs of non-Jews: both individuals (e.g. by delivering the daughter of a Syro-Phoenician woman and a Gerasene demoniac) and groups (e.g. by feeding the 4,000). When preaching the reign of God, Jesus went beyond the frontiers of ethnic and religious separation. The divine kingdom, here and hereafter, was intended for everyone; this kingdom and its

claims knew no frontiers. In his preaching Jesus reached out to all human beings: in his ideals for marriage, his stress on doing the will of God, his parables, the Lord's Prayer, the beatitudes, and the love command.

Luke and Matthew, as we also saw in Chapter 7, adapt some teaching from Jesus about the final banquet, a feast 'for all peoples'. It is not easy to distinguish precisely the theological programmes of the evangelists from what Jesus taught. Yet the evangelists correctly understand what Jesus said and did to prefigure the universal scope of the Church's mission to the world. This mission continued and expanded what Jesus began during his earthly ministry. Matthew recognizes that the ministry of Jesus led on to a period when the followers of Jesus would bring to 'all the nations' their witness to the crucified and risen Lord. Luke also appreciates that Gentile 'outsiders' were invited to share in the final banquet of God's kingdom. John, even if this fourth evangelist in general pictures Jesus as active only among his own people and disengaged from 'outsiders', nevertheless, clearly opens the horizon when the passion came close. He represents Jesus as speaking of his being 'lifted up' on the throne of the cross and drawing all people to himself.

Whether or not Jesus ever literally used this language that we read in John's Gospel, it truly expresses the redemptive intentions of Jesus when faced with death. His violent end would bring, through his resurrection from the dead, the final reign of God and so prove salvific for the whole human race.

(2) Chapter 8 put the case: Jesus not only anticipated a violent death (and resurrection) but also interpreted his end as bringing lasting benefits for all people. There were two steps in this argument. First, Jesus portrayed himself as a 'bridegroom' who would be (violently) 'taken away' from his friends, a prophet who would face a martyr's death, and the 'Son' who would be killed by the tenants of God's 'vineyard'. The prophetic actions of Jesus in entering Jerusalem and cleansing the Temple help explain why he was arrested and executed. His predictions of the suffering, death, and resurrection that awaited 'the Son of man' have an historical core. But we must turn elsewhere to find some indications that Jesus accepted his death as a death for all.

Second, Jesus understood his passion and death not only as resulting from his proclamation of the divine kingdom but also as leading to the final establishment of that universal kingdom. By connecting his approaching death with the coming kingdom, Jesus interpreted that death as somehow salvific for all people. The strongest evidence that he understood his imminent death to benefit all people comes from the Last Supper. There Jesus defined his death as a sacrifice that would atone for sins and initiate a new and lasting covenant between God and all human beings. The Last Supper revealed definitively his saving outreach to everyone.

The characteristic ways in which Jesus had spoken and acted filled his death with meaning. He had shown himself the servant of all, and was ready to die for all, so as to release them from various kinds of servitude. His passion and death were integrated into his mission as a final act of service to all. His martyrdom would set right a moral order disturbed by sin and would bring a new relationship between human beings and God. Faced with death, Jesus interpreted it as a representative and redemptive service for all others.

(3) The death and resurrection of Christ, along with the outpouring of the Holy Spirit, confirmed, clarified, and expanded what his earliest followers took to be his saving impact on the world. As we saw in Chapter 9, the first Christian writer, St Paul, proclaimed the crucified and risen Jesus to be the Reconciler of the whole world, the Agent of the original and the new creation, the New/Last Adam whose obedience redeemed the human race, the Lord (*Kyrios*) of the universe. This salvation extended now to all the nations. Paul himself aimed to announce the good news to as many Gentiles as possible and as soon as possible. To counter the universal ravages of sin, the entire human race needed Christ and his saving grace.

(4) Our sampling of the NT testimony to the universal scope of Jesus' saving impact included Luke's two-part work, his Gospel and Acts (Chapter 10). Here too we heard the claim that the benefits of Christ were and are all-encompassing. Luke presents Jesus as the unique Saviour for all people—the One through whom sins are forgiven and the Holy Spirit is communicated. The blessings of the messianic age are available to all who repent and call upon the name of Jesus (Acts 2: 21, 38–40). We find Luke's primary message in

the words of Peter: 'There is salvation through no one else [than Jesus]; for there is no other name under heaven given among human beings by which we must be saved' (Acts 4: 12).

(5) One could press on and cite further NT witness to the universal extension of the redemptive role of Christ. The Johannine literature uses its characteristic terms to affirm the all-embracing relevance of Christ for revelation ('light', 'way', and 'truth') and salvation ('life'). He is 'the true light that enlightens every human being' (John 1: 9; see 9: 5). In his last discourse Jesus declares: 'I am the way, and the truth, and the life; no one comes to the Father, except through me' (John 14: 6). First John endorses the unqualified nature of this claim ('*the* way, *the* truth, and *the* life... *no one*') in terms of Christ being the sole source of eternal life: 'God gave us eternal life and this life is in his Son. He who has the Son has life; he who does not have the Son of God does not have life' (1 John 5: 11–12).

With its colourful, symbolic language the Book of Revelation makes similar universal claims for Christ. He has died but is alive forever, and has the keys to release those confined within the abode of the dead (Rev. 1: 18). It is his death that has delivered the numberless multitude of the redeemed—'from every nation, from all tribes and peoples and languages' (Rev. 7: 4–17, at v. 9). Since he has brought salvation to all, 'the Lamb' is adored (Rev. 5: 9–10, 12–14) in terms used for the adoration given to God (Rev. 4: 11).

From its earliest to its latest books, the NT did not waver in acknowledging Christ as the one Saviour for all people. The first Christians recognized his redemptive role to be universal (for all without exception), unique (without parallel), complete (as the One who provides the fullness of salvation and the means needed for that end), and definitive (in the sense of being beyond the possibility of being equalled, let alone surpassed in his salvific function). Specifically his redemptive 'work' means that through him sin is forgiven, the life of justification and grace is imparted, a new existence as God's adopted children made available, and a glorious transformation promised in the world to come. This NT sense of Christ's indispensable role for human salvation could be summarized by a fresh axiom: *extra Christum nulla salus* (outside Christ no salvation). His all-determining role in the whole redemptive drama is implied by the fact recalled in the last chapter: the NT gives the title 'Saviour' only to God (the Father) and to Christ.[1]

Undoubtedly those who are not Christians may well find such claims breathtaking, even bizarre. How could a first-century Jew who died by crucifixion determine eternally the salvation of all people of all times and places?[2] Sadly some contemporary Christians find it hard to accept the all-encompassing role of Christ for the salvation of the world. This can happen because they do not accept him as truly divine and hold him to be only a human figure chosen and sent by God. Hence he cannot be *the* Saviour of all humanity; his saving power can only be limited in scope and extension. Whatever their reasons for 'reducing' his saving function to something less than that, they should realize, however, that their views simply do not agree with the faith of NT Christians, the original and normative witnesses to what belief in Christ entails.

THE CHURCH MEDIATES SALVATION

(1) Right from the start, NT Christians were at one in holding that the salvation effected by Christ was mediated by entering the Church and doing so through baptism.[3] Early, perhaps very early, in the story of Christianity, the words of the prophet Joel about YHWH were applied to Jesus: 'everyone who calls on the name of the Lord will be saved' (Joel 2: 32).[4] 'Calling on the name of the Lord' meant invoking

[1] For further material on Christ as universal Saviour, see G. O'Collins, *Christology* (Oxford: Oxford University Press, 1995), 299–303.

[2] J. J. Rousseau enunciated classically this objection: 'You preach to me God, born and dying, two thousand years ago, at the other end of the world, in some small town I know not where; and you tell me that all who have not believed in this mystery are damned' (*Émile or On Education*, trans. Alan Bloom (New York: Basic Books, 1979), 304–5). To be sure, we must discount the idea that all who have not known about and had the chance of believing in this mystery are damned. Nevertheless, Rousseau saw the problem: How could a particular human life—and what is more, one that in many ways was modest and circumscribed—carry eternal consequences for the entire human race? Yet this is exactly what the NT Christians claimed.

[3] See L. Hartman, 'Baptism', *ABD* i. 583–94.

[4] See L. W. Hurtado, *Lord Jesus Christ: Devotion to Jesus in Earliest Christianity* (Grand Rapids, Mich.: Eerdmans, 2003), 179–85.

and venerating Jesus in worship—above all, in the celebration of baptism and the Eucharist. Peter ended his sermon to the Jews in Jerusalem on the day of Pentecost with the invitation: 'Repent, and be baptized every one of you in the name of Jesus Christ, so that your sins may be forgiven; and you will receive the gift of the Holy Spirit' (Acts 2: 38).

Acts presents the same invitation to the Gentiles. Those who believe in the crucified and risen Jesus as the One who brings forgiveness of sins and who is to be the judge of the living and the dead will join the Christian community through being baptized and receiving the Holy Spirit (Acts 10: 34–48; 11: 17–18). Luke takes it for granted that those who accept the message of Christ enter the Church and do so through baptism. This rite of initiation effects purification from sin and entrance into a new, holy 'koinônia', a fellowship with one another created by the Holy Spirit (Acts 2: 41–2). For Luke it is self-evident: faith in Jesus involves joining the Church and accepting baptism, the undisputed initiatory rite of the Church. Does Luke hold that salvation comes *only* to those who in baptism 'call on the name of the Lord' (Acts 2: 21; 4: 12)? We return to this in a later chapter.

(2) Writing earlier than Luke, Paul also cites Joel's text. But first he states the conditions for salvation: 'if you confess with your lips that Jesus is Lord and believe in your heart that God raised him from the dead, you will be saved. For one believes with the heart and so is justified, and one confesses with the mouth and so is saved.' Thus faith in and confession of Jesus are indispensable for justification and salvation. Those conditions do not differ for Jews and Gentiles; they should all call on the name of Jesus, the same generous Lord. Then they will be saved. Paul cites Joel 2: 32 to confirm his teaching (Rom. 10: 9–13). In a previous chapter of the same letter, the Apostle has explained that salvation entails appropriating Christ's death and resurrection by being baptized and then 'walking in newness of life' in the hope of sharing Christ's risen glory (Rom. 6: 3–5). In an earlier letter Paul has spelled out the change of life brought by being cleansed through baptism; this change makes it possible to 'inherit the kingdom of God' (1 Cor. 6: 9–11).[5]

---

[5] See A. C. Thiselton, *The First Epistle to the Corinthians* (Grand Rapids, Mich.: Eerdmans, 2000), 438–58.

For Paul, the saving events of Christ's incarnation, life, death, and resurrection (with the coming of the Holy Spirit) are actualized and made effectively present through the preaching of the gospel and its reception by faith and baptism. Baptism introduces into the community of the Church those who believe in Christ, and thus serves as the efficacious bridge between the past events of salvation and the present moment. Baptism and faith go together in receiving the gift of salvation and 'putting on Christ' (Gal. 3: 25–7)—a metaphor expressing the new conditions of life and radical change of those who share in the 'new creation' (2 Cor. 5: 17). With their sins forgiven, they now belong to Christ, enter a new family to become God's sons and daughters (Gal. 3: 28–9),[6] and through incorporation in the Church share together in the one Holy Spirit (1 Cor. 12: 13). Thus the essential rite of baptism not only draws its power from Christ and his Spirit but also makes the baptized members of the Church.

Clearly what Luke and Paul say or imply about baptism and hence entrance into the Church brings up a painful question about those who are not baptized and do not enter into the community of the Church. The problem this raises for the unbaptized is as big as it gets. If all the blessings that Christ has brought are related to baptism and hence are Church-related, what of those who have never even heard of Christ and hence could not receive baptism and enter the Church? What of those innumerable millions who have never had the chance of sharing in the fellowship of the baptized? It could appear that they are excluded from the new life given by the Spirit through union with Christ and with his body, the Church. In subsequent chapters I will return to this challenge and attempt to show how a close reading of the NT allows us to confront the challenge and deal with it.

(3) Here I wish only to observe that Luke, Paul, and other NT writers take it for granted that human beings need baptism, the rite of passage into the Church, if they are to appropriate the blessings that Jesus has brought. At the end of Matthew's Gospel the risen Jesus commissions the apostolic witnesses: 'make disciples of all nations, baptizing them in the name of the Father, and of the Son, and of the Holy Spirit'. Becoming a disciple or follower of Jesus requires baptism

---

[6] See J. L. Martyn, *Galatians* (New York: Doubleday, 1998), 373–83, 391–2.

and hence membership in the Church. There is no way of embracing such discipleship and learning to live by all the teaching of Jesus without joining the Christian community (Matt. 28: 18–20).

In John's Gospel Jesus puts matters in a shockingly unqualified way: 'no one can enter the kingdom of God without being born of water and the Spirit' (John 3: 5; see 1 Pet. 1: 3, 23). The Letter to Titus fills out the picture by combining the theme of baptismal rebirth with that of sins being washed away: 'he [God our Saviour] saved us, not because of any works of righteousness that we had done, but according to his mercy, through *water of rebirth* and renewal by the Holy Spirit. This Spirit he poured out on us richly through Jesus Christ our Saviour, so that, having been justified by his grace, we might become heirs according to the hope of eternal life' (Titus 3: 5–7). In these terms it seems that there is no salvation, no washing away of sins, no rebirth to new life through the Spirit, and no hope of eternal life for those who do not, through faith and baptism, make the rite of passage into the Church

The Letter to the Ephesians names seven elements that constitute the unity of Christians in one body: 'There is *one* body and *one* Spirit, just as you were called to the *one* hope of your calling, *one* Lord, *one* faith, *one* baptism, *one* God and Father of all' (Eph. 4: 4–6). Baptism unites all believers in the same faith in the one Lord (Jesus). The mediation of the Church is essential to this unity. But what of the millions of 'others'? Without faith in the one Lord Jesus and baptism into the one body of the Church and the reception of the one Spirit, can they hope to enjoy the intimate love and protection of the 'one God and Father of all'?

Luke, Paul, Matthew, John, and the letters to Titus and the Ephesians—not to mention other NT witnesses—highlight the need of baptism and hence the need of the Church if the blessings made available through Christ and the Holy Spirit are to be appropriated by human beings. The same mediating role of the Church also emerges when we recall the Last Supper and the institution of the Eucharist (Chapter 8 above). Jesus celebrated a farewell meal with his core group of disciples. His words (over the bread and the cup) and his actions show that he defined his death as a sacrifice that would atone for sins and initiate a new and enduring covenant with God. But who were/are the beneficiaries of what he did and what he would

suffer? Who were the 'you' of 'this is my body which is broken/given
for you' (1 Cor. 11: 24)? Who were the 'many' of 'this is my blood of
the covenant, which is poured out for many' (Mark 14: 24)? Obviously those followers present at the Last Supper were the immediate
beneficiaries, but also the representative beneficiaries. Through them
Jesus wanted to confer on an indefinite number of others the saving
benefits of his life and impending death. But would those benefits
reach only those who were to participate in the meal fellowship that
Jesus instituted with a core group of disciples? Even when we interpret (correctly) the 'for you' and 'for many' as both pointing to an
indefinitely large group, we still face the question: did Jesus intend
the benefits of his violent death and the new covenant to be conferred
only on those who were sharing and would share (through eating his
'broken body' and drinking from the common cup) in the eucharistic ritual and fellowship that he was creating?

Chapter 8 raised the question: Did Jesus introduce, at least implicitly, a limiting principle: 'outside the Eucharist no salvation (extra
Eucharistiam nulla salus)'? I replied there by arguing that also at the
Last Supper Jesus intended to reach out to everyone. He had done
that in life, and now, faced with death, his saving intentions remained
all-embracing. Yet the immense benefits of the Eucharist in the story
of human salvation will require us to return later to the link between
the Eucharist and the redemption of the non-baptized.

THE ENDURING PLACE OF ISRAEL

Those who acknowledge the Church to be the community that passes
on, through baptism, the Eucharist, and other means, the saving
blessings imparted by Christ and the Holy Spirit must tackle the
issue: what does the NT propose about the ongoing role, if any, of
Judaism?

We have seen in Chapters 9 and 10 how Paul and Luke, respectively, endorse the policy and practice of proposing the message of
Christ first to the Jews and then to the Gentiles. In its own fascinating
way the Book of Revelation maintains this order in its vision of final
salvation. First, it enumerates those who are redeemed 'out of every

tribe of the people of Israel', and lists by name the twelve tribes from Judah to Benjamin—the only time that the NT ever does so. Then comes the numberless 'multitude from every nation, from all tribes, peoples, and languages' (Rev. 7: 4–10). The picture in Revelation is reassuring: the complete number of 144,000 are redeemed from the twelve tribes of Israel; none of the redeemed seems to be missing. The picture from Paul and Luke (and, as we shall see, from Matthew) appears less than reassuring. Some Jews embrace faith in Christ, but very many do not. Christianity appears to have split off from its Jewish matrix. What should Christians think of the place and prospects of Judaism in the ongoing story of salvation? Let us retrieve some replies, while first remarking that, along with notably diverse emphases, the NT in no way authorizes Christians to regard Judaism as somehow 'superseded' and now situated as another religion among the ancient religions of the world. We may not construe post-NT Judaism as being simply a non-Christian religion among other non-Christian religions.

(1) As we saw in Chapter 9, Paul agonizes over the failure of many Israelites to believe in Jesus.[7] How is he to interpret the resistance of his fellow Jews, given the divine election of Israel and the promises irrevocably made by God to the chosen people and their patriarchs? Paul finds no easy and straightforward response to this issue. He argues that God's promise to Israel has not failed (Rom. 9: 6–13). Any rejection by God of Israel is only apparent and not final, especially in view of the 'remnant, chosen by grace'—that part of Israel who accept Jesus and have become Christians (Rom. 9: 27; 11: 1–6). The 'gifts' and divine calling of Israel remain 'irrevocable' (Rom. 11: 29).[8] The temporary resistance to the gospel on the part of many Jews has the providential effect of giving Gentiles the chance to hear and receive the message of Christ (Rom. 11: 7–12). The Gentiles who believe are grafted onto the 'rich root of the olive tree', the ancestors of Israel through whom all Israel was consecrated to God (Rom. 11: 16–17, 28). Paul trusts in the wonderful and mysterious providence of God: all Israel will be saved (Rom. 11:

---

[7] See J. A. Fitzmyer, *Romans* (New York: Doubleday, 1993), 539–635.
[8] Joseph Sievers, 'How Irrevocable? Interpreting Romans 11: 29 from the Church Fathers to the Second Vatican Council', *Gregorianum* 87 (2006), 748–61.

25–36). The chosen people were elected by God and promised salvation; they will be saved through faith in Christ.

In the three chapters where Paul struggles with the very painful issue of many Jews failing to accept Jesus, the highpoint for all people, Jew or Gentile alike, he arrives at the conclusion of his list of the special blessings that God has given to the Jewish people: 'from them, according to the flesh, comes the Messiah, who is God over all, blessed for ever' (Rom. 9: 4–5). It is Jesus the Jew, born of the house of David in his earthly descent and Son of God in his heavenly origin and empowerment by the Holy Spirit through his resurrection (Rom. 1: 3–4), who is over all and works for all. The heart of faith and life for all Christians remains the Jewish Messiah, Jesus. It is to him they all pay worship and from him they all draw life. Because of Jesus, Christianity remains forever Jewish, 'the Israel of God' (Gal. 6: 16), the community whom God calls into existence through the Jewish Messiah.[9]

(2) Any close reading of Acts shows that Luke has no problem with Jewish Christians (including Paul) treating the Temple in Jerusalem as a sacred place and an appropriate place for prayer and acts of piety (e.g. Acts 21: 17–26). That centre will maintain its religious significance, but only until God's judgement falls on the city and its Temple.

The compelling drama of Acts involves Luke's conviction that Peter, Paul, and other Christian leaders are called to restore Israel as a people under its Messiah, the crucified and risen Jesus (Acts 2: 36). The final salvation that God promised to Israel depends on Israel accepting Jesus as Messiah. Or does it? Can God's covenant loyalty to and promises for the Jewish people depend on their accepting here and now Jesus as Messiah? As we saw above, Paul answers in the negative.

Luke seemingly conceives of Israel being reconstituted in that Gentiles are becoming part of Israel. He provides his clearest picture of the post-Pentecost situation through his treatment of the Parable of the Great Dinner (Luke 14: 15–24).[10] When those who have

---

[9] Martyn argues convincingly that Paul wishes to say that the Church as the Israel of God is identified with those who in their lives follow the standards of the new creation (*Galatians*, 567, 574–7).

[10] See the end of Chapter 7 above.

accepted an invitation make last-minute excuses for not coming, the host reacts by first sending a slave to bring in from the streets of the town some poor, crippled, blind, and lame people. The slave is sent out a second time to bring others from the roads and footpaths near the town and so fill up the house for the great dinner. The parable, as Luke presents it, points to three groups. First, there are many Jews at the time of Jesus who decline his invitation to accept firmly an invitation to the messianic banquet. They exclude themselves from the joy of the festive meal, in which 'Abraham, Isaac, Jacob, and all the prophets' will share with 'the people who arrive from east, from north and south' (Luke 13: 28–9). Second, Luke's version of the Great Dinner hints at the less than religiously respectable Jews who come from 'the streets and lanes of the town' to join Jesus and, after Pentecost, enter his Church. Third, there are the Gentiles, those brought in from the roads and footpaths near the town. Luke leaves us with a picture of a reconstituted Israel, an Israel built on the great figures of the past, including many Jews but predominantly from those who are religiously and socially disadvantaged, and now embracing a multitude of Gentiles who come from all points of the compass. A 'reconstituted Israel' seems to summarize what Luke understands to be happening, even though it is not his phrase.

(3) The bleakest picture of post-Pentecost Israel comes from Matthew. In his treatment of the Parable of the Vineyard and the Tenants (Matt. 21: 33–46 parr.), he has Jesus warning 'the chief priests and the Pharisees': 'the kingdom of heaven will be taken away from you and given to a people that produces the fruits of the kingdom'. The evangelist, who is both a Jew and a follower of Jesus, grieves over his nation losing its election; the true Israel, his Church, is now separated from the synagogue.[11] These are the headlines; let us see the small print.

Right from the start of his narrative, Matthew foreshadows the movement of the gospel to the Gentiles: for instance, through the visit of the Magi to the Christ Child (4: 1–12). When Jesus begins his ministry, the evangelist quotes some words from Isaiah and alludes to the coming post-resurrection mission to the nations: 'Land of Zebulun, land of Naphtali, on the road by the sea, across the Jordan,

---

[11] See U. Luz, *Matthew 21–28* (Minneapolis: Fortress, 2005), 13–14.

Galilee of the Gentiles—the people who sat in darkness have seen a great light, and for those who sat in the region and shadow of death light has dawned' (Matt. 4: 15–16). Early in Matthew's story, the faith of a non-Jewish military officer draws not only praise from Jesus but also a sad comment on Israel as a whole: 'many will come from east and west and will eat with Abraham, Isaac, and Jacob in the kingdom of heaven, while the sons [= heirs] of the kingdom will be thrown into the outer darkness, where there will be weeping and gnashing of teeth' (Matt. 8: 5–13). Israel as a whole has proved unbelieving and, as a consequence, will be rejected from the kingdom. In this section of Matthew, the identity of those who oppose or reject the teaching of Jesus is left unspecified; there is no mention of Sadducees or Pharisees, for example. What is said is that the former sons of the kingdom (evidently understood to be Israel as a whole) will be replaced by a new group of sons (the Church).[12] Here Matthew does not include a warning to the new sons of the kingdom: they will not be automatically exempt from the judgement that befell the former sons. Such a warning turns up later in his Gospel.

The Parable of the Vineyard, as we saw in Chapter 8, seems to have come out of controversy between Jesus and some religious leaders. This was the only parable in which Jesus spoke directly about his own activity and fate. It warned of a dramatic change in God's relationship with his vineyard (Israel). Who were the 'others' to whom the vineyard would be given? Seemingly for Jesus himself (at stage one) and clearly for Matthew (at stage three), these beneficiaries would be the Jewish disciples of Jesus and the Gentiles who joined them in the Church, a reconstituted Israel. In this new stage of salvation history, Jesus would remain present to his Church until the end (Matt. 18: 20; 28: 20). Writing after the fall of Jerusalem in AD 70, Matthew understood God's approach to (former, ethnic) Israel to be at an end; that approach had been replaced by the Church's mission to the Gentiles (Matt. 28: 18–20).

Once he has told the story of Jesus entering Jerusalem on 'Palm Sunday' (Matt. 21: 1–11), Matthew includes many passages not only of judgement on Israel but also of warning to the Church. To be called to the Church is not necessarily to be saved.[13] Take, for instance, the way in which the evangelist adapts the original form of the Parable of the Great Dinner and presents it as a wedding banquet staged by a king for his son (Matt. 22: 2–14). Matthew introduces, among other things, an invitation that goes out to everyone, 'good' and 'bad' alike, and a 'wedding robe' that the guests were expected to wear.[14] The invitation to all people does not exempt them from living righteously. To underscore this theme, Matthew throws in a saying from Jesus that apparently had no fixed place in the tradition: 'many are called, but few are chosen'—a Semitic way of saying that all (Jew and Gentile alike) are called, but not all will belong to the elect. The evangelist, while signalling the mission to the whole world, also wants to insist that to be called to the Christian community does not automatically mean to be saved. 'Inside the Church', one might say, 'there is not necessarily salvation.'

Thus we have three somewhat different pictures of the ongoing status of Israel: the most optimistic one from Paul and the most sombre one from Matthew. Paul's reflections tell against those who would speak of Israel being 'superseded', let alone repudiated. As has been well said, 'the Church of the Gentiles is an extension of the promises of God to Israel, and not Israel's displacement'.[15] The Church has not replaced the Jewish people as God's own people. Luke and Matthew seem to portray a 'reconstituted Israel'. For all three NT authors, Christianity is not a new religion that supplants an earlier one. Israel remains at the heart of Christianity, since Jesus was and remains the Jewish Messiah, born of a Jewish woman (Gal. 4: 4). His normative witnesses, the founding fathers and mothers of the Church, were all Jewish, and together make the Church 'apostolic'.

This chapter has attended to the big picture about Jesus, the Church, and Israel. Let us turn now to the heart of the matter, or at least to the heart of this enquiry: a biblical view of the situation of the non-baptized.

---

[13] See Luz, *Matthew 21–28*, 57, 60.

[14] As we noted in Chapter 7, the Book of Revelation also takes up the image of a final, wedding feast, 'the marriage supper of the Lamb', at which the dress will be 'fine linen', understood as 'the righteous deeds of the saints' (Rev. 19: 7–9).

[15] J. H. Beker, *Paul the Apostle* (Philadelphia: Fortress, 1980), 332.

12

The Universal Benevolence of God

We turn now to hear the full range of biblical voices that express the benevolence of God towards everyone. Subsequent distinctions in the election and blessings of particular groups and individuals must be seen against the broader picture of the divine goodwill towards all human beings. Any theology of world cultures and religions that wishes to be faithful to the biblical witness must give prominence to this universal benevolence of God. First of all, what did the chosen people of God (according to the OT) think about the religious situation of 'others', both those who came before the call of Abraham and Sarah and those who, subsequently, did not belong to their community of faith?

FROM ADAM AND EVE TO ABRAHAM AND SARAH

The OT scriptures yield a rich picture of the origin, nature, and destiny of human beings. The Bible begins with a range of figures and stories that express the unity of humankind and God's gracious concern for all human beings.

(1) The Book of Genesis depicts symbolically the past origin and present sinful state of all humanity—of every man and every woman (Chapter 1 above). 'Adam' and 'Eve' portray the whole human community: their creation through the powerful goodness of God and then their fall into sin that initiates the subsequent story of sin. Made in the divine image and likeness (Gen. 1: 26; 5: 1–3), all human

beings are defined in terms of their relationship with God. They are 'crowned with glory and honour' (Ps. 8: 5), and enjoy an unconditional dignity. God has granted them the privileged task of being his stewards, who will preside in the divine name over the rest of creation. As the psalmist says to God, 'you have given them dominion over the works of your hands; you have put all things under their feet, all sheep and oxen, and also the beasts of the fields, the birds of the air, and the fish of the sea' (Ps. 8: 6–8).

Humanity collectively enjoys a favoured status vis-à-vis the rest of creation, but relies totally upon God for this status and indeed for life itself. Humanity is likewise responsible collectively in its obedience to God, and should obey the commands of God—in particular, the command not to eat any fruit 'of the tree of the knowledge of good and evil' (Gen. 2: 16–17). Hence when 'the man' and 'the woman' disobey the divine commands, their rebellion affects the whole human community. Far from enhancing their life, sin leaves every man and every woman less than they should really be, and ushers in destructive consequences. The most distressing consequence concerns death. Disobedience to God has changed the experience of death for sinful human beings; death has become a troubling fate, a painful sign of sin.

Despite the sad consequences of sin, God continues to cherish the original human beings; their disobedience cannot render void the special relationship between God and the human race. Human sin cannot do away with divine mercy. Even after their sin, human beings continue to display the divine image and likeness and to experience the loving concern of God. God clothes the disobedient 'man' and 'woman' with 'garments of skin' (Gen. 3: 21). He will put a protective 'mark on Cain, so that no one who came upon him would kill him' (Gen. 4: 15). The benevolence of God brightens a situation darkened by human sin.

(2) After the disobedience of Adam and Eve, the picturesque Genesis story shows human beings opting against God and one another and so shaping a whole situation of sin that needs 'cleansing' through the flood to allow for a new beginning (Gen. 9: 1–2). By means of Noah and his descendants, God establishes a covenant with the whole of humanity and with all creation. The blessing originally given to both human beings and non-human creatures

(Gen. 1: 22, 28) is now renewed: 'Be fruitful, multiply and fill the earth' (Gen. 9: 1). Unlike the later covenants made with Abraham and Sarah (Gen. 17) and with the Israelites at Mount Sinai (Exod. 24), the covenant with Noah is *universal* in its scope. The three sons of Noah are regarded as the ancestors of all peoples (Gen. 9: 18; 10: 1–32). The entire human race is understood to share forever in the covenant made with Noah and to inherit the divine blessings of the new age. God's loving care extends to everybody and does so for all time.

Through this cosmic covenant all people form a single family under God, share the same basic blessings from God, and are called to observe a universal moral law. Any further elections, covenants, or other blessings cannot supplant this primary relationship of all human beings with God and with one another that has been established through the covenant with Noah.

(3) With Abraham and Sarah, the story of the chosen people begins. But this special election does not involve terminating the universal divine benevolence. While Abraham and Sarah are to become the ancestors of 'a great nation', their new relationship with God will benefit everyone: 'in you all the families of the earth will be blessed' (Gen. 12: 1–9).

Various stories about Abraham and Sarah (e.g. Gen. 15: 1–21; 18: 1–15) show them enjoying an intimate relationship with God in prayer. But that access to God is never understood to be limited to them and to later 'insiders', their descendants who will constitute the chosen people. In his gracious goodness, God is and remains accessible to all human beings. Even a murderer, like Cain, can converse with God in prayer (Gen. 4: 9–16), and so too can the Philistine king, Abimelech (Gen. 20: 3–7).

DEUTERONOMY, AMOS, AND JONAH

(1) As we saw in Chapter 2, Deuteronomy, while rejecting image worship and idolatry, made a bold attempt to place the other nations, their religions, and their gods within the one plan of God—called 'Lover of the peoples' in an alternative reading for Deuteronomy

33: 3. An address by Moses allows a certain legitimacy at least to astral religion, along with a command to the Israelites not to share in that religion (Deut. 4: 19; see 29: 6; 32: 8–9).

Thus the followers of astral religion exist in some relationship with YHWH through the religious experience that occurs in the context of their own religion. To the extent that their religion properly develops the basic gift of YHWH, the things he has 'allotted to all the peoples everywhere' (Deut. 4: 19), it will prove a road to truly experiencing salvation. This Deuteronomy text interprets such astral religion as a gift from the Lord and a sign of his all-loving concern for all peoples and nations.

The problem, however, was that presenting YHWH as the High God with a court of lesser divine beings looked unacceptably polytheistic. The imagery of the divine court of lesser (astral) deities and the (subordinate) legitimacy of astral religion were not pursued in the OT. The attempt was generous, but jeopardized by its polytheistic implications.

(2) Two prophetic books (see Chapter 3) help to fill out vividly the divine concern for all peoples. First, the prophet Amos, even if he fiercely indicts Israel for its sins and injustice, does not challenge the election of the chosen people. Israel has been chosen from 'all the families of the earth' (Amos 3: 2). Yet this does not mean that God has rejected the other nations of the world. In fact, Amos connects the special election of Israel with the universal rule and benevolence of God. To make his point, the prophet picks out three peoples: the Ethiopians, the Philistines, and the Arameans or Syrians. They are all blessed by God. In particular, God was involved in the migrations of the Philistines and Arameans, just he was involved in the Israelite exodus from Egypt (Amos 9: 7). The divine care and guidance extended and extends to all peoples.

The teaching of Amos on the benevolence of God is strikingly universal. Yet this universal teaching turns up almost incidentally and is not developed. In the Book of Jonah, however, the 'others' and the merciful love God exercises towards them are central to the plot.

(3) Jonah tells the story of God's word being addressed to a foreign nation through an obstinate and narrow-minded prophet. That prophet runs away from the mission that YHWH has given him, is miraculously saved from drowning, preaches repentance to the

wicked people of Nineveh, and then sulks when his hearers instantly repent. Jonah has to learn that God's saving love goes out to everyone, even to the horrendous and hated Ninevites. The instant and wholesale conversion of the Ninevites involves a moral change of life, and not as such a shift to worshipping YHWH and adopting the Mosaic law and practice (Jonah 3: 4–10). God is content to let the Ninevites remain what they are religiously, provided they undergo a *moral* conversion from their 'violence and evil ways'—a reasonable description of Ninevite behaviour until their dominion ended at the close of the seventh century BC.

It was Jonah who needed to change his *religious* views. The last chapter of the book is devoted to him. He began by being 'angry' that his preaching in Nineveh had instantly brought moral results. He did not want that to happen. He explained to God that he had initially fled by ship because he refused to become the human instrument of the divine mercy towards the hateful Ninevites: 'I knew that you are a gracious God and merciful, slow to anger, and abounding in steadfast love, and ready to relent from punishing.' Jonah did not wish to see these Assyrians spared by a loving, gracious God. He shrank from his prophetic obligation to care about their interests, and showed no concern or compassion for Nineveh. But God made it clear to him that the divine love embraced every creature in the universe. The merciful concern of God knew no frontiers (Jonah 4: 1–11).

ISAIAH

As we saw in Jonah, there is no question of the Ninevites accepting the worship of YHWH and taking part in a great procession to Jerusalem. What God expects of them is moral conversion and that is instantly forthcoming. Here the divine benevolence takes a decentralized form. A benevolence that is centralized seems, however, the normal expectation in the Book of Isaiah (Chapter 4 above).

(1) Chapters 40–66 of Isaiah are usually divided into Second Isaiah (40–55) and Third Isaiah (56–66). These two sections view at times very positively the religious situation and future of the nations. Yet such an open-minded view is not lacking in First Isaiah (1–39).

In a new age the nations will 'stream' to Zion and say: 'Let us go to the mountain of the Lord, to the house of the God of Jacob, that he may teach us his ways and we may walk in his paths' (Isa. 2: 2–3)—a strong hint of the inseparable revelatory (teaching) and salvific (walking in God's paths) aspects of the divine self-communication. To be sure, First Isaiah contains many oracles against the nations. But wedged into this predominantly negative section several verses foretell a coming relationship of Egypt and Assyria with YHWH. At that time 'the Egyptians will worship with the Assyrians', and Israel will be a blessing to the nations. 'Israel will be third with Egypt and Assyria, a blessing in the midst of the earth, whom the Lord of hosts has blessed, saying, "Blessed be Egypt my people and Assyria the work of my hands, and Israel my heritage"' (Isa. 19: 24–5). In a remarkable statement of divine benevolence, these verses put Egypt and even Assyria (both denounced elsewhere for oppressing Israel) on a par with Israel, as 'my people' and 'the work of my hands'. Such expressions of God's intimate graciousness are elsewhere reserved for Israel itself. Yet there is no question in this context of Egypt and Assyria being assimilated to Israel; they keep their own cultural and religious identity.

More of this vision of divine benevolence towards 'others' recurs in the theme of a final banquet for all nations: 'On this mountain [Zion] the Lord of hosts will make for all peoples a feast of rich food, a feast of well-aged wines.' Then 'the Lord God will wipe away the tears from all faces' (Isa. 25: 6–8). This promise that God will feed and comfort all peoples expresses movingly the divine concern for the true and final welfare of everyone.

(2) In Second Isaiah the mysterious figure of the 'Servant' (Israel as a whole or an individual or both) has the mission of bringing the divine teaching and justice to all people (Isa. 42: 1–4) and so being 'a light to the nations' (Isa. 49: 6). The songs of the 'Servant' reach their climax with the fourth song (Isa. 52: 13–53: 12). His vicarious suffering will atone for the sins of the 'many' and bring them God's blessings. Whatever shape we give the details when interpreting this moving passage, clearly the Servant will benefit the wider world and restore people to God.

God's gracious outreach to the nations through the 'Servant' has two, inseparable dimensions. It will bring revelation (teaching and light) and salvation (atonement for sin and justice).

(3) Among the most vivid texts about divine salvation being extended to the whole world is a poem in Third Isaiah that pictures the restoration of Jerusalem: 'Arise, shine, for your light has come, and the glory of the Lord has risen upon you... Nations shall come to your light, and kings to the brightness of your dawn' (Isa. 60: 1–3). The closing chapter of Third Isaiah offers a classic message about God's active love towards all people: 'I am coming to gather the nations of every language. They shall come and see my glory' (Isa. 66: 18). The divine plans are so open-minded that God even intends to select some persons from among the Gentile nations and make them serve as 'priests and levites'—an expression typical of Israel but now applied to non-Israelites.

The author(s) of Third Isaiah never suggested that the special gifts and privileges that God had given his chosen people were now in doubt. But God was greater than any of his gifts. Through the chosen people YHWH aimed to create a new community for all people. The divine love was shockingly generous and universal. As far as God was concerned, there were no outsiders. With Israel, the nations will assemble in Jerusalem, and a great chorus of praise will ceaselessly arise to the throne of God (Isa. 66: 22–3).

WISDOM LITERATURE

The OT wisdom literature is particularly rich for those who reflect on God's gracious benevolence towards all people (Chapter 5 above). For the most part, wisdom literature remains general in its religious approach and so helps us to appreciate that there are blessings for everyone. God, personified as Lady Wisdom, cherishes and seeks out all human beings.

(1) The unexpected and unmerited sufferings of a holy non-Israelite, Job, reach their turning-point when God puts impossible questions to Job. He draws him deeper into the divine mystery until Job acknowledges an intimate communion with God: 'now my eyes see you' (Job 42: 5). God has revealed himself in his power over the created world and not as the God of Jewish history. The wise God is disclosed in his cosmic majesty, and yet as intimately involved in the life and destiny of human beings.

(2) Sirach proclaims that divine Wisdom dwells in Jerusalem, and yet 'holds sway' over 'every people and nation' (Sir. 24: 3–11). Associated in a special way with Israel, Wisdom is also powerfully present everywhere. Wisdom proves a source of life and nourishment for everyone.

(3) According to the Wisdom of Solomon, the last of the OT books to be written, God blesses with immortality all just persons and not merely just Israelites. Wisdom makes herself accessible to all those 'worthy of her' (Wisd. 7: 22–8: 1). Unquestionably, Wisdom is portrayed as involved in protecting the Jewish patriarchs and people (Wisd. 10: 1–11: 4). Nevertheless, her involvement in the particular salvation history of Israel does not exclude her role in the lives of all 'those on earth', human beings at large who can experience her light and saving power (Wisd. 7: 18).

In summarizing some OT data that draw attention to the universal benevolence of God, this chapter has highlighted testimony to that benevolence being exercised towards groups rather than individuals. The next chapter will take up the story of various individuals. Before doing that we need to hear some of the witness of the NT to the universal benevolence of God.

THE PASTORAL EPISTLES

For those concerned with plotting the NT testimony about the universal saving outreach of God, the Pastoral Epistles (the two letters to Timothy and the one to Titus) offer a promising start. As Jerome Quinn stated, 'God's will and plan to save all men and women, universally and without exception, is a controlling theme' in these Pastoral Epistles.[1] Normally dated to late in the first century and so having a generation of belief behind them, these letters reflect a situation when the original missionary journeys have resulted in established Christian communities that are led by 'episcopoi (overseers)', 'presbyteroi (elders)', and 'diakonoi (ministers)'. Clearly the message about Jesus Christ has won many adherents, but there are

---

[1] J. D. Quinn, *The Letter to Titus* (New York: Doubleday, 1990), 162–3.

still very many Jews and innumerable Gentiles who have not heard the gospel and accepted baptism. What is to be said about their present and future prospects in the saving plan of God? Some statistics suggest the concern of these letters with the issue of human salvation. The verb 'save' turns up seven times; the noun 'salvation' is used twice and the adjective 'saving' once. The title 'Saviour' is given ten times, either to God (the Father) or to Jesus Christ. We begin with a passage in Titus (2: 11–3: 7).[2]

The Letter to Titus describes the coming of Christ as 'the grace of God appearing' or 'the goodness and loving kindness of God our Saviour appearing' (2: 11; 3: 4). An indissoluble link is established between this first appearing and the last appearing, 'the glorious manifestation of our great God and Saviour, Jesus Christ' (2: 13). A parallel link is also drawn between what has already been accomplished for human salvation (2: 11, 14; 3: 5–7a) and what is yet to happen (2: 13; 3: 7b). What are the prospects for those who have not or have not yet become Christians? The passage begins by declaring that 'the grace of God' is 'saving for all human beings'. But then it quickly turns to take into account only 'us', Christians who, thanks to '*our* Saviour', have been reborn through baptism, renewed by the Holy Spirit, and now wait for 'the glorious manifestation of *our* great God and Saviour, Jesus Christ'.[3] But what of those who have not heard the good news of Christ and remain unbaptized? What is to be said about their situation before God? Are 'the goodness and loving kindness of God our Saviour' actively at work to achieve their salvation? For even a partial answer we must look to another letter.

---

[2] On salvation in the Pastoral Epistles, see ibid., 304–15.

[3] The opening chapter of 2 Timothy also applies the language of Christ's 'appearing' to his incarnation (v. 10), as well as speaking of his second coming (v. 12). The saving impact of Christ's first 'appearing' is summarized negatively (*through* his appearing he 'abolished death') and positively (he 'brought life and immortality to light *through* the gospel'). The repeated 'through (dia)', set clearly in parallel, indicates first how Christ embodied God's saving purposes and second how the medium (the gospel) makes those purposes of 'life' and 'light' effective (v. 10). The passage depicts how salvation has occurred for Christian believers who have responded to the gospel with faith. This limited group ('we') is also indicated by talking of how God 'has saved us and called us with a holy calling' (v. 9). Nothing is said in these verses from 2 Timothy about 'life' and 'light' reaching those who have not heard the message of Christ.

The First Letter to Timothy has the relatively limited purpose of providing guidance for the administration of Christian communities and for opposing false teaching. Nevertheless, it offers a broad horizon for understanding what 'Christ Jesus, the one Mediator between God and human beings' achieved when 'he gave himself as a ransom for all'. Christ's human life and redemptive death demonstrated the universal scope of God's saving plan: 'God our Saviour desires all human beings to be saved and to come to the knowledge/recognition of the truth' (1 Tim. 2: 3–5). This affirmation underlines the universal extent of the divine will to effect the salvation of all human beings. They cannot save themselves, but need 'to be saved'.[4] The affirmation also hints at the two inseparable dimensions of this deliverance: 'God our Saviour desires everyone to be saved' (salvation) and 'come to the knowledge of the truth' (revelation). A certain reciprocity between God and human beings is also indicated. God offers salvation and human beings respond by 'coming to the knowledge of the truth'. (We return below to the possible meaning(s) of this phrase.) God is called '*our* Saviour' (i.e. the Saviour of Paul, Timothy, and the community of Christian believers), but the divine plan of salvation embraces everyone. God 'desires all human beings to be saved'. Yet nothing is said here either about *how* this salvation might work out in the case of those who are neither evangelized nor baptized, or about *how* they might 'come to the knowledge of the truth'.

The same letter returns, more briefly, to the theme of a universal plan of salvation, by writing of 'the living God, who is the Saviour of all human beings, especially (in particular) of believers' (1 Tim. 4: 10). The reference to 'believers' is not intended to modify the universal scope of God's saving plan, but to strengthen the confidence of Christians. Since God wants to save everyone, believers in Christ (in particular) can be all the more confident that they will share in the salvation planned by God. Yet this brief statement does not shed any light on how those who are not Christians might be 'saved and come to the knowledge of the truth'.

---

[4] The affirmation may primarily express God's will that all 'belong to the people he is forming in the world', but does not exclude the broader meaning: God wills that all human beings be saved. See L. T. Johnson, *The First and Second Letter to Timothy* (New York: Doubleday, 2001), 191.

In several passages the Pastoral Epistles invoke 'knowing/recogniz-ing the truth'.[5] One of these further examples which seems pertinent to our question turns up later in 1 Timothy. Some false teachers are forbidding legitimate marriage and demanding abstinence from cer-tain foods. But marriage and food should be 'received with thanks-giving by those who believe and know/recognize the truth'. They believe and know/recognize that 'everything created by God is good' (1 Tim. 4: 3–4). Here Christian faith and knowing/recognizing the truth are closely associated, almost as if they were equivalents. A similar association, albeit made in general and not directed to a specific moral challenge, occurs when the Letter to Titus begins by invoking 'the faith of God's elect and the godly knowledge of the truth' (1: 1). In this context 'God's elect' are undoubtedly Christian believers, identified by their faith in Jesus. Nevertheless, something of more general application may emerge. Let me explain.

Coming to the knowledge of the truth at the start of Titus implies coming to faith, recognizing who Jesus really is, and expressing a special relationship to him. In the case of adult Christian converts, knowing the truth, believing, and being baptized coincide in a public fashion. But what of those who have never heard the message about Jesus and yet accept faithfully the divine overtures for their salvation? What is happening in their case? The association (made in 1 Tim. 4: 3–4 and Titus 1: 1) between faith and knowing the truth can suggest some answer—at least, if we apply this association by combining 1 Timothy 2: 4 ('God desires everyone to be saved and come to the knowledge/recognition of the truth') with the classical teaching from Hebrews: 'without faith it is impossible to please God. For whoever would approach him must believe that he exists, and that he rewards those who seek him' (Heb. 11: 6). Combining these two verses, we can reach this position. Salvation occurs by knowing and believing the truth that God exists and judges all people fairly. Those who somehow grasp in faith the knowledge of this truth will be saved. Joining and reading these two classical verses together amounts to

---

[5] Another example of 'knowing the truth' in the Pastoral Epistles is not closely relevant to our issue. The writer comments sadly on the false teachers who lead astray women who are 'always trying to learn and can never arrive at a knowledge of the truth' (2 Tim. 3: 7). On the knowledge of the truth in the Pastoral Epistles, see Quinn, *The Letter to Titus*, 276–82.

expanding 1 Timothy 2: 4: 'God desires everyone to be saved and this happens through their coming in faith to the knowledge/recognition of the truth of the existence and justice of God, and thus through their responding in faith to this minimal revelation of God.' (This chapter has dwelt on 1 Timothy 2: 4; a later chapter will take up in greater detail Hebrews 11: 6.)

Without putting matters too strongly, I would suggest two further meanings that could also be conveyed by 'coming to the knowledge/recognition of the truth' (1 Tim. 2: 4). First, an association is made between coming to know/recognize the truth and *repentance* on the part of those who have been led astray by youthful lusts and senseless controversies (2 Tim. 2: 22–6). Here 'coming to the knowledge/recognition of the truth' has strong overtones of a moral *conversion*. Something of such a moral conversion is required if human beings in general are 'to be saved' (1 Tim. 2: 4). The Pastoral Epistles regularly link truth and virtue, as opposed to error and vice. Knowing the truth will issue in good conduct, and vice versa. There is a 'symbiotic relationship' between good conduct and true understanding and coming to know the truth.[6]

Second, in the context of the Pastoral Epistles 'coming to the knowledge/recognition of the truth' may well imply *coming to know/recognize Christ*. Completed a few years later, the Gospel of John identifies Christ as Truth, the divine Truth in person (John 14: 6). Coming to Christ and believing in him is then the equivalent of coming to know/recognize the Truth, and vice versa. The Pastoral Epistles contain passages that are close to affirming this equivalence. After expounding 'the mystery of the faith', 'the faith in Christ Jesus', and the 'truth' and 'mystery' of Christ (3: 9, 13, 15–16), 1 Timothy recalls at once how the Holy Spirit had announced that in the period before the day of the Lord, 'some will renounce the faith'—that is, the whole way of life centred on the person of Christ. Faithful Christians, however, believe and know/recognize the truth—that is, Christ himself (4: 1, 3). Several passages in 2 Timothy speak of 'missing the mark concerning the truth' (2: 18), 'opposing the truth' (3: 8), and 'turning from listening to the truth' (4: 4). All that seems roughly equivalent

---

[6] See ibid., 279.

to saying, 'missing the mark concerning Christ', 'opposing Christ', and 'turning from listening to Christ'. Timothy himself is to 'explain [or delineate accurately] the word of truth [or gospel]' (2: 18), and that sounds close to saying that he should explain Christ, who is the Word of God and divine Truth in person. Thus there is a certain plausibility about interpreting 'coming to the knowledge/ recognition of the truth' as 'coming to the knowledge/recognition of Christ'.[7]

These two further meanings of 'coming to the knowledge/recognition of the truth' do not mutually exclude each other. The NT regularly links repentance (along with forgiveness) and believing in Christ and his message. Mark's Gospel, for instance, presents the programme of Jesus that way: 'repent and believe in the good news' (Mark 1: 15). Repenting or conversion opens one up to accepting the truth of the good news and coming to Jesus, who is himself the good news in person.

Whether or not we take it with reference to the person of Christ, unquestionably what the phrase 'coming to the knowledge/recognition of the truth' entails for those not (or not yet) evangelized remains very mysterious. But it is obviously more than 'knowing the truth' in a generic sense. Some kind of 'opening up of the divine world and its claim' is involved.[8] Hence I hold that more should be said than what James Dunn envisages: 'salvation includes a knowledge, both intellectual and existential, an awareness and acknowledgment of the reality of oneself and of the world'.[9] At first sight, this seems a little like a latter-day version of the Greek ideal 'know yourself', as if 1 Timothy were to say: 'Know yourself and you will be saved.' Surely the author of this letter understands 'a knowledge of the truth' to go beyond a mere awareness of oneself and the world and include a real *ac-knowledging* of God in the moral conduct of one's life? Perhaps Dunn implies this by referring to 'the reality of the

---

[7] See ibid., 281.

[8] See E. Käsemann, *Commentary on Romans* (Grand Rapids, Mich.: Eerdmans, 1980), 38; this is a comment on Rom. 1: 18 and those who wickedly try to 'suppress the truth'.

[9] J. D. G. Dunn, 'The First and Second Letters to Timothy and the Letter to Titus', in *The New Interpreter's Bible*, xi (Nashville: Abingdon Press, 2000), 798.

world'; God is, after all, the heart of the world in which we live and move and have our being. But it would be good to state this clearly. A better reflection comes from Dunn when he subsequently remarks: 'God's ultimate purpose is ultimate and, therefore still unknown, as well as the divine means of achieving that purpose.'[10] One must concur. Data from their lives may allow us to say something about how the non-evangelized 'come to the knowledge of the truth', as desired by God. But ultimately their salvation is shrouded in divine mystery, as in many ways is the salvation of Christians.

JESUS AND THE KINGDOM

Where the Pastoral Epistles represent something close to the final stages in the establishment of NT Christianity, the preaching of God's kingdom by Jesus constituted the launching-pad for the Church, set going fully by the resurrection and the outpouring of the Holy Spirit. The central theme for my book concerns, as stated in the preface, the world situation in which the Catholic (and, more broadly, the Christian) community finds itself now as it faces the question: What form(s) does the universal benevolence of God take towards the several billion human beings who have not heard or accepted the message about Jesus? The earthly ministry of Jesus took place before the situation that was beginning to emerge at the time of the Pastoral Epistles and would continue even after the stunning, fourth-century Christian growth: a minority Church living in a world of non-Christians. Nevertheless, much of the record of Jesus' ministry for the kingdom (Chapter 7 above) prefigures or at least illuminates the situation we know today.

(1) Embodying personally the extravagant love of God, Jesus embraced, with his words and deeds, all human beings. Even if the primary thrust of his ministry was towards the reform of Israel, he showed a gracious openness and kindness towards Gentiles. On a visit to non-Jewish territory, he delivered the daughter of a Syro-Phoenician woman from the suffering caused by a demon. Within

[10] Ibid., 800.

the borders of Galilee he healed the son (or servant) of a non-Jewish military officer. The powerful benevolence towards Gentiles shown on these two occasions was further highlighted by the fact that the Gospels do not record any other healings 'at a distance'. Only Gentiles were the beneficiaries of such exceptional gestures.

Perhaps the most sensational exorcism described by any of the Gospels was that of a non-Jewish demoniac in Gerasa (or Gadara) (Mark 5: 1–20). Unlike the Syro-Phoenician woman and the centurion, apparently he had never heard of Jesus beforehand; certainly he did not ask Jesus for a cure. Nor did relatives or friends bring him to Jesus and seek help. Rather, Jesus spontaneously took the initiative to liberate this Gentile outcast from his desperately evil condition, freed him from demonic possession, and restored him to normal society. When the ex-demoniac wanted to join his company, Jesus sent him away: 'Go home to your friends, and tell them how much the Lord has done for you, and what mercy he has shown you' (v. 19). The man responded immediately by going around the Decapolis, a group of predominantly Gentile cities, and 'proclaiming' to the amazement of 'everyone' 'how much Jesus had done for him' (v. 20).

In the case of the Syro-Phoenician woman (and her daughter) and the centurion (and his son or servant), we learn nothing of what these Gentile outsiders did after their dramatic meeting with Jesus. They encountered him at moments of extraordinary need in their lives, and were powerfully helped by him. And that was it, as far as the Gospel record goes. In the case of the ex-demoniac, however, he is remembered as having become a vigorous witness to Jesus in a notable group of Gentile cities. Perhaps the man later joined the Christian community, but there is no hint of that. He is recalled as an 'outsider' who was dramatically blessed by Jesus and 'proclaimed' this to the people of the region where he lived. Does this man symbolize anything or anyone for us today? Might we see him as a forerunner of those people who in various ways have been touched by the teaching and story of Jesus but do not enter the Christian community?

(2) It would be misleading to look for precise teaching from Jesus about the religious situation of those who remain non-Christians today. His ministry took place *before* the Church began fully and

publicly. Nevertheless, the story of Jesus continues to raise vital questions and suggest possible answers.

Take, for instance, the parable that bears the name of 'the Good Samaritan' (Luke 10: 30–7). A Jewish priest and a Levite (one of those designated to be lay-associates of the priests) fail to stop for a wounded traveller. It is a Samaritan, an outsider presumed to be hostile to Jews and hardly expected to show them much sympathy, who generously takes care of the wounded man, presumably a Jew. It is the Samaritan outsider who proves a role model for those ready to help people in terrible need. Certain modern preachers have drawn attention to a contemporary parallel. Some Christians, including some Christian leaders, come across people, even their fellow Christians, in dreadful distress, but pass by on the other side. 'Outsiders', adherents of other religions or followers of no particular religion at all, can be the 'good Samaritans' who stop and help. At times it is they rather than the official followers of Jesus who show themselves to be the human instruments of God's benevolence.

Jesus, by and large, preached only to his fellow Jews, but his message of the kingdom was for everyone. The kingdom of God and its claims knew no frontiers. Jesus based, for instance, his distinctive command to love even one's enemies (Matt. 5: 43–7) on the love of God which embraces all: 'your Father in heaven makes his sun rise on the evil and on the good, and sends rain on the righteous and the unrighteous'. All human beings share a common origin in a most benevolent God; therefore, they should be graciously loving to all others, including their enemies and persecutors.[11] Here Jesus clearly intended concrete deeds of love, and not mere friendly feelings. He proclaimed an unrestricted love of God, which should find its counterpart in the life of every human being. As Ulrich Luz puts matters, 'acts of love towards enemies are, in Jesus' view, an expression of the unconditional yes of God to human beings for their own sake'.[12] This was the way Jesus expected everyone to live, then and later.

[11] Luke's version of this teaching spells out even more the theological foundation: 'love your enemies, do good, and lend, expecting nothing in return. Your reward will be great and you will be children of the Most High; for he is kind to the ungrateful and the wicked. Be merciful, just as your Father is merciful' (6: 35–6).

[12] *Matthew 1–7: A Commentary* (Minneapolis: Augsburg, 1989), 351; trans. slightly corrected.

In his life and ministry Jesus embodied the loving benevolence of God, a benevolence that was limitless. Of course, he was surrounded by the disciples who followed him on his travelling ministry; from among them he had chosen a core group of twelve for a leadership of service. But that choice took nothing away from the unique openness he showed to all men and women, especially those whom 'normal' society disqualified in various ways. As far as Jesus was concerned, there were neither 'insiders' nor 'outsiders'. All were children of the one loving Father, 'Abba'. The benevolence of God was all-embracing, and yet it was also shockingly demanding. It required real love exercised not only towards personal enemies but also towards anybody in terrible need, as the Parable of the Good Samaritan and the criteria for the final judgement of all people (Matt. 25: 31–46) made clear.

Since all were children of the same divine Father, all were encouraged to pray, or—as Jesus put it—to ask, seek, and knock. Jesus left things as open as possible. He did not specify what human beings might ask for and seek, nor did he guarantee when their requests might be answered. He did not say, 'ask and it will be given to you at once'; nor did he say, 'seek and you will find immediately'; nor did he assure his hearers that the door would be opened without delay to those who knocked. But he did guarantee that their prayers would be answered, since these prayers were addressed to an infinitely loving Father. Jesus appealed to 'the—admittedly—ambiguous experience of the love of earthly fathers' as a 'helpful pointer to the heavenly Father'.[13] 'Is there anyone among you', Jesus asked, 'who, if your child asks for bread, will give a stone? Or if the child asks for a fish, will give a snake? If you then, who are evil, know how to give good gifts to your children, how much more will your Father in heaven give good things to those who ask him!' (Matt. 7: 7–11).

The Lord's Prayer was/is *the* prayer of the kingdom and summarized what Jesus preached (Matt. 6: 9–13; Luke 11: 2–4). Once again there was no question of any insiders or outsiders. All could and should enjoy through this prayer an intimate and privileged relationship to a loving and merciful Father. It was and is a prayer that invites us to share this relationship with all human beings; for all men and

[13] Ibid., 422.

women are our brothers and sisters. A vertical relationship to a loving 'Abba' must be matched by a horizontal relationship with all the human beings who inhabit the planet earth.[14] The limitless divine benevolence asks nothing less of us. To be sure, the Lord's Prayer has been the special prayer of Christians, in their public worship and private devotion. Nevertheless, its open quality takes this prayer beyond the Church and her members to the entire community of human beings. They all live in a world that is under the power of God's kingdom but still awaits its full coming. One may not be a Christian, but still pray—in these or equivalent words—'thy kingdom come'.

The open benevolence of God shines through a number of 'whoever' statements coming from Jesus. He set about founding a new family or new final community and did so on a remarkably open basis: 'whoever does the will of God is my brother and sister and mother' (Mark 3: 35). Any man or woman who did what God wanted to be done qualified for admission to this new community and became, whether he or she knew it or not, truly related to Jesus in the kingdom of God. In Chapter 7 we retrieved a number of 'whoever' statements such as those about welcoming children and the real greatness of being the servant of others. Such statements spell out some typical deeds of those bent on doing the will of God, and apparently could be applied to anyone, even to those who have never even heard of the name of Jesus. All those who pray with sincerity 'thy will be done' and live accordingly qualify to be members of Jesus' family, even if their identification as such remains mysteriously hidden. The preaching of Jesus encourages one to recognize in the kingdom of God, which already exists in our world, innumerable brothers, sisters, and mothers of Jesus, whose identity will be known in the glorious kingdom to come.

(3) After sampling the activity and teaching of Jesus for the kingdom which enacted an effective divine benevolence towards all, we come to his death in the cause of the kingdom. The record of the Last Supper and further testimony from the Gospels showed us (Chapter 8 above) that Jesus hoped and intended that his violent death would bring God's final reign and prove salvific for the whole

---

[14] See G. O'Collins, *The Lord's Prayer* (London: Darton, Longman & Todd, 2006).

human race. The message of the kingdom, as we saw, led more or less straight to the mystery of the passion. Jesus associated his approaching death with the salvation of human beings in the coming kingdom of God. All people were to be the beneficiaries of his sacrificial self-giving and of the new covenant it inaugurated. Faced with death, Jesus reached out to everyone in his redemptive intentions. He had lived and preached a universal vision of salvation. At the end he died a representative and redemptive death for all people.

PAUL AND THE NON-EVANGELIZED

What did Paul think about the religious situation of those many Jews and innumerable Gentiles who had not (or had not yet) joined the emerging Church (Chapter 9 above)? As we saw, he held that Christ and the Holy Spirit were and are all-determining for the salvation of every human being. But what of all those Gentiles who, for one reason or another, remained and would remain unbaptized?

Paul struggles with a different issue. He agonizes over the failure of many of his fellow Jews to believe in Jesus. In Romans 9–11 he argues that God's promise to Israel has not failed and Israel's apparent rejection by God is not final. But what of the Gentiles who have not—to use Paul's imagery—become branches grafted into the olive tree, which is and remains Israel? Nevertheless, without violating the Apostle's original meaning, we can reread appropriately some of his texts in our new contexts and find a plus-value that illuminates, for instance, the role of the Holy Spirit in the situation of contemporary non-Christians.

(1) We saw how, despite his list of terrible sins committed by Gentiles, Paul recognized that there were also morally responsible Gentiles who 'do by nature what the law requires'. Their conduct prompted the Apostle to draw the conclusion: 'they give proof that what the law requires is written on their hearts' (Rom. 2: 14–15). Later in the same letter he insisted that doing what God wants necessarily requires being helped by God in the struggle against the evil power of sin (7: 14–8: 4). With that help, some Gentiles

conscientiously performed what the law 'written on their hearts' summoned them to do.

This language about 'writing on the heart' echoes some passages from Jeremiah and Ezekiel. The first communicated a promise that God would convey a knowledge of the divine will written on human hearts (Jer. 31: 33). Ezekiel promised the gift of a new spirit and new (responsive) hearts that would allow the Israelites to keep the divine ordinances (Ezek. 11: 19–20; 36: 26–7). The language of Paul in Romans seems to extend these promises to the Gentiles. In Romans 2, he presumably has in mind a divine 'Writer' as the One who writes on the hearts of the Gentiles and empowers them to practise the essential requirements of the divine law. Should we recognize the Holy Spirit to be the One who touches the hearts and lives of these 'outsiders' who show themselves ready, with divine help, to follow God's law? Paul's language encourages us to recognize the Holy Spirit at work in the hearts and lives of Gentiles. Thus they can live according to the Spirit and not according to the flesh (or dominated by selfish passions and incapable of submitting to God's law) (Rom. 8: 5–11).

Galatians 4: 1–7 can prompt us, as we saw in Chapter 9, to think of the invisible mission of the Holy Spirit in the hearts and lives of all human beings. To what we glean from Romans 2 and Galatians 4, we might add Paul's testimony to the life-giving Spirit in Romans 8: 1–27. Some of what Paul writes there applies specifically to Christians, but he also highlights the life-giving power of the Spirit that touches all human beings. They are all being brought by the Spirit to the final fulfilment of the entire universe.

(2) The all-embracing language about Christ that we summarized in Chapter 9 readily suggests the powerful presence of Christ in the existence of all human beings, baptized or otherwise. The reconciliation brought by Christ affects the whole of humanity and, indeed, the whole created world. The presence of Christ as universal 'Reconciler' touches all human beings. And so too does his sovereign rule as agent of creation, the One 'through whom all things exist' (1 Cor. 8: 6). Paul also pictures Christ at the Last Adam, a corporate figure whose benefits bless all people. Lastly, the Apostle acknowledges the risen Christ as the exalted Lord of the entire universe. His sovereignty extends to everyone.

In summing up, we could say that, while Paul consistently talks of baptized Christians being 'in Christ' and the Holy Spirit being 'in them', his teaching allows us to extend this language to everybody. In some sense all human beings are 'in' Christ, and the Holy Spirit is 'in' them. A later chapter will take up this question of the universal presence of Christ and the Spirit.

LUKE AND THE NON-EVANGELIZED

Chapter 10 illustrated the central message of Luke and Acts: human beings are saved only through the crucified and resurrected Christ. What then might Luke say or at least imply about the situation and prospects of those who have not (or have not yet) heard the good news of Jesus and responded to him in faith? The evangelist presents the Christian community as *the* place where, through repentance and baptism in the name of Jesus, sins are forgiven and the Holy Spirit is communicated. The blessings of the messianic age are available for all who repent and call upon the name of Jesus (Acts 2: 21, 38–40). What then does Luke think, or at least imply, about those who continue to worship and live in other ways? Is sharing in the Spirit and in Christ limited to those Jews and Gentiles who repent of their sins and accept baptism?

Our answer can take shape around episodes in Acts which involve an Ethiopian eunuch, a Roman centurion, the people of Lystra, and Paul's audience in Athens. Without doing violence to what Luke wishes to communicate, we can find a plus-value in his texts which sheds light on the situation of the non-evangelized.

(1) The Ethiopian, *before* he asked Philip to baptize him, worshipped the one, true God of Israel (and today we should add, of Islam), read the scriptures prayerfully, and, in particular, was moved, as a marginalized outsider, by the mysterious prefiguring of Jesus in the Suffering Servant of Second Isaiah. The Ethiopian represents all those who are touched by suffering and in prayer are drawn to seek for the meaning of what they and others suffer. He seems emblematic of those who, without yet knowing clearly what is happening, are led to seek (and sometimes find) Christ in their struggle with the mystery of suffering.

(2) The episode of Cornelius the centurion is told at greater length. We begin with him as an unbaptized Gentile whose piety is exemplary. He leads his household by his life of constant prayer and generous almsgiving. He is favoured with a vision in which an angel of God brings him a message that will change his life and that of innumerable others. Luke, as we saw, reports three times this vision of someone who is neither Jewish nor Christian—a way of showing readers how the religious experience of such 'outsiders' may bring them into close intimacy with God. This 'outsider', along with his family and close friends, is then blessed with an outpouring of the Holy Spirit; this also happens *before* any of them receive baptism. In Luke's view, divine visions and the manifest presence of the Spirit are not limited to the members of the Christian community. Furthermore, such 'outsiders' can have very significant things to teach Christians in general but also the leaders of the Church in particular. After he has heard from Cornelius an account of his vision, Peter remarks that he now clearly understands that 'God shows no partiality. But in every nation anyone who fears him and does what is right is acceptable to him' (Acts 10: 34–5).

Anyone who treasures the authority of the NT scriptures dares not take a less generous view than Luke's convictions about the religious experience of non-Christians and their possibilities. Jesus is not merely Lord of the Jewish people (Luke 2: 11), but also Lord of all people (Acts 10: 36). His authority applies to all, and his benefits are open to all (Acts 10: 42–3).

(3) Before summarizing the theological import of Luke's account of Paul's stay in Athens, we should pause to assess the lasting significance of what Paul and Barnabas say to people in Lystra, who (unlike the Ethiopian eunuch and Cornelius but like the Athenians) share neither the Jewish faith in one God nor their scriptures (Acts 14: 15–17). Paul and Barnabas highlight the fruitfulness of nature which witnesses to the goodness towards all exercised by the Creator of the universe. All human beings alike have been the beneficiaries of the generous benevolence and providential care for everyone that God reveals through nature.

Paul and Barnabas say nothing about Jesus in their brief speech. They are content to appeal to the 'book of nature' and the universal benevolence of the one, true God. The testimony of nature to the divine benevolence can be 'read' and accepted by all people every-where.

(4) The speech Paul makes in Athens yields at least four pointers for those concerned with the salvation of the millions of people who either have never heard of Christ or have not (yet) accepted the message about him. First, the speech inculcates a respectful appreci-ation of other cultures and religions. As Luke pictures him, Paul looks for what is true, valuable, and worthwhile in the culture and religion of 'others'. In fact, they are not really 'others'. All human beings are God's 'offspring' (Acts 17: 28–9) and make up the one family of God. Second, all human beings live enveloped by God: 'in him we live and move and have our being'. Their search for God depends on God and comes from the very radical relationship to God which determines their entire being. A third lesson from the Areopa-gus speech hints at the way all human beings are open to the infinite; they have a primordial desire to know and love God, who is the very fullness of being. Every human person shares the same basic hunger in their minds and hearts—a deep hunger of God. Fourthly and finally, Paul does not want to introduce into the cultural and reli-gious context of his hearers a 'foreign' or alien deity. Even if hitherto not explicitly known, the 'God Unknown' has already been present among the Athenians. Paul gives a face and name to the divine Anonymous One: the resurrected Jesus who will come in glory to judge all people at the end of world history.

In the Book of Acts Luke certainly endorses a clear and compelling mission to evangelize the world. At the same time, as we have seen, he encourages a generous and respectful openness to those who are not or not yet Christian believers. For individual examples of such people, we can find a wide range in the OT.

13

Holy 'Outsiders'

The previous chapter probed the whole Bible for its witness to the universal benevolence of God. Beyond question, it is always possible to abuse the scriptures to support a present-day agenda, including the urgent desire to have some pointers towards grasping the situation of those who have not yet been evangelized or who, for various reasons (including honourable ones), have not accepted the message of Christ. Yet the biblical record can help us with this issue. It presents a range of 'outsiders' who are remembered with respect for what they did in priestly, prophetic, or other ways. What we glean about them from the OT can raise useful and even disturbing *questions* for Christians today.

Every spiritual tradition treasures the power of the question. In Zen practice, for instance, a 'koan' is a question to check the rational mind's attempt to control reality. Moreover, questions do not erect barriers the way answers can sometimes do. Christians too must treasure questions, not least because of what they read in the Gospel of John. The very first words of Jesus take the form of a question: 'What are you looking for?' (John 1: 38). Many other wonderful questions follow, right through to the final, triple question: 'do you love me?' (John 21: 15–17).

PRIESTLY ACTIVITY

From the Book of Genesis and beyond, the OT records notable, marginal figures who perform priestly or at least cultic acts which clearly win the divine approval. They include Noah, Melchizedek, Jethro, the sailors in the story of Jonah, and Naaman the Syrian.

(1) In the story of the great flood, when it subsides, God commands Noah to disembark from the ark, along with his wife, sons, daughters-in-law, and 'the families' of animals and birds. Noah does what he is told. But he does something further by building 'an altar to the Lord' and making on it 'burnt offerings' of 'clean' animals and birds. After 'the Lord smells the pleasing odour', he 'says in his heart' that he will never again curse the ground and bring destruction (Gen. 8: 15–22). When Noah builds an altar and offers this sacrifice of thanksgiving, he does so spontaneously and, obviously, without intending to follow any prescriptions about burnt offerings and other offerings understood to have been introduced later by God through Moses (Lev. 1–7).

Obviously we read here a legendary story, concerned with primeval times. But it enjoys its special value, since Noah was reckoned to be the second founder of the human race. Do the sacrificial gestures of Noah retain any significance for later times? Do they even suggest that some value can still attach to priestly worship among the descendants of Noah who still follow religious ways of life other than Christianity? Or should we respect the truth and value of what Noah does but simply deny that it points to any enduring value among the religions of today?

(2) A little later in the Book of Genesis, as we recalled in Chapter 1, Abraham meets Melchizedek, a mysterious figure who blesses Abraham and does so in the name of 'God the Most High' (Gen. 14: 19–20).[1] In the story Melchizedek turns up for only two verses, but he enjoys an extraordinary, even unique, 'afterlife'. This ancient Canaanite priest-king of Jerusalem will be pictured in a royal psalm as a forerunner to the king of Israel. The new king, who also bears the dignity of priesthood, will be deemed 'a priest forever according to the order of Melchizedek' (Ps. 110: 4). The Letter to the Hebrews will go much further by interpreting the priesthood of Christ himself 'according to the order of Melchizedek' (Heb. 5: 10; 6: 20). Melchizedek prefigures the Son of God who is superior to the

---

[1] See M. C. Astour, 'Melchizedek', *ABD* iv. 684–6.

Levitical priests and holds his priesthood permanently. From the end of the second century AD, the bread and wine offered by Melchizedek would be seen as a type of the Eucharist and in this connection he was introduced into the Roman Canon of the Eucharist (dating probably from the fourth century): 'Look with favour on these offerings, and accept them as once you accepted the gifts of your servant Abel, the sacrifice of Abraham our father in faith, and the bread and wine offered by your priest Melchizedek.'

Melchizedek is a 'liminal' figure, one who shows up briefly on the margins of the story of Abraham and Sarah. He does not have further contact with, let alone join, the central narrative of the formation of God's people. Yet this 'outsider', and not some personage from the story of Israel, serves to interpret the eternal priesthood of Christ. At one point when addressing God, the Roman Canon calls Melchizedek 'your priest'. Has the importance of this 'liminal' priest-king changed or even been lost with the passage of time, so that Christians should rule out the possibility of meeting and receiving a blessing from such an 'outsider', a latter-day Melchizedek? Or is Melchizedek more than a forerunner of Christ, more than 'merely' someone who participated in advance in the priesthood of Christ? Is he a person to be permanently treasured as a possible pointer to the existence today of other priest-kings of 'God the Most High' who would somehow participate in the one priesthood of Christ?[2] Could we imagine situations today in which contemporary figures do things like Melchizedek and so mediate the blessings of God?

---

[2] By associating 'your servant' Abel with Melchizedek, the Roman Canon echoes the fact that not only Melchizedek but also Abel has a part in the Letter to the Hebrews, albeit a minor one. Abel heads the roll call of heroes and heroines of faith; Hebrews notes his sacrifice and death (11: 4). The roll call ends with the supreme example of Christ, 'the pioneer and perfecter of faith', who endured the cross and like Abel shed his blood (12: 2–4). Thus Abel and Christ create a kind of 'inclusion', modified by the fact that the blood of Jesus, 'the mediator of a new covenant', is superior to that of Abel (Heb. 12: 24). In both cases an innocent victim is killed. But the murder of Abel cries out for vengeance (Gen. 4: 10), whereas the blood of Jesus provides mercy and seals a new covenant with God; see R. S. Hess, 'Abel', *ABD* i. 9–10. Even more legendary than Melchizedek (who is tied into popular history by being priest-king of Jerusalem and meeting Abraham), Abel at least raises the question: could there be in today's world 'Abels' whose faith, offerings, and death 'please' God?

(3) A further 'liminal' priestly figure in the OT is Jethro, the father-in-law of Moses.[3] A Midianite priest, he came back on the scene after the Exodus to visit Moses in the wilderness, give him advice on the administration of the law, and offer a sacrifice to God (Exod. 18: 1–27). Even if the Midianites worshipped idols, Jethro surprisingly recognized YHWH: 'Blessed be the Lord (YHWH) who has delivered you from the Egyptians and from Pharaoh. Now I know that the Lord is greater than all gods, because he delivered the people from the Egyptians.' Then Jethro 'brought a burnt offering and sacrifices to God; and Aaron came with all the elders of Israel to eat bread with Moses' father-in-law in the presence of God' (vv. 11–12).

Did this priest of Midian already regularly worship YHWH? (That is left unclear.) What 'rubrics' and 'rules' did he follow in making his cultic offering and celebrating a sacred meal with Aaron and all the elders of Israel? Or is that a hopelessly anachronistic question? At all events we meet here in the Exodus narrative, shortly before the Sinai theophany and the making of the covenant, a somewhat unexpected openness to a priestly 'outsider'. Of course, as the father-in-law of Moses, Jethro cannot be reckoned to be simply an 'outsider'. It was partly within the story of the chosen people that he played out his brief, 'liminal' role. That said, Jethro and his priestly activity leave us with the question: could Catholics and other Christians imagine Jethro-style priests still operating on the threshold of the Church? Or is there no place nowadays for a Jethro to be active, even as a visiting preacher or celebrant? Do all priestly operations depend on someone being regularly baptized, confirmed, and ordained to the priestly ministry? Whatever else we say about the father-in-law of Moses, Jethro invites us to perform some thought experiments and imagine the reception (or non-reception) in the Church of some figure like him turning up and making his 'burnt offering and sacrifices to God'.

(4) We looked earlier at other cases of cultic acts of worship practised by 'outsiders' and obviously approved by God. The sailors who have reluctantly thrown Jonah out of the boat make sacrificial offerings to YHWH when they are rescued (Chapter 3 above). Unlike

---

[3] See J. C. Slayton, 'Jethro', *ABD* iii. 821; G. E. Mendenhall, 'Midian, Midianites', *ABD*, iv. 315–18.

Noah, Melchizedek, and Jethro, they remain an anonymous group. Unlike Melchizedek (who encounters Abraham) and Jethro (who meets the Israelites under the command of his son-in-law), they are neither 'liminal' characters involved with the central story of the OT, nor even people with a priestly status recognized by some public. Their worship of YHWH, at least as the story goes, seems a transitory episode. In the narrative it shows how, even though he is running away from his primary mission (that of preaching repentance in Nineveh), Jonah cannot help doing the will of God. Despite himself, he has become a missionary to a bunch of sailors and been the occasion of their acknowledging and worshipping YHWH at least in an emergency.

Even if the text supplies no further details, Naaman the Syrian on his return to Damascus evidently intended to practise some kind of cultic worship of YHWH (Chapter 2 above). After his cure from leprosy, he took home 'two mule-loads of earth' from Israel. He believed that YHWH, like other deities, could not be worshipped apart from his own land. He would be widely separated from Israel, but somehow in touch with the God of Israel. Does the case of Naaman even hint at contemporary possibilities of offering genuine worship to God 'at a distance' and not publicly and visibly 'within' the confines of official Christianity?

PROPHETIC ACTIVITY

Chapter 3 observed the way in which Balaam, a Mesopotamian diviner, was somewhat unfairly vilified in the NT. In the full story about him (Num. 22: 1–24: 25), he clearly exemplifies how an 'outsider', who never joins the people of God, can pronounce genuine prophecies about the destiny of Israel, its royal leader, and Jesus himself. Could we imagine such prophetic activity continuing today among those who do not belong to the Church?

One might readily think here of 'positive' figures such as Martin Buber (1879–1965), Mahatma Gandhi (1869–1948), and the Dalai Lama (b. 1936). But what of such notoriously 'negative' figures as Sigmund Freud (1856–1939), Karl Marx (1818–83), and Friedrich

Nietzsche (1844–1900). Merold Westphal entertained that possibility in his *Suspicion and Faith: The Religious Uses of Modern Atheism*.[4] Westphal explored brilliantly the abiding challenges that Freud, Marx, and Nietzsche pose to believers, who slide into various forms of self-deception. Without changing anything, he might have given his book another subtitle: *The Prophetic Uses of Modern Atheism*. What would it be like to take the case of Balaam as an encouragement to look for prophetic figures, both positive and negative, in the modern world? St Augustine of Hippo (354–430) recognized the presence not only of 'hidden saints' but also of 'prophets' among the Gentiles (*Contra Faustum* 19. 2; *De catechizandis rudibus* 22. 40). He declared roundly that 'prophecy was extended to all nations (omnibus gentibus dispensabatur prophetia)' (*In Ioannem* 9. 9).

Of course, one might argue that God raised up Balaam-style prophets during the time of the OT, but further examples of such prophetical operations are ruled out by the coming of Christ. Nevertheless, the case of Cornelius (Chapters 10 and 12 above) presents us with someone who, while not yet a Christian, received a very significant communication from God through a vision and led St Peter to acknowledge some enormously important elements in the universal availability of the salvation effected by Christ. One might also cite the case of Caiaphas, the high priest, who remarks about Jesus: 'it is better for you to have one man die for the people than to have the whole nation perish'. John comments: 'He did not say this on his own, but being high priest that year, he prophesied that Jesus was about to die for the nation, and not for the nation only, but to gather into one the children of God who had been scattered' (John 11: 50–2). Caiaphas is an institutional figure who unconsciously delivers a dramatic prophecy. Cornelius, however, receives and mediates his message on an individual basis. Could there be individual or institutional people in our modern world, like Cornelius or Caiaphas, who do not or do not yet belong to the Church and yet, either consciously or unconsciously, have prophetic messages to communicate to Christians?

---

[4] New York: Fordham University Press, 1998.

OTHER INDIVIDUALS

Thus far this chapter has raised questions about the enduring significance of biblical figures of a priestly or prophetic kind. What of other personages who do not belong in either category? There are those like Abimelech, who intersects twice with the story of Abraham and Sarah (Chapter 1 above), and the widow of Zarephath, who was blessed by God through Elijah (Chapter 2 above), but who do not then enter the mainstream story of Israel. Then there is Ruth the Moabite, who enters the history of Israel and becomes an ancestor of King David and of Jesus himself (Chapter 2 above). They too provide case studies to be examined under the aegis of 2 Timothy, which says of the OT: 'all scripture is inspired by God and is useful for teaching' (3: 16). What do these figures have to teach Christians today—both those who remain 'outsiders' and those like Ruth who become 'insiders'?

Perhaps the most poignant of the OT cases is that of Ishmael, his descendants, and the children of Abraham's second wife, Keturah.[5] The son of Abraham's concubine Hagar, Ishmael has an ambiguous press in the OT. On the one hand, he is called 'a wild ass of a man'— perhaps with reference to the freedom of the wandering Ishmaelites in the southern wilderness (Gen. 16: 12; see 25: 16–18). On the other hand, God promises: 'As for Ishmael . . . I will bless him and make him fruitful and exceedingly numerous; he shall be the father of twelve princes, and I will make him a great nation' (Gen. 17: 20; see 21: 13, 18). The Ishmaelites are said to be organized, like later Israel, into twelve tribes, each with a tribal prince (Gen. 25: 12–18). As for the descendants of Abraham through Keturah, they make up the Arabian tribes, including Midian (Gen. 25: 1–6; Exod. 2: 15–22; 18: 1). What is one to make of these descendants of Abraham, who are spun off from the mainstream of his descendants? The figure of Ishmael is troubling. It is said that 'his hand shall be against everyone, and everyone's hand against him, and he shall live at odds with his kin' (Gen. 16: 12). Yet, after living 'in the wilderness' (Gen. 21: 20), he returns to join Isaac in ensuring that their father Abraham is buried

---

[5] See E. A. Knauf, 'Ishmaelites', *ABD* iii. 513–20; id., 'Keturah', *ABD* iv. 31.

properly alongside Sarah in the field that Abraham had purchased (Gen. 25: 9–10). Both Islam and Judaism regard Ishmael as the ancestor of Arab peoples.[6]

In thinking about the troubling and complex picture of Ishmael and his descendants—not to mention those of Keturah—I feel driven back to that wonderful sentiment in 1 John: 'God is greater than our hearts, and he knows everything' (3: 20). The OT yields a bewildering variety of cases that invite our detailed study. How do they fit into the one, overall plan of God for the salvation of the whole human race? What light might they shed on the situation of the equally bewildering variety of religions today? Some patient and modest reflection on the variety of ways in which God is effectively present may guide us somewhat in our quest for understanding.

---

[6] See H. A. R. Gibb and J. H. Kramers (eds.), *Shorter Encyclopedia of Islam* (Ithaca, NY: Cornell University Press, 1953), 'Ismâ'îl', 178–9.

14

The Universal Presence of Christ and the Spirit

The concluding verses of the Book of Exodus invoke two exquisite symbols to depict the divine presence in the tabernacle, the portable sanctuary that accompanied the Israelites on their journey: 'the cloud covered the tent of meeting, and the glory of the Lord filled the tabernacle' (40: 34). The glorious presence of God, as rabbis and scholars later appreciated, could be closer and more intense, or seemingly more distant and less felt.[1] Salvation was experienced through the personal and powerful presence of God. In his first address in Deuteronomy, Moses asked: 'What other great nation has a god so *near* to it as the Lord our God is whenever we call to him?' (4: 7). Here we come close here to the heart of the divine blessings lavished on Israel.

In the second century of the Christian era, St Irenaeus (d. around 200) acknowledged the universal scope of the divine action for human salvation: 'the Word of the all-powerful God . . . on the invisible plane is co-extensive with the whole of creation', 'rules the universe', and as the Son of God 'has traced the sign of the cross on everything' (*Demonstratio* 34). In the third century Origen (d. around 254) also highlighted the universal saving presence: 'Christ is so powerful that, although invisible because of his divinity, he is *present* to every person and extends over the whole universe' (*In Ioannem* 6. 15; italics mine). This was not to deny that Christ was present in a special, fuller way in the lives of the baptized. But that fuller presence did not mean an absence elsewhere.

---

[1] See S. Terrien, *The Elusive Presence: Toward a New Biblical Theology* (San Francisco: Harper & Row, 1978).

Many centuries later Pope John Paul II (1920–2005) said something similar, while letting the theme of the Holy Spirit shape the way he expressed matters. He proclaimed, of course, that the full means of salvation are available for the followers of Christ. But this faith did not mean denying the Spirit's powerful presence everywhere. As John Paul II put matters in his 1990 encyclical *Redemptoris missio*, the universal '*presence* and activity' of the Spirit 'affect not only individuals but also society and history, peoples, cultures, and religions' (no. 28; italics mine). Through the Spirit's presence the 'others' participate in their own ways in the one divine plan for human salvation.

In their different ways, some OT texts, Irenaeus, Origen, and John Paul II can suggest that presence and its varieties form the key for thinking about how divine salvation reaches all people. We live in a 'world of grace', a world in which in various ways Christ powerfully demonstrates his personal presence through the Holy Spirit.[2] Reflecting on St Paul (Chapter 12 above), I suggested one way of unpacking this gracious presence: in some sense all human beings are 'in' Christ and the Holy Spirit is 'in' all human beings. To fill out this suggestion I need first to analyse what is meant by 'presence' and how this obviously personal category can be used.

A PHILOSOPHY OF PRESENCE

A major challenge to be faced in employing 'presence' comes from the fact that philosophers offer little help. Over the centuries theologians have often been able to take advantage of the way philosophers have clarified a whole range of concepts, which—with the necessary adjustments made—could then be pressed into service to express Christian faith coherently and systematically. With the notion of presence, however, little philosophical analysis is available. This neglect is documented by the fact that major encyclopedias and dictionaries of philosophy rarely carry an entry on 'presence'. From the time of Augustine, when developing a doctrine of God,

---

[2] See L. J. O'Donovan (ed.), *A World of Grace: An Introduction to the Themes and Foundations of Karl Rahner's Theology* (New York: Seabury, 1980).

philosophers and theologians have discussed the question of the divine omni-*presence*. In their theories of knowledge the medievals treated the presence of the object (and of truth) to the mind, the primordial unity between the subject knowing and the object known. Edmund Husserl (1859–1938) and other phenomenologists have paid some attention to the theme of presence. But, all in all, the topic has often been left alone by philosophers (and theologians) and handled rather by mystical and spiritual authors, who write of experiencing and cultivating the divine presence. One can puzzle over and speculate about this relative silence from the philosophers.[3] Whatever the explanations, we need first to spell out at least some of the essential components of presence before applying it to the universal presence of Christ and the Holy Spirit.

(1) Among the most obvious characteristics of presence is the way it implies 'presence to'. Being present always means being present to someone, something, or some event. 'I was present at the baptism of my niece'; 'I was present when the bridge collapsed and ten people died.' In other words, presence entails 'being to' or 'being in relation with', and not simply 'being in itself' or existence as such. Presence is not being but a mode of being.

This 'being to' also covers one's presence to oneself, 'das Bei-sich-sein' as German philosophers would put it, or that being present to oneself in any experience and coming to oneself which forms the nub of Thomist interpretations of knowledge.[4] The higher one's being, the

---

[3] On this silence of philosophers (and, to some extent, of theologians) see the documentation I provided in *Christology: A Biblical, Historical, and Systematic Study of Jesus Christ* (Oxford: Oxford University Press, 1995), 310. To that documentation one could add other recent works which lack any entry on 'presence'—e.g. two ten-volume works: D. M. Borchert (ed.), *Encyclopedia of Philosophy* (Farmington Hill, Mich.: Macmillan, 2nd edn., 2006); E. Craig (ed.), *Routledge Encyclopedia of Philosophy* (London: Routledge, 1998). There are discussions of 'presentness' or *temporal* existence: e.g. W. L. Craig, 'Is Presentness a Property', *American Philosophical Quarterly* 34 (1997), 27–40. For Martin Heidegger (1889–1976) being determined by a definite mode of time was identified as presence.

[4] On cognitional presence according to Thomas Aquinas, see J. Maritain, *Degrees of Knowledge* (New York: Scribner, 1959); A. Maurer, 'Reflections on Thomas Aquinas' Notion of Presence', in J. Long (ed.), *God of Abraham: Essays in Memory of James A. Weisheipl, O.P.* (Toronto: Pontifical Institute of Mediaeval Studies, 1911), 113–28; K. Rahner, *Hearers of the Word* (London: Sheed & Ward, 1969).

more one can come to or return to oneself in knowledge. 'Self-knowing' and 'being' thus form a primordial 'presence to'.

In these terms, consciousness means being self-possessed or present to oneself—in that concomitant knowledge that knowers have of themselves and their acts in the process of knowing something other than themselves. Along with this presence to oneself, knowledge also involves the presence of the known object in the knower (something similar to the presence of the beloved in the lover). Whenever we come to know someone or something, the object known becomes present in us, and so related to us. There is a mutual presence of the perceiver in the perceived.

(2) Whether we deal with conscious self-presence (a relation of identity) or presence to others (a relation of difference), 'presence' is relational and 'happens' in relationship. That is tantamount to naming presence as essentially personal. Only persons can, properly speaking, be present, even if one must admit that faithful dogs can imitate and supply some of the better features of human presence.

Many who reflect on personal existence argue that it should be primarily understood as being constituted by relationship to other persons.[5] The personal self can be self only in relation to other selves. Being personal means being relational, and here we may add: being personal means being present to other persons. Being in relation and being present express what it is to be personal. 'Presence' picks up two essential characteristics of being personal: the togetherness or relationship to the other(s) and, at the same time, the distinction between each other. Without this distinction the communion and proximity would collapse into identity, and we would no longer have two or more persons present *to* each other. In brief, presence signifies 'being with' but not 'being identical'.

(3) As a (or rather the) form of self-bestowal, presence implies a free act, the exercise of our personal freedom that communicates a loving, non-invasive presence. We are truly present to those with whom we genuinely wish to be present; in other words, we are present and remain present to those whom we love. We are 'there' because of our urgent desire to give and receive love.

---

[5] See O'Collins, *Christology*, 234–6.

(4) The free self-giving that constitutes interpersonal presence denotes a breaking into 'my' life that discloses fresh possibilities and a being acted upon in ways that may even profoundly change the direction of my existence. Such presence can bring a new communion of life and love. The relationship of spouses to one another and that of parents to children spring to mind as paradigm examples of the loving communion of life brought about by interpersonal presence. Such active presence means disclosing oneself, sharing one's presence, and making others 'at home' with an unconditional hospitality that gives and enhances life.

Where death signifies absence, life signifies presence and vice versa. One might adapt John 10: 10 and make it read: 'I came that they may have my presence and have it abundantly.' To enjoy the Lord's bountiful presence must mean to be acted upon by him and to receive life from him in abundance. Whether they are aware of this or not, the life of all human beings can be seen as a longing for the presence of Christ. Their history entails struggling for life in his presence, suffering from the experience of his absence, and yearning for his definitive, face-to-face presence.

(5) One should also mention the 'cost' of presence. Sheer physical distance may keep us apart from people and means that making ourselves personally present to them (instead of being content to phone them or send them e-mail messages) costs time and money. The psychological distance between ourselves and others, from whom we are separated by misunderstandings or worse, may call for real sacrifice when we decide to seek them out and attempt to re-establish personal relations on a new footing. In our world of so much violence that is monstrously destructive, simply unjustified, and even senseless, making ourselves present to those in terrible need can be fraught with danger. In innumerable ways presence can be 'costly', even to the point of risking our lives. Vulnerability shows itself to be a recurrent feature of personal presence.

(6) Various examples offered above repeatedly imply a sixth aspect of presence: it has something bodily or spatial about it. Since human persons can be described as embodied spirits, the free exercise of their freedom to make themselves present inevitably involves some element of the body. Obviously there is more to authentically human presence than mere bodily or spatial proximity. Nevertheless, we

persistently and necessarily experience presence as involving our bodies and occurring in some particular place. The mutual presence of people entails their being close and within one another's 'field of view'.

This raises the question: how then can God, being purely spiritual and non-spatial, be present to human beings and so, in that sense, be located in space and time? One can and should respond that in all cases the beneficiary, being human, supplies the bodily, spatial factor. God is permanently related to the spatial–temporal creation, even if not related in a spatial–temporal way. God may be beyond space and time, but continuously interacts with agents in space and time. On the side of the recipient, the presence of God proves to be bodily.

Furthermore, by personally assuming the human condition, the incarnate Son of God provided the bodily, spatial–temporal element also on the divine side. Through the earthly body of his human history and then through his risen, glorious body, Christ has supplied the bodily 'requirement' on the side of God. Because of his incarnation, the Son of God assumed a 'bodily place' in time and eternity. Thus the incarnation provided a new way for a divine person to be present somewhere and (through the transformation of his resurrection) everywhere.

This chapter also deals with the presence of the Holy Spirit—both in baptized Christians and other persons. The Holy Spirit has not taken on the bodily human condition through an incarnation. The distinctive mission of the Spirit is attested by Paul (Chapters 9 and 12 above) and Luke (Chapters 10 and 12 above), along with other NT authors. But surely, unlike the visible mission of the Son, the Spirit's mission must be called 'invisible' and hence non-bodily and non-spatial? To call the mission of the Spirit simply invisible would not seem correct, and that for two reasons. First, there is a certain visibility to this mission, inasmuch as the Spirit aims to sanctify bodily, human beings and transform the material universe. The Spirit, Paul insists, produces visible effects 'for the good of all' (1 Cor. 12: 7) Second, the Spirit's mission may be proper to the Spirit, but is inseparably joined with the visible mission of the Son. That consideration also justifies recognizing some bodily visibility in the mission of the Spirit, which takes place in space and time.

(7) The mediation of presence calls for some attention. Our experience shows how presence can be mediated through words, events (e.g. meals and embraces), and things (e.g. flowers and photographs). Between the divine persons of the Trinity presence is communicated immediately. But where presence involves human beings, it happens symbolically—through the mediation of our voices, our actions, and things which have some special connection with us. Presence, in the case of human beings, is always, even when its intensity makes it seem intimately immediate, in some sense mediated and never a strictly and exclusively immediate presence.

(8) As much as or more than anyone else, Gabriel Marcel (1889–1973) highlighted the differing qualities and modes of presence.[6] The relationships involved seem endlessly various: interpersonal presences can always be closer, more intense, more freely chosen, and more productive of an ever richer communion of life. A seemingly infinite variety of form and intensity characterizes the presences we experience; 'presence' is a radically analogous term and reality. We never face a simple alternative, presence or absence. It is always a question of what kind of presence and what kind of absence, or how someone is present or how someone is absent. Every presence, short of the beatific vision of the final encounter with God, is always tinged with absence.

Given the stunning variety and qualitative differences that characterize human presence, we should be ready to acknowledge an endless variety in the qualitatively different possibilities of divine presence and activity. To allege anything less would be strangely at odds with the loving freedom of an infinitely creative God. It seems weirdly arrogant to limit possibilities in the case of the divine presence and activity. Below we will examine the strikingly new modes of divine presence to humanity and the world that the missions of the Son and the Holy Spirit brought.

(9) Finally, reflection suggests a feminine dimension to presence. Our first experience of human presence was a maternal one, when we were each umbilically bonded to our mother who harboured and protected us. After birth her presence continued to shelter and

---

[6] On presence and its varieties see G. Marcel, *Homo viator* (London: Victor Gollancz, 1951); id., *The Mystery of Being* (London: Harvill Press, 1950–1).

nurture us. It is no wonder then that there is a receptive, nurturing, and maternal feel to the presence of God, in whom 'we live and move and have our being' (Acts 17: 28). Inasmuch as it creates a quiet 'space' in which to breathe and grow, human and divine presence wears a maternal, feminine face.

This working account of presence comprises nine elements. As relational, personal, and free, presence creates communion. It comes across as vulnerable and bodily. Mediated symbolically among human beings, it bespeaks an endless variety of possibilities. While obviously not exclusively so, it emerges as primordially feminine. What light can this account shed on the presence of all human beings 'in' Christ and the presence 'in' them of the Holy Spirit?

THE REVEALING AND SAVING PRESENCE
OF CHRIST

Major items expounded in previous chapters can be re-articulated through the nine themes in my account of presence and so throw light on the universal, saving presence of Christ. Let us begin with the ministry of Jesus. (1) Chapter 7 expounded Jesus' preaching of and activity for the kingdom of God. In his earthly ministry Jesus, implicitly but clearly, proclaimed himself as inseparably connected with the divine kingdom that was breaking into the world. He was and is the kingdom in person, the 'autobasileia' as Origen put it (*In Matt.* 24. 7; on Matt. 18: 23). With and through his personal presence (in his life, death, and resurrection), the rule of God has become already present and will come in its fullness at the end of all history. Since the kingdom of God touches everyone, the revealing and saving presence of Christ, the heart of the kingdom, must do likewise. No human beings, whether they are aware of this or not, can escape living in the presence of Christ. Whatever occurs, occurs in the presence of Christ. Whoever acts, acts in the presence of Christ, even if he or she does not discern and acknowledge his presence.

(2) Joining Paul in identifying Christ as the last Adam and thus head of the new humanity, means acknowledging him as present to and related with all men and women, wherever they may be.

Likewise, acknowledging him to be the Reconciler of the world, the divine Agent of creation and new creation, and exalted Lord of the universe entails recognizing his all-pervasive presence and activity in the whole created world. There neither is nor can be any situation 'outside' or 'without' Christ and 'outside' his free self-giving that effects, however mysteriously, a communion of life and love with him. One must allow for an endless variety of qualities and modes in this cosmic presence of Christ. To say less would not seem compatible with mainstream Christian faith in him.[7]

(3) From the time of St Justin Martyr (d. around 165), St Irenaeus and later church Fathers regularly identified Christ as the divine Logos (Word) or Wisdom, who, by creating and sustaining the world, intimately accompanies everyone and everything. Hence they understood the Logos to permeate the body of the world. No place or person lies 'far from' God's creative Logos or Wisdom. The Logos was and is universally present to and related with everyone and everything.

In explaining this universal presence, Justin and Irenaeus portrayed the Logos as the unique source of religious knowledge—a knowledge shared in differently by Christians, Jews, and others. According to Justin, on the one hand, 'the seeds of the Word' are everywhere and in every person (*Second Apology* 8. 1; 13. 5). On the other hand, even though 'the whole human race shares' in the Logos (*First Apology* 46. 2), some people live only 'according to a fragment of the Logos'. Christians live 'according to the knowledge and contemplation of the whole Logos, who is Christ' (*Second Apology* 8. 3). One can translate this language in terms of the endless variety and modes not only in the presence of the Logos but also in the knowledge that he communicates.

In his concern to protect the utter transcendence of God the Father, Justin developed the intermediary roles of the Son as Logos and 'Angel'. As Logos he mediates and is present in all creation. As Angel he revealed the divine will in the OT theophanies (*Dialogue* 56. 1, 4).

---

[7] In this context it is worth recalling Col. 1: 19 where God is the presupposed but unexpressed subject ('it was the will that all the fullness dwell in him [Christ]'. In *Colossians* (New York: Doubleday, 1994), M. Barth and H. Blanke comment: 'the presence of God exists now only in Christ' (p. 212), to which one must add: 'and that presence is now found everywhere'.

He was the One who spoke to Abraham, Jacob, Moses, and others in those theophanies, which in effect become Christophanies. Irenaeus, while not continuing the 'Angel' Christology of Justin, agreed that it was the Logos who was manifested to Adam in the garden and to Noah at the time of the great flood. In the third century Origen endorsed this view: the books of 'the law and the prophets' record the encounters between the OT saints and the pre-incarnate Logos (*In Ioannem* 6. 4. 19–22).

Irenaeus summed up the Son's universal role in revelation as follows: 'From the beginning, the Son reveals (*revelat*) the Father to all whom the Father desires, at the time and in the manner desired by the Father' (*Adversus haereses* 4. 6. 7). No one is left out when the Son discloses the Father. Yet the timing and manner for this universal revelatory activity depend on God and not on human beings. What matters *primarily* is God's searching for us through his Son rather than any human search for God. As Irenaeus put matters: 'no one can know God, unless God teaches: that is, without God, God cannot be known' (ibid. 4. 6. 4).

Salvation belongs inseparably to this revealing activity of the universally present Son/Logos. To quote once again a key passage from Irenaeus: 'the Word of the all-powerful God . . . on the invisible plane is co-extensive with the whole of creation', 'rules the universe', and as Son of God 'has traced the sign of the cross on everything' (*Demonstratio* 34). While Irenaeus held that, from the very beginning and in every part of the world, the Son has in one way or another revealed the Father to every person, he saw that this universal revelatory activity involved salvation for the non-baptized. The Son, he wrote, 'came to save all' (*Adversus haereses* 2. 22. 4; see 3. 18. 7; 4. 22. 2).

(4) The incarnation, when the Logos became flesh, brought a fresh stage in his revealing and saving presence. This event put Christ in a material solidarity with all human beings and their world. Present now in a bodily, human fashion, he offered and offers new possibilities for mutual, interpersonal relationships.

He drew near to all human beings and, in a particular way, to their sufferings. His presence made him fatally vulnerable; it cost him his life. The body of Christ on the cross expressed for all time his mysterious but truly redeeming presence to those who suffer anywhere and at any time. His death on Calvary between two criminals symbolized forever his close solidarity with those who suffer and die, an identification with human pain expressed also by the criteria for the last judgement (Matt. 25: 31–46). The final blessings of the kingdom will come to those who, without recognizing Christ, meet his needs in the people who suffer by being hungry, thirsty, strangers, naked, sick, or imprisoned (Chapter 7 above). Pascal's reflection ('he is in agony to the end of the world') has classically articulated the crucified Christ's enduring presence in the mystery of all human suffering.[8] To express the worldwide presence of Christ in all who suffer, we could well say: 'ubi dolor, ibi Christus (wherever there is suffering, there is Christ)'.

(5) Christ's resurrection from the dead ushered in a dramatically new, life-giving sharing of his presence, or—to put it another way—a situation in which his loving, reconciling presence remains definitively and universally present. This post-Easter presence is reflected in Luke's liking for the language of life when speaking of the resurrected Christ (e.g. Luke 24: 5, 23; Acts 1: 3), and in John's subsequent identification of Jesus with life itself (e.g. John 11: 25; 14: 6). Risen from the dead, Christ is actively present everywhere as the source of eternal life for everyone. This new presence meant that Christ not merely was with us (through creation and incarnation) and for us (through his ministry and crucifixion), but also is in us, inviting us to respond to his presence (Col. 1: 27).

His personal self-bestowal, made possible through a glorious transformation that lifts him beyond the normal limits of space and time, has effected a presence which St John typically describes as 'Christ-in-us and we-in-Christ' and St Paul as 'we-in-Christ'. Where John's Gospel represents this new presence as mutual indwelling, Paul usually depicts it as our dwelling 'in Christ' as in a corporate personality.[9] In an unprecedented way the risen Christ, through

---

[8] Listed as *Pensée* 552 in such editions as W. F. Trotter's trans. (New York: E. P. Dutton, 1958), which follow the standard Brunschvicg edition, this *pensée* is numbered 919 in A. J. Krailsheimer's trans. (Harmondsworth: Penguin Books, 1966), which adopts the order of the *Pensées* as Pascal left them at his death in 1662.

[9] Very occasionally Paul varies his normal usage and writes of 'Christ/Jesus in us/me' (e.g. Gal. 2: 20).

the mission of the Holy Spirit, enables all human beings to share in his saving presence and live 'in him'. This presence is real and effective, but need not be a felt presence. It can remain a hidden presence—throughout the lives of innumerable human beings.

This new saving presence differs according to one's location in the world of various cultures and religions. For the baptized, the Church's worship, teaching, and whole life bodies forth the living presence of the risen Christ. She forms the visible verification of his invisible but actively real presence. He exercises the primary ministry in and through all the sacraments. Whenever the sacraments are administered, the risen Christ is personally and effectively present. In commenting on St John's Gospel, St Augustine summed up this sacramental ministry and presence of the risen Lord: 'when Peter baptizes, it is Christ who baptizes. When Paul baptizes, it is Christ who baptizes. When Judas baptizes, it is Christ who baptizes' (*In Ioannem* 6. 7).

In other cultures and religions the risen Christ is also redemptively present in varying ways and degrees. To echo Irenaeus, Christ's invisible and powerful presence is literally spread everywhere. In other religions he is also actively 'there', even before any contact with the gospel message has taken place. These other religions have proved a matrix in which his saving revelation has been effectively present and so has mysteriously but really brought people to live 'in him'. Here we might cite again and extend what Augustine wrote about the presence in the six ages of the world of 'hidden saints' (*De catechizandis rudibus* 22. 40) and 'prophets' among the Gentiles (*Contra Faustum* 19. 2). 'Prophecy', he declared, 'was extended to all nations' (*In Ioannem* 9. 9). These 'hidden saints', 'prophets', and— we should add founders—did not and do not operate independently of Christ. Without knowing this, they have all been delegates and agents of the risen Christ and help bring people to a mysterious, real existence in him.

Obviously this language of 'saints', 'prophets', and 'founders' should be understood analogously. Here, even more than elsewhere, 'one size does not fit all'. There is, for instance, a difference of kind and not merely of degree between the risen Christ as Founder (upper case) of Christianity and the founders (lower case) of various world religions.

We can extend the language of Luke about 'the unknown God' (Acts 17: 23) to speak of the unknown Christ who has been and is effective everywhere, for everyone, and in the history of all cultures and religions—albeit often hiddenly. He may be unknown, but never absent. He has mediated the fullness of revelation and salvation through particular historical events, and continues to mediate to all the revelatory and saving self-communication of God. Yet he is more than simply a reality *within* the temporal and spatial order. He proves effectively present in all creation and history, and yet not in a way that depersonalizes him and reduces him to being a mere 'Christ idea' or universal principle. Salvation and revelation are communicated personally—through the divine person who became incarnate, died, and rose from the dead as Jesus of Nazareth.

Some object to such a vision of Christ being present truly, but yet less visibly, in the lives of those who adhere to other religions. Such critics often belong to two sharply different groups. Some find it hard to share the generous and justified views of Irenaeus, Origen, Augustine, and other church Fathers about everything (and that includes the religions of the world) being under the influence of Christ. They try to argue that adherents of the world religions can be saved, *despite* their religion, ignoring (or denying) the possibility of Christ acting in and through the 'saints' and 'prophets' who shaped and shape such religions. Other critics dismiss the idea of a more vivid and powerful presence of the risen Christ in the Church as an arrogant claim that Jesus, more or less arbitrarily, favours some over others. Such an objection does not reckon with the way in which the love of Jesus resembles human love by not being exercised in an identical way towards all cultures, religions, and individuals. The risen Jesus lovingly interacts with the whole world, and that means he interacts in ways that are different. He is absent from nobody, but he interacts differently with everybody.

In the post-resurrection situation, the whole story of the world unfolds as a drama of cosmic and human reconciliation. By means of its vivid scenarios and apocalyptic images, the Book of Revelation invites its readers to discern and contemplate the victory of the suffering Christ not merely in the Christian community but also in human history at large. In the 'signs of the times' Christians note and seek to interpret current indications of the risen Christ's personal presence and influence. That presence assumes a multiform diversity that allows us to acknowledge him as present everywhere and active in an endless variety of ways.

Beyond question, this Christian affirmation may seem to many 'others' an appalling piece of arrogance. They give their allegiance to other religions, or to none, and will resist and even vehemently reject claims about Jesus present everywhere and lovingly interacting with everybody. Yet we should recall three points. First, this claim is personal and not institutional; it maintains the universal impact of Jesus himself and not of the Christian Church as such. Second, we should not forget that some other religions (e.g. Islam and some forms of Hinduism) honour Christ and include him in one way or another in their faith. They do not endorse the universal significance of Christ that is proposed here, but they certainly do not deny all significance to him. Third, while Christians should not ignore the claims of other religions, they should not play down or misrepresent their own claims about Jesus universally present to mediate salvation and revelation everywhere. In my experience, adherents of other faiths find such dissimulation, even when adopted by Christians for 'the best of reasons', dishonest and even disrespectful towards partners in inter-religious dialogue.

(6) In analysing above the various facets of presence, I drew attention to its feminine, maternal features. Nowadays to distinguish feminine and masculine characteristics is to face controversy at almost every turn. However, we should respect and develop the data from scripture and tradition.[10] The Jesus of the Synoptic Gospels applies to himself a very homely, feminine image (Luke 13: 34 par.). He is present like a mother hen to shelter her chickens when they run back under her wings. Reading what is now numbered as Psalm 102, Augustine recalls Christ's picture of himself as a mother hen, and draws on an ancient legend of the pelican who sheds her blood over her dead offspring and so dies by bringing them back to life (*Enarrationes in Psalmos* 102. 8). Augustine encouraged later writers (and artists) to take up the image of Christ as 'the loving pelican', who has died for all people. Whether we picture Christ as

---

[10] On this see further my *Christology*, 319–21.

hen or pelican, in both cases we deal with the image of a mother with her young. It seems easier to apply the second image to the case of Christ's relationship with and presence to the non-baptized. Since he 'died for all' (2 Cor. 5: 14), we should extend the image of Christ the Pelican to all human beings, and not limit it, for instance, to those who receive him in the Eucharist.

In Chapter 10, I put the case for taking in a maternal way Paul's words about God as the One 'in whom we live and move and have our being' (Acts 17: 28). The text can yield a plus-value when we apply it in terms of the common experience of human beings. During the first nine months of our existence, we each live, move, and have our being within our mother, on whom we radically depend for life, sustenance, and growth. I do not see why this image may not also be applied to the risen Christ whose all-encompassing presence forms the 'place' in which the entire human race, including those who do not yet explicitly acknowledge his presence, live, and move, and have their being.

Julian of Norwich expressed this presence as follows: 'Jesus is in all who will be saved, and all who will be saved are in Jesus.'[11] This sense of mutual indwelling went hand in hand with Julian's wonderful sense of 'Christ our Mother'[12] and with Julian's hope for the salvation of all. She prayed and expected that all would be saved through Christ, who is Mother to all without distinction.

(7) Thus far I have been exploiting various themes from my analysis of presence to articulate the relationship between the risen Christ and those who have not or have not yet heard the message about him. To express his all-determining presence at the end of history, we can draw on points 3, 4, and 8 to speak of what will happen then as (3) the supreme form of self-bestowal that will bring (4) an eternal communion of life and love through (8) a qualitatively supreme form of his presence. Christ's rising from the dead has already initiated the presence of the end. But at his final coming human beings and their world will be raised and transformed

---

[11] Julian of Norwich, *Showings*, ch. 51, trans. E. College and J. Walsh (New York: Paulist Press, 1978), 276.

[12] In a wonderful paradox she wrote: 'Our Saviour is our true Mother, in whom we are endlessly born and out of whom we shall never come'; ibid. (ch. 57), 292.

(1 Cor. 15: 20–8)—in an ultimate gathering into the divine presence. Then through Christ human beings will be 'with God' forever.

We may give this vision of the final future further shape by invoking the bodily character of presence (point 6). Christ is 'there' for us, whenever we encounter the body of the created world, various embodiments of the kingdom of God, all human bodies (especially of those who suffer), the body of the Church, the body of world religions. Every body and everybody mediate his presence here and now in an endless variety of ways and with varying degrees of clarity and intensity. At the consummation of all things, everyone and everything will be drawn together in his glorious, eschatological body to enjoy the unconditional divine hospitality which is eternal life.

Augustine was second to none when it came to envisaging the final presence of all in Christ. He summoned Christians to their future life: 'be united in him alone [Christ], be one reality alone, be one person alone (in uno estote, unum estote, unus estote)' (*In Ioannem* 12. 9). From incorporation in Christ, Augustine moved to a profound solidarity with him, and even to a personal assimilation. Augustine, while defending and expounding the resurrection of individuals to eternal life,[13] also insisted on their being drawn in the closest imaginable way into the presence of Christ: 'and there will be one Christ loving himself (et erit unus Christus amans seipsum)' (*In Ep. Joh.* 10. 3).

Augustine also expressed the final communion of life in the divine presence through the theme of praise: 'there we shall praise; we shall all be one, in him [Christ] who is One, oriented towards the One [the Father]; for then, though many, we shall not be scattered (ibi laudabimus, omnes unus in uno ad unum erimus; quia deinceps multi dispersi non erimus)' (*Enarrationes in Psalmos* 147. 28). Addressing the triune God, Augustine also wrote: 'and without ceasing we shall say one thing, praising You [the Trinity] in unison, even ourselves being also made one in You [the Trinity] (et sine fine dicemus unum laudantes te in unum, et in te facti etiam nos unum)' (*De Trinitate* 15. 28. 51).

---

[13] See G. O'Collins, 'Augustine on the Resurrection', in F. LeMoine and C. Kleinhenz (eds.), *Saint Augustine the Bishop: A Book of Essays* (New York: Garland, 1994), 65–75.

Right from the early second century, such praising of God with Christ had been set forth as *praying* or *singing* together. Thus St Ignatius of Antioch (d. around 107), when using musical metaphors to depict the unity and harmony between a bishop and his clergy and/ or congregation, wrote: 'and may each of you remain joined in chorus, that being harmonious in concord, receiving God's variation in unity, you may sing with one voice through Jesus Christ to the Father, that he may both hear you and recognize you through what you do well, as members of his Son' (*Ephesians* 4. 2).[14] In classical Greek literature and later, the image of the chorus was applied to the harmony of the cosmos, to the political concord of a city, to union within a family, and to similar situations where peace reigned.[15]

Talk of believers praying and singing in chorus to the Father through and with Christ turned up among ancient Christian writers, especially when they commented on praying or singing the psalms.[16] Thus in his *Enarrationes in Psalmos*, St Augustine reflected: 'it is the one Saviour of his [mystical] body, our Lord Jesus Christ, Son of God, who prays for us, who prays in us, and who is prayed to by us. He prays for us as our priest; he prays in us as our head; he is prayed to by us as our God. Let us therefore recognize in him our voice and in us his voice' (85. 1). Augustine understood the psalms to be 'the voice of the whole Christ, head and body/members (vox totius Christi capitis et corporis)'.

A modern version of this metaphor turned up in the 1963 Constitution on the Sacred Liturgy, *Sacrosanctum Concilium*, of the Second Vatican Council: 'Christ Jesus, high priest of the new and eternal covenant, by assuming human nature, introduced into this earthly exile that hymn which is sung throughout all ages in the halls of heaven. He joins the entire community of human beings to

[14] Trans. from W. R. Schoedel, *Ignatius of Antioch* (Philadelphia: Fortress, 1985), 51. As Schoedel points out, 'it is likely that the reference in this context to the Ephesians as "members" ($\mu\acute{\epsilon}\lambda\eta$) of God's Son is to be understood as a play on words: they are also his "melodies" ($\mu\acute{\epsilon}\lambda\eta$)', (ibid., 53).

[15] Ibid., 51–3.

[16] On the psalms being 'the voice of Christ to the Father (vox Christi ad Patrem)', as well as 'the voice of the Church about Christ to the Father (vox Ecclesiae ad Patrem de Christo)' and 'the voice of the Church to Christ (vox Ecclesiae ad Christum)', see B. Fischer, 'Le Christ dans les Psaumes', *La Maison Dieu* 27 (1951), 86–113.

himself, and associates it with himself in singing together this divine canticle of praise' (no. 83; trans. my own). The 'canticle of divine praise' is presumably directed to God the Father, and is understood to be a hymn sung by all creatures in heaven. Christ in his priestly role is represented as having inaugurated the singing of the divine praises on earth, by assuming the human condition in his incarnation. He is pictured as joining not merely those who come to know and believe in him but also the whole human community to himself in a chorus, of which he is obviously the leader. This passage strikingly portrays the active presence of Christ to all human beings. This unity of the whole human race in him, which began with the incarnation, must be understood to be strengthened and perfected through the resurrection. Finally, it will be consummated when human beings reach 'the halls of heaven'. This picture of Christ the Cosmic Choir Master serves brilliantly to symbolize the union in him of all, baptized and non-baptized alike. Long before they become aware of this, even those who have never heard his name are mysteriously but truly in the hands of Christ the Choir Master of the world.

THE UNIVERSAL PRESENCE OF THE HOLY SPIRIT

For those who challenge the presence of the Spirit in all human beings, the short answer could be: the universal presence of the Spirit accompanies and enacts the presence of the risen Christ which is a universal presence. Since the co-Sender of the Spirit (the risen Christ) is always inseparably there with the Sent (the Holy Spirit) (Chapter 10 above) and since Christ is present everywhere and in every human life, the Spirit must also be present everywhere and in every human life. People do not have to be aware of living in the presence of Christ and the Holy Spirit for this to be the case. *Being present* does not as such imply *being known to be present*. A longer answer should begin with the function of the Spirit in and for the Church.[17]

---

[17] See G. O'Collins, *Jesus Our Redeeemer: A Christian Approach to Salvation* (Oxford: Oxford University Press, 2007), 200–17.

(1) As the 'soul' or vital principle of the Church (see 1 Cor. 6: 19), the Holy Spirit mediates the dynamic presence of Christ to the Church through the sacraments, the scriptures, preaching, teaching, and other ministries of this new Easter community. It is the Eucharist that shows the primary thrust of the Spirit's mission. With the first eucharistic invocation (*epiclesis*) and the words of institution, the Spirit descends on the gifts to change them and bring about the most intense and real presence of Christ for the Church and the world. Through the second *epiclesis* the Spirit is invoked to transform the members of the worshipping community by strengthening their identity as believers, who call God 'Abba', share in Jesus' loving relationship to the Father, and serve his suffering brothers and sisters.

While being the primary agent in carrying out the mission of the Church, the Holy Spirit also works to transform everyone and everything in the world. Baptism, the Eucharist, and other outward signs of the Church's life do not circumscribe and limit the operations of the Spirit. In its invisible mission the Spirit offers everyone the possibility of being changed by the saving grace brought through Christ's dying and rising from the dead. The Spirit communicates life to everyone and illuminates the pilgrimage of all humanity towards God, a pilgrimage which will bring human beings everywhere to make up the one body of Christ. Earlier chapters recalled the (explicit and implicit) witness of Paul and Luke to this activity of the Holy Spirit beyond the Christian community.

(2) Paul's language in Romans 2: 14–16 encourages us to recognize the Holy Spirit at work in the hearts and lives of Gentiles (Chapters 9 and 12 above). The Spirit 'writes' on the hearts of these 'outsiders' and enables them to practise the essential requirements of the divine law. Thus they can live 'according to the Spirit' and not 'according to the flesh' (or dominated by selfish passions and incapable of submitting to God's law). Moreover, the Spirit imparts life and the hope of fulfilment not only to all human beings but also to the entire created world. The Spirit is the divine principle of the new order created by God through Christ, or the universal, enabling power by which to live (Rom. 8: 1–30). Thus the invisible mission of the Spirit extends far beyond the visible members of the Church to be powerfully present in the whole of creation.

(3) In his scene of the first Pentecost, Luke gathers together representatives 'from every nation under heaven' to witness and experience the outpouring of the Spirit who calls all people into the community of Christ (Acts 2: 5–11). Luke will go on to provide specific stories of the worldwide activity of the Spirit. The story of the Roman centurion Cornelius (Chapters 10 and 12 above) illustrates how someone who is neither Jewish nor Christian can experience the intimate presence of God—even in a most significant vision. This 'outsider', along with his family and close friends, is blessed with an outpouring of the Holy Spirit. This happens *before* any of them receive baptism. In Luke's view, divine visions and the manifest presence of the Spirit are not limited to actual members of the Christian community.

(4) When we move to what later Christians had to say in interpreting and applying the witness of Paul and Luke, one particularly instructive example turns up in 1 Corinthians 12: 3: 'no one can say "Jesus is Lord" except by the Holy Spirit'. In the context of this letter Paul was perhaps offering advice about ways of discerning episodes of ecstatic prayer. The Corinthians could be sure that those who cried out 'Jesus is Lord' were doing so under the impulse of the Holy Spirit. Possibly the reference was to a very brief 'credo' on the occasion of baptism. Yet it seems more likely that Paul had in mind a confession made in times of persecution. Through the agency of the Spirit believers were empowered to confess Jesus as 'my/our/the Lord' (see Matt. 10: 17–19), rather than apostatize and declare under pressure that 'Jesus is cursed' and 'cursed is the Lord'.[18]

When commenting on this passage in the fourth century, an anonymous author who eventually came to be distinguished from Ambrose of Milan and known as 'Ambrosiaster' wrote: 'whatever truth is said by anyone is said by the Holy Spirit (quidquid enim verum, a quocumque dicitur, a Sancto dicitur Spiritu'.[19] In the form of 'everything that is true, no matter by whom it is said, is from the Holy Spirit (omne verum, a quocumque dicatur, a Spiritu Sancto

---

[18] See A. C. Thiselton, *The First Letter to the Corinthians* (Grand Rapids, Mich.: Eerdmans, 2000), 916–27.

[19] *In Epistolam B. Pauli ad Corinthios Primam* 12. 3; *Patrologia Latina* 17, col. 245B; the passage is also found in CSEL 81, pars 2, 132.

est)', this expression turns up eighteen times in the works of Thomas Aquinas.[20] In the late twentieth century John Paul II gave the expression a twist that was fresh but that put it back in the original context of prayer, albeit authentic prayer that can go up to God anywhere and not simply prayer within a meeting of ecstatically gifted Christians.

In his 1979 encyclical *Redemptor hominis* (the Redeemer of the human person), John Paul II supported 'coming closer together with the representatives of the non-Christian religions' through 'dialogue, contacts, and *prayer in common*' (no. 6; italics mine). In October 1986, he boldly broke new ground by doing just that, and going off to Assisi with the Dalai Lama and other heads or representatives of the world's religions to pray for peace. Some Catholics, including some members of the Roman Curia, were harsh in their judgements of this event in Assisi as if it somehow betrayed Christian faith in Jesus. The Pope replied to his critics in his Christmas address to the Roman Curia, delivered on 22 December 1986. He echoed and adapted the dictum of Ambrosiaster and Aquinas to speak not of truth but of prayer: 'every authentic prayer is called forth by the Holy Spirit'. For good measure, he added that the Spirit 'is mysteriously present in the heart of every person'.[21] That same year the universal activity of the Holy Spirit had already been firmly put on the agenda of papal teaching.

John Paul II dedicated a long encyclical letter *Dominum et vivificantem* (Lord and giver of life), published at Pentecost 1986, to the Holy Spirit active in the life of the Church and in the whole world. According to God's plan of salvation, the 'action' of the Spirit 'has been exercised in every place and at every time, indeed in every individual'—an action which, to be sure, is 'closely linked with the mystery of the incarnation and the redemption' (no. 5). That is to say, the universal activity of the Spirit is inseparably connected with what the Son of God did for all human beings by taking on the

[20] E.g. *Summa theologiae* II–II, q. 172, a. 6 arg. 1. Like others, Thomas thought that the saying came from St Ambrose of Milan.
[21] *Acta Apostolicae Sedis* 79 (1987), 1082–90, at 1089. The full text of the address was published by the Secretariat of Non-Christians (renamed in 1988 the Pontifical Council for Interreligious Dialogue), *Bulletin* 64/22/1 (1987), 54–62. The key passages are found in ND, nos. 1049–52.

human condition, by dying and rising from the dead, and by sending the gift of the Holy Spirit from the Father.

As a Roman Catholic I found this papal teaching not only illuminating and helpful in the inter-faith context of our world but also genuinely developing what Paul and Luke suggest about the religious situation of those who are not (or not yet) Christians. I welcomed as a further development of NT teaching what I was to read in a 1990 encyclical *Redemptoris missio* (the mission of the Redeemer). There John Paul II insisted that, while manifested 'in a special way in the Church and her members', the Spirit's 'presence and activity' are, nevertheless, 'universal'. He understood the Spirit to operate 'at the very source' of each person's 'religious questioning'. He went on to write: 'the Spirit's presence and activity affect not only individuals but also society and history, peoples, *cultures and religions*' (no. 28; italics mine). These were two momentous statements.

First of all, the Holy Spirit is actively operating in and through the questions which sooner or later arise for everyone: Where did I come from? Where am I going? What is the meaning of life? What do suffering, sin, and evil mean? What will come after death? Who is the God in whom I live and move and have my being (see Acts 17: 28)? As far as John Paul II was concerned, the Holy Spirit is actively present and operating not only whenever anyone prays authentically but also whenever anyone faces the profound religious questions of life. One might coin a new expression along the lines of Ambrosiaster and Aquinas: 'every truly religious question, no matter by whom it is raised, is from the Holy Spirit (omnis quaestio vere religiosa, a quocumque moveatur, a Spiritu Sancto est)'. No human being exists outside the powerful presence of God the Holy Spirit. The Spirit is the mysterious companion and religious friend who raises the deep and necessary questions in the life of every human being. When we share this picture, we are not too far from the way in which Luke in Acts 17 describes Paul engaging the Athenians through their questions and desire to know (Chapter 10 above).

Second, the Pope appreciated how the presence and activity of the Holy Spirit also affect the wider human society and all human 'history, peoples, cultures, and religions'. In other words, the Spirit acts in and through the cultures and religious traditions of our world. This activity is inseparable from the salvation that Christ has brought about; it is an activity that aims at bringing all people, sooner or later, to Christ. But in the meantime the Spirit is present and operative in and through all that is true and good in various cultures and religions around the world.

This vision of the universal presence of the Holy Spirit requires a rich view of the nature of personal presence. Here too we should not think in terms of a sharp alternative: the Spirit is either totally present or completely absent. That would be to forget what we saw earlier in this chapter about the vast variety of ways in which personal agents are present. Personal presence can assume many forms and exhibit a great variety of intensity. What is true between human beings is all the more true of the endless variety of ways in which the Holy Spirit is present to human beings as individuals and in their various cultures and religious traditions. To be sure, the Spirit is present in a quite special and intense way within the Christian Church. But that does not allow us to say: 'outside the Church there is no Holy Spirit'. There is no such thing as being 'outside the Holy Spirit'. No place, person, culture, or religion is simply 'outside' the Holy Spirit. We need here a broad vision of presence—in particular of that active presence of the Holy Spirit which can assume indefinitely many modalities and intensities.

CONCLUSION

This chapter has aimed at exploiting the language of 'presence' to throw some light on the mysterious activity of Christ and the Holy Spirit in our entire world. Characteristically St Paul pictured the life of Christians as their being 'in Christ' and the Holy Spirit being 'in them'. Unless we rigidly insist that 'one size fits all' and that this 'being in' can only come in one shape or form, there is ample room left to acknowledge that the Holy Spirit is also 'in' those who have not been baptized (all the Corneliuses of our world) and that these non-baptized can also in some real sense 'be in Christ'. In this case it is worth developing the theme of the universal presence of divine Wisdom.

15

Universal Wisdom

Outside Christ there is neither salvation nor revelation. As one could say in Latin: 'extra Christum nec salus nec revelatio'. But, as we argued in the last chapter and earlier, there is no way to be 'outside Christ', and no zone beyond him. The one Mediator of revelation and salvation, he conveys saving revelation to all (1 Tim. 2: 5). The corollary of this position is that no one can experience revelation or salvation, without experiencing, however obscurely, the presence of Christ.

From the second century AD, believers articulated the universal presence of Christ in terms of his being the creative, revealing, and redemptive Word (Logos), active before Christianity came into being and active in the world beyond the visible Christian community. In dialogue with the Graeco-Roman culture, Justin, Irenaeus, Origen, Athanasius, and other church Fathers pressed into service various themes connected with the Logos. Occasionally they spoke of Christ as the divine Wisdom present everywhere.[1] But generally, at least in Western Christianity, when they attended to the universal presence and roles of Christ, they named him as Logos or as Son of God. Thus Irenaeus stated: 'the Son from the beginning is the Revealer (enarrator/$E\xi\eta\gamma\eta\tau\eta s$) of the Father to all' (*Adversus haereses* 4. 20. 7). The Nicene Creed of 325 confessed the Son, through whom 'all things were made' and who 'for our salvation' came down from heaven.

Julian of Norwich was one of the few Western Christians to treasure Christ as divine Wisdom and, for good measure, one of the very few to acknowledge him in maternal language: 'God all

---

[1] Athanasius of Alexandria, *Against the Arians* 2. 78–9.

Wisdom is our loving Mother.'[2] Such language reached back to the
OT and Sirach's picture of the blessings granted to a man who sought
Wisdom with resolute intensity: 'She will come to him like a mother,
and like a young bride she will welcome him' (Sir. 15: 2). We will
return below to the feminine, maternal face of Wisdom. But, first
of all, what advantages might there be in reflecting on Christ's all-
encompassing impact by pursuing the line of Wisdom? At least six
advantages suggest themselves.

(1) BIBLICAL ATTENTION TO WISDOM

One obvious, rather formal, advantage of exploring our issue
through Wisdom is that the OT offers a rich storehouse of sapiential
literature. To be sure, the OT contains some material on divine
sonship, but that language was applied to angelic beings, the chosen
people, their king, and righteous persons. Surprisingly 'son of God'
was not an OT messianic title; evidence from Qumran suggests that
this messianic title might have been emerging right at the time of
Jesus.[3] The Word (Logos) of God may look more promising. 'Word'
repeatedly expresses God's active power and self-revelation in and
towards the created world. John's Gospel opens with the majestic
pronouncement, 'In the beginning was the Word, and the Word was
with God, and the Word was God'. One can understand how early
and later Christians have treasured this title.[4] Nevertheless, there are
no OT books dedicated to the theme of the Logos. This personification of the divine activity turns up here and there: in Genesis, the
Psalms, Second Isaiah, and elsewhere. But it does not receive anything like the attention dedicated to divine Wisdom, the theme of
several OT books and sections of books (Chapter 5 above). This
personified agent of God's activity stands out not only quantitatively
but also qualitatively, endowed with vivid personal characteristics as

---

[2] Julian of Norwich, *Showings*, ch. 58, trans. E. College and J. Walsh (New York:
Paulist Press, 1978), 293.
[3] See G. O'Collins, *Christology: A Biblical, Historical, and Systematic Study of Jesus
Christ* (Oxford: Oxford University Press, rev. edn., 2004), 116–18.
[4] Ibid., 40–4.

Lady Wisdom. Before reflecting on what this feminine, nurturing image might convey about Christ's revealing and saving function for all people, we should note a second, 'public' advantage.

(2) WISDOM AS A BRIDGE

When we interpret Christ's role as universal Revealer and Saviour through the image of wisdom, we can exploit a very visible fact in our world. The Jewish-Christian scriptures and religion do not enjoy a monopoly on wisdom. In one way or another, at least some wise teachings and wise ways of life turn up in all cultures, societies, and religions. Being found everywhere, sapiential modes of thought and living make an obvious bridge between the adherents of Christianity and others.

The formal presence of the wisdom genre in the Book of Job is limited to one hymn (28: 1–28). Yet what the presence of that chapter celebrating Wisdom signals is her role in the life of 'outsiders'. Some sapiential literature to which we will come below (e.g. Sirach) clearly emerges from the life of the chosen people. What the presence of Wisdom in Job, a long work about a non-Israelite and his non-Israelite friends, establishes is that the same divine Wisdom also illuminates and shapes their lives. Wisdom and her teaching forms a bridge between these 'others' and the people of God.

This bridge-building function of Wisdom also crops up in Proverbs, as we saw in Chapter 5. A second collection of proverbial sayings in that book (22: 17–24: 34) depends in some way on an Egyptian sage, Amen-em-ope. Thus the Book of Proverbs shows that 'others' not only can receive Wisdom but may also prove a source of wisdom teaching for Israel herself. This example from Proverbs is a spectacular example of how the people of God learned from outsiders about the appropriate life of human beings and their relationship with God.

(3) WISDOM AS UNIVERSAL AND PARTICULAR

A third rich theme to be drawn from the sapiential books concerns the universality and particularity of Wisdom. Let me explain. On the one hand, Wisdom enjoys a universal presence and dominion—'over all the earth' and 'over every people and nation' (Sir. 24: 6). On the other hand, God chose a special place for her to dwell: 'I was established in Zion. Thus in the beloved city he [God] gave me a resting place, and in Jerusalem was my domain' (Sir. 24: 10–11). Wisdom is present universally—everywhere and to everyone—and also has a special, privileged home chosen by God. But that particular divine choice does not mean that Wisdom is absent elsewhere in the world and hence unavailable for the whole human race.

This OT language about Lady Wisdom yields a helpful pattern for thinking about Christ's presence in the world. In a special way he is present to believers who through baptism are incorporated into him. They recognize in him the full revelation of God and the source of the abundant means of salvation that they are offered in the life of the Church. But acknowledging all this, far from excluding Christ's universal presence in the world, requires Christians to discern and accept the revealing and saving presence of Christ in genuine wisdom, wherever it is found. 'Where there is wisdom', we should say, 'there is Christ (ubi sapientia, ibi Christus)'. To deny to others and their religions any true knowledge of God and mediation of salvation would be to belittle the scope of Christ's activity as universal Wisdom.

It is at our peril that we neglect the universal quality of Christ's role in the worldwide history of revelation and salvation. In innumerably varied ways he works as divine Wisdom in the lives of people who adhere to other religions, honour their founders, and thus receive knowledge of God and salvation. In one way or another all people experience Christ as divine Wisdom in person, and express what they experience in their lives, cultures, and religions. This universality of Christ as Wisdom takes nothing away from the particularity of his presence in the Christian community, and vice versa.

To reject this vision of Christ as universal Wisdom would undercut our right to see him prefigured in the language of Sirach. The same would be true of the Wisdom of Solomon. Written last among the OT books, Wisdom combines brilliantly a particular and a universal thrust. On the one hand, the anonymous author of this book portrays Wisdom as saving the ancestors of Israel. This author reinterprets Israelite history by assigning to Wisdom the saving deeds normally assigned to YHWH. It was Lady Wisdom who protected the patriarchs, and brought the people 'over the Red Sea, and led them through the deep waters' (Wisd. 10: 5–21). On the other hand, the involvement of Wisdom in the particular salvation history of Israel in no way rules out her role in the lives of human beings at large. They too can know the light and saving power of Wisdom, since she pervades all creation and the whole human story. 'She renews all things; in every generation she passes into holy souls and makes them friends of God and prophets' (Wisd. 7: 22–7).

In this classic passage in Wisdom 7, it seems that no limits are placed on the activity of Wisdom. She 'renews all things' and in 'every generation' turns 'holy souls' into 'friends of God' and even into 'prophets'. 'All things' and 'every generation' clearly imply that this activity of Wisdom is not restricted to the particular history of the people of God. There is more than a hint here of the activity of Christ in creating the 'hidden saints' and 'prophets' that Augustine wrote about (see last chapter). The language of this book helps us to appreciate and spell out both the universal and the particular aspects in the activity of Christ, divine Wisdom in person.

(4) WISDOM AS REVEALING AND SAVING

Wherever it occurs, the divine self-communication exhibits two distinguishable but inseparable dimensions: revelation and salvation. On the one hand, God's self-revelation is always salvific. To experience and know God, however it happens, changes and even transforms us. On the other hand, divine salvation does not take place in darkness. God casts light on our lives and provides illumination for our journey home. To appreciate and evaluate the religious situation of Christians and others, one needs to hold together persistently the revelatory and saving activity of God—that illumination which liberates people from darkness and brings them into the divine communion of love. In the language of St John's Gospel, Christ is both 'truth' and 'grace', both 'light' and 'life'. His being 'the Light of the world' belongs inseparably with his being 'the Life of the world'.

What the OT says about Lady Wisdom matches these two dimensions of the divine self-communication. Wisdom persistently provides understanding, illuminates human beings, and helps them to live wisely and relate to God and to one another. The blessings of Wisdom go beyond precepts for the conduct of everyday life (e.g. Sir. 4: 20–5: 8). They include a knowledge that will make righteousness possible and even bring the gift of eternal life (Wisd. 3: 1–5). Sirach vividly pictures the revelatory and salvific response of Wisdom to the man who seeks her with resolution and intensity: 'She will feed him with the bread of learning, and give him the water of wisdom to drink. He will lean on her and not fall, and he will rely on her and not be put to shame' (Sir. 15: 3–4).

In a famous scene Lady Wisdom invites the simple or unwise to a banquet; her 'bread' and 'wine' will enable them to 'walk in the way of insight' (Prov. 9: 1–6). She teaches and brings life. In an earlier chapter of Proverbs she is called 'a tree of life to those who lay hold of her; and those who hold her fast are called happy' (Prov. 3: 18).

At the end of the OT, this picture of Lady Wisdom and her banquet becomes more personalized. Her invitation now runs: 'Come to me, you who desire me, and eat your fill of my fruits. For the memory of me is sweeter than honey, and the possession of me sweeter than the honeycomb. Those who eat of me will hunger for more, and those who drink of me will thirst for more' (Sir. 24: 19–21). Here Sophia presents her very self as food and drink. She is now the source of nourishment and life, and not merely a source of understanding about what it is to live a wise life.

A classic prayer (Wisd. 9: 1–18) draws together the role of Wisdom as a guide to God and a saving power; she is, one might say, the self-revelation of God that brings true life. Wisdom both teaches and saves. Hence addressing God the prayer ends by saying: 'and thus the paths of those on earth were set right, and people were taught what pleases you, and were saved by wisdom'.

Inasmuch as he is divine Wisdom in person, Christ is both light and life. One might put this in Latin: 'ubi sapientia, ibi lux et vita (where there is wisdom, there is light and life)'. One could illustrate this vision of divine Wisdom's double role by extending the application of an inscription traced on some early Christian tombs in Asia

Minor.[5] On those tombs we find combined in a cross two Greek terms, '*Φως*' (light) and '*Ζωη*' (life), two words that turn up over and over again in John's Gospel. '*Φως*' runs down the inscription and intersects with '*Ζωη*' which runs across. The two words intersect in the last letter of the Greek alphabet, 'omega'—a reminder that Christ who died for us on the cross is also the omega point, our final and utterly worthwhile destiny on whom everything converges. Those early Christians, inhabitants of what is now part of modern Turkey, knew that the relatives and friends whom they were burying had confessed the Christian faith, in which Jesus was their light and life. Now they hoped that these beloved relatives and friends would find, with and through Christ, the fullness of light and life forever. We might take up and extend the meaning of that inscription. Not only for those who live and die as Christians but for everyone who comes into this world (see John 1: 9), as divine Wisdom Jesus is light and life. He is the Light of the world and the Life of the world. He is the omega point or utterly satisfying goal for all people, the goal of everlasting light and life to which they are all called.

(5) THE BEAUTY OF WISDOM

The beauty of Lady Wisdom ranks high among her characteristics. A lyrical passage, after listing her twenty-one (3×7) attributes, presses on to call her 'a pure emanation of the glory of the Almighty', 'a reflection of eternal light', and 'a spotless mirror of the working of God'. Not surprisingly the passage declares: 'she is more beautiful than the sun, and excels every constellation of the stars' (Wisd. 7: 22–9). Since God is the very 'author of beauty' (Wisd. 13: 3) and since Lady Wisdom is 'a pure emanation of the glory (= beauty) of the Almighty', the quality and level of her beauty are set very high indeed.

It is no wonder that King Solomon falls in love with her and desires her as his bride and teacher: 'I loved her and sought her from my youth; I desired to take her for my bride, and became

---

[5] See R. Bultmann, '*Ζαω*', in G. Kittel *et al.* (eds.), *Theological Dictionary of the New Testament*, ii (Grand Rapids, Mich.: Eerdmans, 1964), 832–75, at 841 n. 66.

enamoured of her beauty' (Wisd. 8: 2). He knows that 'companion-
ship with her has no bitterness, and life with her has no pain, but
gladness and joy' (Wisd. 8:16). As always, beauty attracts us, evokes
our wonder and joy, and arouses a flood of delight. Not surprisingly
when Solomon succumbs to the beauty of Lady Wisdom, he wants to
stay in her presence and live with her forever. The impact of her
beauty is not only lasting but also total. His whole existence is
illuminated by her beauty.

The NT, when identifying Christ as divine Wisdom in person,
attends at times to the central characteristic of beauty. He is, for
instance, 'the radiance of the glory (beauty) of God' (Heb. 1: 3). The
Book of Revelation begins by evoking the awesome beauty of the
risen Christ: his 'face was like the sun shining with full force' (Rev. 1:
16). St Paul writes of the glory of God on the face of the risen Christ.
He connects our chance of knowing this radiant glory with the
primeval act by which God first created light: 'it is God who said,
"let light shine out of darkness", who has shone in our hearts to give
the light of the knowledge of the glory of God in the face of Jesus
Christ' (2 Cor. 4: 6). From its first chapter John's Gospel writes of the
revelation of Christ's 'glory', which is tantamount to the revelation of
his beauty: 'the Word became flesh and lived among us, and we have
contemplated his glory' (John 1: 14).

Unlike the Synoptic Gospels, John does not record the episode of
the transfiguration. In a real sense the whole of this Gospel portrays
Jesus revealed in his glory (e.g. 2: 11). His self-description as 'the good
shepherd' (10: 14) could also be rendered 'I am the beautiful shepherd'.[6] According to the Synoptic Gospels, Peter, James, and John
went up a high mountain with Jesus and saw him 'transfigured', as
divine glory streamed through him. His face shone like the sun, and
two heavenly figures (the prophet Elijah and the lawgiver Moses)
talked with him. The disciples reacted not only with astonished awe
but also with a desire to prolong the vision of the radiantly beautiful
Lord that they were experiencing (Mark 9: 2–8 parr.).

The Synoptic Gospels likewise report words of Jesus which imply
that, in the joyful time of salvation, he had come as 'the bridegroom'

---

[6] Although it is normally translated 'good', the Greek adjective 'kalos' also means
beautiful. It is applied in the Book of Wisdom to Lady Wisdom; she is both beautiful
and good.

for his followers (Mark 2: 19–20 parr.; see Chapter 8 above). The parable of the wise and foolish bridesmaids, which presented the future kingdom in terms of the coming of the bridegroom and the need to be prepared (Matt. 25: 1–13), left its hearers with the question: Who is this mysterious bridegroom if not Christ himself? This language evokes many OT passages, such as an ode for a royal wedding. Psalm 45 highlights the glory, majesty, and beauty of the king: 'you are the most handsome of men; grace is poured upon your lips' (Ps. 45: 2). The NT ends with the promise of marriage between the gloriously beautiful Christ and his Church (Rev. 21–2).

Down the centuries Christians have celebrated the beauty of Christ, even if they did not always associate this beauty with his being the divine Wisdom in person. When commenting on the royal wedding song that we know as Psalm 45, St Augustine of Hippo declared: 'He [Christ] is beautiful in heaven; beautiful on earth; beautiful in the womb; beautiful in his parents' arms; beautiful in his miracles; beautiful under the scourge; beautiful when inviting to life . . . beautiful in taking it up again; beautiful on the cross; beautiful in the sepulchre; beautiful in heaven' (*Enarrationes in Psalmos* 44. 3). A nineteenth-century poet, Gerard Manley Hopkins (1844–89), in 'The Windhover' catches the beauty of a falcon in flight, and then takes us to the crucified and risen Jesus, who is 'a billion times told lovelier'. In a famous sermon on Christ, Hopkins said: 'There met in Jesus Christ all that can make a man lovely and loveable.' No wonder then that he went on to admit: 'I look forward with eager desire to seeing the matchless beauty of Christ's body in the heavenly light.' Yet 'far higher than beauty of body', Hopkins added, 'comes the beauty of his character'. He ended his sermon by urging the congregation to praise the beautiful Christ over and over again in their hearts.[7]

As the incarnate and resurrected Wisdom of God, Christ lets his beauty shine everywhere. Hopkins preached his sermon on Christ's beauty to a Christian community but he knew that this beauty is reflected everywhere. In his poem 'As Kingfishers Catch Fire', he wrote: 'for Christ plays in ten thousand places,/ Lovely in limbs, and lovely in eyes not his/ To the Father through the features of men's faces'. Looking at human beings anywhere and everywhere, one might well

[7] See Christopher Devlin (ed.), *The Sermons and Devotional Writings of Gerard Manley Hopkins* (Oxford: Oxford University Press, 1959), 34–8.

join Hopkins and say: 'where there is beauty, there is Christ (ubi pulchritudo, ibi Christus)'. In the commentary on Psalm 45 that we cited above, Augustine was concerned with the impact of the glorious beauty of Christ on people in need of redemption. Those who experience that need are in fact all human beings. Often mysteriously but always really, the beauty of Christ touches all lives and does so in a redemptive way.

In *The Idiot* Dostoevsky has two characters refer to the saintly, Christlike hero Prince Myshkin the words: 'beauty will save the world'. We can add: 'It is the beauty of Christ that is already saving the world.' It is through his beauty, even if it is only obscurely glimpsed, that human beings are led to truth and goodness. As Solomon sensed in the Book of Wisdom, this beauty does not depend on us but comes as pure gift. The beautiful Christ invites human beings to open themselves up, stay in his lovely presence, and let the impact of his unique beauty shape their lives, now and forever.

Before leaving this fifth theme, we might reflect briefly on its value for inter-religious dialogue: it could encourage an 'aesthetic' approach to 'other' religions and cultures. Often those Christians who consider the values of such 'other' religions and cultures do so in terms of the truth and goodness they find there. They raise such questions as: how much truth do I detect and respect in the portfolio of beliefs that constitute the doctrinal heart of this religion? What comes across as genuinely worthwhile in the moral code of this religion? In other words, other religions are commonly evaluated by standards of truth and goodness. Perhaps it is time to try or even privilege an aesthetic approach. What elements of beauty strike me in these other religions? Appreciating what is beautiful in their way of life, worship, and teaching might lead me more easily to recognize the elements of truth and goodness that they embody. There, as elsewhere, beauty may be the most helpful path to truth and goodness.

(6) WISDOM AS FEMININE

The feminine image of Lady Wisdom, precisely as feminine, also helps to suggest the universal role of Christ, who invites and draws all to share in the divine banquet—like Lady Wisdom in Proverbs and Sirach. The Christian community has long been identified as 'Holy Mother the Church'. Within this visible, feminine community Christ has been primarily identified by his masculine qualities—as the 'Spouse' of the Church (e.g. Eph. 5: 21–33; Rev. 19: 7, 9; 21: 9). But beyond the visible community of his followers, the feminine image of Lady Wisdom catches his role in drawing, healing, and receiving, albeit anonymously, human beings around the world.

In the last chapter I drew attention to some feminine, maternal features of Christ. Any attempt to distinguish feminine and masculine characteristics will be controversial and deeply conditioned by one's culture. But let me do so, using in part the reflections of Walter Ong.[8] Following his lead, I would see masculinity as differentiating, moving outward, set on change, breaking idols, competitive, and restlessly earning its identity through struggle. The contrary, feminine qualities include being receptive, nurturing, interior, self-assured, self-possessed, dealing peacefully with conflict and change, and not needing constant contest to earn and maintain one's identity. Being present belongs unmistakably to this list. Both in 'real' life and in literature women are persistently 'there'—from birth (necessarily) to death (by choice) in a way that men do not match. Men have often avoided these situations, perhaps through insecurity and a fear of being absorbed by the feminine.

What do the Gospels record about Jesus' masculine and feminine qualities? One can risk correlating Christ's modes of action and discourse with characteristically masculine and feminine styles. Unquestionably we come across adversarial, masculine language and characteristics. He looks with anger on those who would condemn his healing a handicapped person because they have made an idol of Sabbath observance; he challenges them by restoring the man's withered hand (Mark 3: 1–6). He presents his mission in combative and divisive terms: 'you must not think that I have come to bring peace to the earth; I have not come to bring peace but a sword. I have come to set a man against his father, a daughter against her mother, a daughter-in-law against her mother-in-law' (Matt. 10: 34–5 par.). The sense

---

[8] Walter Ong, *Fighting for Life: Contest, Sexuality and Consciousness* (Ithaca, NY: Cornell University Press, 1981).

of masculine divisiveness turns up in another saying common to Matthew and Luke: 'he who is not with me is against me, and he who does not gather with me scatters' (Matt. 12: 30 par.). Jesus is set on radically changing the environment he has encountered: 'I have come to set fire to the earth' (Luke 12: 49). His identity as the bearer of God's final kingdom emerges in his struggle with the forces of evil (Matt. 12: 22–9 parr.). John's Gospel, while remaining silent about Jesus' exorcisms or delivering people from the grip of demonic powers, expresses this masculine struggle through the theme of light clashing with darkness (John 1: 4–5; 9: 1–41).

Alongside such masculine characteristics we can easily uncover feminine ones. Jesus receives little children into his presence and nurtures them (Mark 10: 13–16 parr.). He is remembered as constantly cultivating the inner life through prayer (e.g. Mark 1: 12–13, 35; 6: 46). The struggle in Gethsemane comes across as the more surprising, since hitherto Jesus had seemed so self-assured about his mission and identity. His sayings include some that seem downright feminine or at least do not find support in male, adversarial logic: for instance, 'whoever wants to save his life will lose it, but whoever loses his life for my sake and for that of the gospel will save it' (Mark 8: 35). 'Seek and you will find; knock and the door will be opened to you' (Matt. 7: 7 par.) sounds masculine and a way to win. But letting go and losing because one hopes to be saved converges with the non-violent, feminine strength-in-surrender or power-in-vulnerability with which Luke portrays the death of Jesus: 'Father, forgive them . . . Father, into your hands I commend my spirit' (Luke 23: 34, 46). These words suggest a self-giving humility that is not self-destructive.

A striking testimony to the untroubled, feminine delicacy of Jesus' language emerges when we recall the image of female prostitution used at times by OT prophets to focus the disobedience of God's people. The vivid, ugly allegories of sexual infidelity developed by Ezekiel (16: 1–63; 23: 1–49) more than hint at the male insecurity and dominance of that priest-prophet. The Jesus of the Synoptic Gospels never needs to indulge in such language. On the contrary, he does not flinch from applying to himself a very homely, female image (Luke 13: 34 par.). He is present like a mother hen to shelter her chickens when they run back under her wings. Like Lady Wisdom he invites his audience: 'come to me, all you who labour and are heavily burdened, and I will give you rest' (Matt. 11: 28). John's Gospel develops its feminine version of Jesus in various ways: for instance, through the discourse on the bread of life which evokes Lady's Wisdom's banquet (John 6: 22–58) and the allegory of the branches which dwell in the receptive vine and bear much fruit through that welcoming presence (John 15: 1–10).

Thus the feminine image of Lady Wisdom, further elaborated by feminine characteristics from the record of Jesus' life, can suggest something of the mysteriously welcoming and nurturing impact of Christ the divine Wisdom on human beings everywhere. At the end of *Faust*, Part II, Johann Wolfgang von Goethe (1749–1832) unconsciously conjured up something of this impact: 'das Ewig-Weibliche zieht uns hinan (the eternal feminine draws us upwards)'. What Goethe had in mind was the inspiration he had received throughout his life from women. One might freely adapt these words and say: the feminine, maternal Christ, eternally transformed and made gloriously and universally effective, draws all people, albeit often hiddenly, forwards and upwards throughout their lives to their final destiny with him in the everlasting life of God.

This chapter has aimed at filling out what is involved in acknowledging the universal impact of Christ as divine Wisdom in person. Without alleging this as the only possibility, I have proposed six advantages in developing this theme. I set myself to tell the story of Christ's activity in the world as the universal story of divine Wisdom. This story remains intertwined with the Holy Spirit, just as the earthly story of the historical Jesus, right from his conception, was defined by the Spirit. The glorified Christ's activity as universal Wisdom is played out through the power and presence of the Holy Spirit. Before concluding this chapter, we must make room for a tribute to the Spirit who empowers the continuing story of Wisdom.

WISDOM AND THE HOLY SPIRIT

In setting out the nature and beneficial works of Lady Wisdom, the Book of Wisdom flags her twenty-one attributes (7: 22–8: 1). Some of these attributes highlight her power: she is 'irresistible', 'all-powerful', 'more mobile than any motion', 'penetrating all things', 'renewing all things', and 'ordering all things well'. This language prefigures the universal operation of Christ, the divine Wisdom in person. It also foreshadows the power that 'carries' that story—the inseparable energy of the Holy Spirit. Although he does not develop this thought, the title that Gary Badcock chose for his book on the Holy Spirit, *Light of Truth and Fire of Love*, proves suggestive about the relationship between the Spirit and divine Wisdom.[9] Where the glorious Christ acts universally as truth and love, the empowering Spirit is the light of that truth and the fire of that love. In a lyric passage Isaiah sketches the characteristics of the messianic king, with 'the spirit of the Lord resting upon him' and 'the spirit' immediately identified with 'the spirit of wisdom' (Isa. 11: 2). We can take up this language and speak of the Holy Spirit as light and fire 'resting upon' the divine Wisdom, since this luminous and 'fiery' Spirit always belongs with Wisdom.

As OT personifications of the divine activity, 'wisdom' and 'spirit' could be set in parallel to each other and show themselves as functionally equivalent. For instance, in a prayer to God Solomon asks: 'Who has learned your counsel, unless you have given *wisdom* and sent your *holy spirit* from on high?' (Wisd. 9: 17).[10] The incarnation and all that followed yielded a clearer answer to the question: Who and what is God? Wisdom and Spirit emerge as distinct divine persons. Without merging into one another and being personally identified with each other, Christ the divine Wisdom and the Holy Spirit are intimate and inseparable companions. We might express this relationship by saying : 'where there is Wisdom, there is the Spirit (ubi Sapientia, ibi Spiritus)'.

Faced with this inseparable relationship, we can and should apply to the Spirit the characteristics we have recognized in divine Wisdom. We can begin with the themes of particularity and universality.

(1) There is a *particularity* and a *universality* to the presence of the Spirit. The particular life of the Church is steeped in the power and

---

[9] G. Badcock, *Light of Truth and Fire of Love: A Theology of the Holy Spirit* (Grand Rapids, Mich.: Eerdmans, 1997).

[10] Some passages speak of 'the spirit of wisdom' (e.g. Isa. 11: 12; Deut. 34: 19), almost as if 'the spirit' were to be identified with 'wisdom'.

presence of the Spirit, above all the Church's preaching, teaching, and the celebration of the sacraments. Yet this special presence does not rule out the universal presence of the Spirit in the worldwide kingdom of God. One could say: 'Where there is the kingdom of God, there is the Spirit.' There is no zone that can be 'outside the Holy Spirit'. As Yves Congar puts matters, 'like Wisdom, the Spirit of God is at work everywhere'.[11] The Spirit is not only the mysterious companion and religious friend in the life of every human being but also fills the universe to gather everything in it for the glory of the Father. In the words of Congar, 'the Holy Spirit, who fills the universe and who holds all things in unity, knows everything that is said and gathers together everything that, in this world, is for God'. The Spirit 'ties the sheaf together in a hymn of cosmic praise through, with, and in Christ', the Wisdom of God in whom 'everything is firmly established'.[12]

Thomas Aquinas obviously treasured a saying that went back to an anonymous fourth-century author, known as Ambrosiaster: 'every truth, no matter who says it, comes from the Holy Spirit (omne verum, a quocumque dicatur, a Spiritu Sancto est)'. The expression turns up eighteen times in the works of Aquinas.[13] One could well expand the dictum and say: all goodness, beauty, and authentic prayer, no matter where they are found, come from the Holy Spirit. Truth, goodness, beauty, and prayer are found universally in our world and are charged with significance—precisely as signs of the Spirit's presence. The Holy Spirit is the divine principle that inspires all true knowledge, all goodness, all beauty, and all authentic prayer. Witnesses to this conviction have turned up among Christian believers, right down to modern times. Cardinal Henry Edward Manning (1808–92), for instance, wrote in 1875: 'It is true to say with St Irenaeus, "ubi ecclesia ibi Spiritus (where the Church is there is the Spirit)", but it would not be true to say, "where the Church is not, neither is the Spirit there". The operations of the Holy Ghost have always pervaded the whole race of men from the beginning, and they

---

[11] Y. M. J. Congar, *I Believe in the Holy Spirit*, 3 vols. (New York: Seabury Press, 1983), ii. 218.

[12] Ibid., 224.

[13] E.g. *Summa theologiae* II–II, q. 172, a. 6 arg. 1.

are now in full activity even among those who are without the Church.'[14] Bishop John V. Taylor called the Spirit 'the Go-Between God', that is to say, the One who acts as a kind of divine broker, subtly reaching everywhere and creating true relationships. The Holy Spirit, he wrote, is 'that unceasing, dynamic communicator and Go-Between operating upon every element and every process of the material universe, the immanent and anonymous presence of God'—in short, the 'creative-redemptive action at the heart of everything'.[15]

(2) As the divine Wisdom, Christ is both the Light of the whole world and the Life of the whole world. The Holy Spirit, the inseparable companion of Wisdom, likewise plays this double role by revealing the divine reality and leading all people and things to the fullness of salvation. These twofold blessings allow us to describe the Spirit as also being the Light of the world and the Life of the world (or 'the Giver of life' in the language of the Nicene-Constantinopolitan Creed). The 'Veni Creator Spiritus', a hymn that goes back at least to the seventh century, cherishes the universal functions of the Spirit in communicating the divine revelation and salvation. The Spirit is called on to come as 'a living fountain, fire, and charity (fons vivus, ignis, caritas)'. The hymn asks that the Spirit grant not only light but also strength and love.

Here one should also invoke the 'Veni Sancte Spiritus', a sequence for Pentecost, which dates to the late twelfth century and was probably written by Stephen Langton, an Archbishop of Canterbury who died in 1228. High technical skill expresses the deep religious feeling of this sequence, which asks for both 'light for [human] hearts (lumen cordium)' and the help of saving grace: 'wash what is dirty, water what is dry, heal what is wounded (lava quod est sordidum, riga quod est aridum, sana quod est saucium)'.

(3) Both the OT personification of Lady Wisdom and Christ, the incarnate and glorified Wisdom of God, display *beautiful* and *feminine* characteristics. Beauty has been called 'illuminated being'— something that is pre-eminently true of the Holy Spirit. Both the

---

[14] Manning, *The Internal Mission of the Holy Ghost* (New York: P. J. Kenedy, 1875), p. v.

[15] J. V. Taylor, *The Go-Between God* (London: SCM Press, 1972), 64.

'Veni Creator Spiritus' and the 'Veni Sancte Spiritus' catch something of the luminous radiance of the Holy Spirit.

The beauty of Christ, the glorious Wisdom of God, reflects the beauty of the Spirit. St Paul understands the resurrection of Christ to have been effected by the Father through the power of the Holy Spirit (e.g. Rom. 1: 4; 8: 11). The Apostle also points to the lovely 'fruits of the Spirit' to be seen in the lives of faithful Christians (Gal. 5: 22–3). The beauty of Christ and his followers displays something of the beauty of their heavenly 'cause', the Holy Spirit. At least analogously, the old adage applies here: 'every agent effects something similar to itself (omne agens agit sibi simile)'. In this indirect way, the beauty of the Spirit shows up, and encourages us to coin the phrase: 'where there is beauty, there is the Spirit (ubi pulchritudo, ibi Spiritus)'.

St Cyril of Alexandria understood the Spirit to effect such a change. Commenting on the words of the risen Christ, 'receive the Holy Spirit' (John 20: 22), Cyril wrote of the Spirit restoring the loveliness which human beings had lost through sin. When creating Adam, 'God gave him the most perfect beauty—making him share in his spirit'. After the resurrection, 'Christ breathed on us, renewing the former beauty' (*In Matthaeum* 24c–d). A new beauty is created in those who share in the Spirit. This theme from Cyril can and should be extended beyond the community of the baptized to the whole world. We might say: 'where the Spirit is, there is beauty (ubi Spiritus, ibi pulchritudo)', and add at once: 'The Spirit is present everywhere and available to everyone.'[16]

Yves Congar documented the long-standing Christian conviction that the Holy Spirit exercises a motherhood towards all the baptized.[17] The Spirit is also active as 'Mother' beyond the visible community of the Church. In 'God's Grandeur' Gerard Manley Hopkins celebrated the Holy Spirit as the source of unquenchable vitality, light, and beauty for the whole universe: 'the Holy Ghost over the bent/ World broods with warm breast and with ah! bright wings'. Hopkins extolled the Spirit as the universal source of beauty and life, and did so in a maternal key. Like and with Christ, the divine

---

[16] See G. O'Collins, *Jesus Our Redeemer: A Christian Approach to Salvation* (Oxford: Oxford University Press, 2007), 205–7.

[17] Congar, *I Believe in the Holy Spirit*, iii. 155–64.

Wisdom, the Holy Spirit enjoys an all-encompassing, life-giving impact and does so in a motherly way.

This chapter has put the case for recognizing the universal power and presence of those seamlessly intertwined companions, divine Wisdom and the Holy Spirit. What remains now is the task of saying something about the *response* to this hidden Wisdom and Spirit made by those who do not belong through baptism to the visible Christian community.

16

Saving Faith and 'Outsiders'

The universal presence of Christ as divine Wisdom in person leaves us with the question: how does this presence impinge on those who may never have even heard his name? Is his presence somehow disclosed to such 'outsiders' and able to change their lives? In the light of all that has gone before in this book, how should we construe the 'facts' in their case and the possibility of saving faith somehow being available to them? Does it make sense to speak of their being through faith in the kingdom of God but not (yet) in the Church? To answer such questions, we need to linger for a moment on those who have acknowledged and accepted Christ's offer of light and life, and through faith and baptism have found in the power of the Holy Spirit communion with Christ and one another. But first let me insert something about faith.

Christian 'faith' is understood here as an act that involves the whole person, an obedient commitment that includes but is not limited to an intellectual assent given to the divine self-revelation. St Paul (1) relates faith closely to obedience (Rom. 1: 5; 16: 26), recognizes that faith entails (2) confessing the truth of God's self-disclosure in Christ (e.g. Rom. 10: 9) and (3) entrusting our future to God (e.g. Rom. 6: 8), and teaches that faith (4) is made possible through the power of the Holy Spirit (e.g. 2 Cor. 3: 16–18).

In the case of those who do not adhere to Christianity and, for that matter, of OT figures who lived before Christianity, it is relatively easy to see how elements (1), (3), and (4) apply. Abraham and Sarah, venerated also by Christians as ancestors in faith, obeyed the divine call, entrusted their future to God, and, without realizing this, were empowered in their faith by the Holy Spirit. But the second item in our account of faith could not apply: from their place in history they were not in a position to confess the divine revelation communicated through the life, death, and resurrection of Christ. They could not even share the future confession of Israelites about God's saving action in delivering his people from Egypt and bringing them into the promised land (Deut. 26: 5–10). Obviously limits in the confession of faith cannot be decisive in recognizing the existence of saving faith. Otherwise, Abraham and Sarah could not be reckoned examples, let alone outstanding examples, of shining faith. Thus the profile of faith we glean from Paul leaves it open for 'outsiders' to be blessed by saving faith. But, as we will see below, the account of faith from Hebrews 11 opens up matters even more dramatically for those who do not belong to the Christian community.

THE CHURCH AND THE KINGDOM

Mainstream Christians agree that the fullness of the means of revelation and salvation is to be found in the Church—in particular, but not exclusively, through their faith being nourished by the proclamation of the word and the basic sacraments of baptism and the Eucharist. Even if many Christians do not consistently and consciously live their lives in the presence of Christ, that presence is there for them—often as a quiet background experience and sometimes as a spectacular occurrence that creates a turning-point in their existence. Either way, they know that faith in him gifts them with possibilities here and hereafter that they could never attain by themselves.

The NT twice utters the momentous truth, 'God is love' (1 John 4: 8, 16). Many Christians would be ready to transpose this statement in terms of Christ. He is love, incarnate love—present to them and for them as creative, self-giving, and life-creating love. Christ makes a difference in their lives, and they can discern this difference and do so even vividly. At least from time to time they sense his presence to be the presence of his divine-human love for them. But what of the others?

For all Christians the reign of God should be a decisive point of reference. The Church exists for this wider, universal reality and at its service. Even if not a separate reality, the Church is distinct from the kingdom. It is simply 'not true' that the NT authors 'substituted the Church for the kingdom as preached by Jesus of Nazareth'.[1] It was and is Jesus himself, rather than Christian believers, who enjoys a 'special and particularly close connection' with the kingdom of God.[2] The incarnate, exalted, and omnipresent Christ was more or less equated with the kingdom of God. In the NT and the post-NT period, even when Christians did not explicitly invoke the kingdom, to acknowledge the *Lord* Jesus Christ implied the kingdom of God and vice versa. To receive salvation through Christ meant living in the kingdom of God and so being in God's presence.

As we saw in Chapters 7 and 8, Jesus preached the kingdom of God, that wider, albeit hidden, reality which embraces the whole of humanity. He accepted a violent death in which his blood was poured out for all men and women. From what he said and did when celebrating the Last Supper, we found enough to show that his new covenant and the coming kingdom enfolded all people. The institution of the Eucharist expressed in a supreme way his desire to bring revelation and salvation to all. Since the Eucharist 'embodied' and 'embodies' that desire, one can well say that 'outside the Eucharist there is no salvation (extra eucharistiam nulla salus)'. One must add at once that in that deeper sense there is no 'outside the Eucharist', inasmuch as Christ instituted it with the intention to save all.

In the worship of the Church the eucharistic prayers distinguish between the invocation of the Holy Spirit to maintain the holiness and unity of the faithful and the intercessions for innumerable burdened and afflicted human beings throughout the world (intercessions which do not take the form of an invocation or 'epiclesis' of the Spirit). Some distinction is made between the Church's role for the salvation of her members and her role for the salvation of 'the others'. Nevertheless, the power of prayer ('for others' or, for that matter, for anybody) should not be underplayed, as if prayer were

---

[1] K. L. Schmidt, 'Basileia', in G. Kittel *et al.* (eds.), *Theological Dictionary of the New Testament*, i (Grand Rapids, Mich.: Eerdmans, 164), 579–93, at 589.

[2] Ibid., 588.

'merely a moral' cause. The effect of intercessory prayer should not be written off in that way. All baptized Christians are called to intercede lovingly for the whole world. By their prayers for all people, including bad rulers, Christians express and live up to God's will to save all (1 Tim. 2: 1–4). These prayers play their part in effecting the salvation of 'the others'. Christians have received the astonishing gift of faith in Jesus, a gift that creates an essential responsibility to be fulfilled towards 'others'—not only through action but also through persevering prayer. But how can the 'others' receive the gift of faith?

The Letter to the Hebrews makes the unqualified statement: 'without faith it is impossible to please God' (11: 6). This teaching leaves behind any talk about merely human (religious) *beliefs* elaborated through an unaided human search for God. Without responding in *faith* to the revelation mediated through the Son of God and the Holy Spirit, no one can 'please God' and receive salvation. Putting this positively, we can say that the offer of light and life to everyone makes possible, respectively, faith and salvation. Christ takes the initiative as both universal Revealer and universal Saviour. The divine quest for all human beings, rather than any human quest for God, should be utterly basic for every version not only of redemption but also of revelation.

Often enough when discussing other religions, modern writers have more or less concerned themselves only with Christ's saving role for all, with that 'one salvation' which Irenaeus highlighted (*Adversus Haereses* 4. 6. 7). But the same Irenaeus dealt also with the one revelation offered to all through the Son, who 'from the beginning reveals the Father to all' (ibid. 4. 20. 6–7). Christ is the source and agent of revelation for the whole world, no less than he is the source and agent of salvation for the whole world. He offers the truth to all, so that they may share in the divine life of the Trinity. Experiencing the truth and light which comes from Christ and is personally identical with him who is *the* Truth and *the* Light, all people are called to faith in him and to salvation through him and his Spirit. But where does that leave all the 'others', who often have never learned of Christ? Should we leave their lives and destiny to the loving, mysterious providence of God? Or can we say something, perhaps only a little, about their situation?

STRUCTURES FOR FAITH

Chapter 15 put the case for the universal presence of Christ and the Holy Spirit. Since the divine persons are present everywhere and to every one, they cannot fail to act everywhere and do so lovingly towards all. They exercise their divine love 'in an infinite series of unique acts of love, each new and different from all the others'.[3] But Christ and the Spirit do not necessarily and always make their presence consciously felt. It is, in any case, a matter of common experience that 'we experience many things without knowing *what* we experience or *how* we experience them'.[4] To this we might add that we can experience personal agents without necessarily knowing *whom* we experience. We may never, for instance, be in a position to know the identity of some mysterious stranger who proves particularly helpful to us. Against the background of this presupposition, we turn to a classic passage on faith: Hebrews 11: 1–12: 27.

The passage opens by declaring: 'Now faith is the assurance of things hoped for, the proof of things not seen. By this [faith] the elders [our ancestors] received approval. By faith we understand that the universe was fashioned by the word of God, so that from what cannot be seen that which is seen has come into being' (11: 1–3). A further verse closely concerns our enquiry: 'without faith it is impossible to please God; for whoever would approach him must believe that he exists and that he rewards those who seek him' (11: 6).[5]

The opening three verses describe faith but say very little about its content. The passage hints at the future. Divine promises (presumably of some eternal inheritance) have aroused the hope of human beings and their trust that God will keep these promises, which concern future 'things which are not seen'. Faith also involves a view of the past. We understand by faith the unseen origin of the world; it 'was fashioned by the word of God'. Just as people of faith

---

[3] I. U. Dalferth, *Becoming Present: An Inquiry into the Christian Sense of the Presence of God* (Leuven: Peeters, 2006), 147.

[4] Ibid., 115; italics mine.

[5] On these and the other relevant verses on faith, see C. R. Koester, *Hebrews* (New York: Doubleday, 2001), 468–553.

rely on the word of God about the *genesis* of the universe, so too do they rely on the word of God's promise when considering the *goal* of the world and their existence now and in the future. Both in their view of the past and their hope for the future, the lives of those who have faith are entwined with the life of the invisible God.

Faith cannot prove the 'unseen things' of God; rather faith itself is 'the proof' of these things. As C. R. Koester comments, 'the unseen realities of God give proof of their existence by their power to evoke faith'.[6] It is the divine reality that creates faith, not faith that 'creates' the divine reality. The divine 'object' of faith and hope 'can be known by its effects on human beings'.[7] The invisible power of God evokes faith and hope, and directs men and women towards invisible ends. One cannot see God and the word of God, but one can know them from their results. Both faith and the created universe witness to the invisible power of God and the reality of the unseen world of God.

The opening description on faith makes no mention of Christ. He will appear later, when the list of the heroes and heroines of faith runs right up into the case of 'Jesus, the pioneer and perfecter of faith' (12: 2), who was one might say 'faith personified'. The opening verses of Hebrews 11 invoke 'the elders' or 'ancestors', people who have been honoured and approved by God for their perseverance in faith. Then follow examples of those who have lived on the basis of faith, with particular attention paid to Abraham, Sarah, and Moses. Some of those who exemplified faith (Abel, Enoch, and Noah) existed prior to Abraham, Sarah, and the formation of the chosen people. One figure of faith is 'Rahab the prostitute', an outsider who belonged to the story of the conquest of the promised land. Abel and Noah are identified as 'righteous'—a useful reminder that their faith *and* righteousness responded, respectively, to the revelatory and salvific dimensions of the self-communication of God. They found in God the light of faith and the life of a righteous existence.

Even though it does not explicitly do so, the opening account of faith allows us to glimpse the human questions to which faith supplies the answer. (1) Is there anything beyond the visible world? Are we bonded with things unseen or, rather, with the unseen God?

---

[6] Ibid., 480.   [7] Ibid.

(2) Where do we and our universe come from? Has 'that which is seen' come 'into being from that which cannot be seen': that is to say, from God and his creative word? We come into a world that is not of our making. Do we nourish faith in the invisible Creator from whom all things have come? Such faith is close to gratitude towards the unseen Giver, a gratitude for the past from which we have emerged and for the future to which we have been summoned. (3) Does it matter how we behave? Should we imitate our 'ancestors', approved by God for their persevering faith? Should we live as pilgrims afflicted by various sufferings,[8] but always hoping for 'a better country' (11: 16) and yearning for a God-given life to come? In short, may we and should we trust God as the One who 'rewards those who seek him'?

These questions are not limited to Christians but belong to everyone. They yield a vision of the questions that the Holy Spirit can stir in the hearts of people everywhere and so open them to the hidden but powerful presence and activity of Christ. Hebrews 11: 6 lets us glimpse the shape that the faith of outsiders can take.

THE FAITH OF GOD'S OTHER PEOPLES

Five elements show up and then are clarified somewhat by related statements elsewhere in Hebrews. (1) First, subsequent exhortations fill out what 'pleasing God' entails: 'let us give thanks, by which we offer God worship in a pleasing way with reverence and awe' (12: 28). Such grateful worship of God issues in acts of kindness that build up community: 'do not neglect to do good and to share what you have; for such sacrifices are pleasing to God' (13: 16). A further verse draws together such 'pleasing God' in terms of doing the divine will: 'May

---

[8] Right from the example of Abel (11: 4) through to the end of the list of named or unnamed heroes and heroines of faith (11: 38), sufferings of various kinds afflict those who persevere in faith. This feature of Hebrews 11 calls to mind results from the Religious Experience Research Unit, established in Oxford by Sir Alister Hardy and later directed by David Hay, which found that people, over and over again, reported deep religious experience occurring along with great suffering. Suffering seems profoundly connected with faith and with the experience of the mysterious God who encounters human beings vividly in the midst of their pain.

the God of peace . . . make you complete in everything good that you may do his will, working among us that which is pleasing in his sight' (13: 20–1). We could sum up what this view of 'pleasing God' entails: it envisages a faith that gratefully offers to God a reverent worship and does his will through deeds of kindness and service of others. Obviously explicit faith in Christ will vigorously empower the life of faith. Yet a vertical relationship with God (through grateful worship) and a horizontal relationship with other human beings (through self-sacrificing kindness) call for the invisible support of the Holy Spirit, but do not as such depend on a conscious relationship with Christ. A faith that pleases God is a possibility open to all.

(2) Various other passages in Hebrews illustrate what the 'drawing near to God' (11: 6) involves. It means approaching God in prayer and worshipping God. Thus the anonymous author writes of 'drawing near to the throne of grace' (4: 16). Christians will be conscious of doing this through Jesus, 'since he always lives to make intercession for them' (7: 25). But approaching God in prayer and worship does not demand an awareness that such 'drawing near' depends on the priestly intercession of the risen and actively present Christ. That intercession functions, whether or not the worshippers are conscious of the presence of Christ when they approach God in prayer.

(3) Obviously those who approach God in prayer display faith that he *exists*. They answer the question 'is there anything beyond the visible world?' by bonding with the invisible God. Their faith inevitably involves accepting that the world is made by God, whom they worship as the unseen Creator from whom all things have come and towards whom all things are directed. God is both the origin and the goal of the world (see 2: 10).

(4) In faith God is accepted not only as the origin of the universe but also as the One who 'rewards those who seek him'. This means letting God be the future goal of one's existence. God is accepted as just and faithful to his promises, however they are construed. In some way those with faith live as pilgrims who hope for 'a better country'. Obviously those who embrace faith do not always enjoy the 'normal' (material) blessings in this life. It is precisely that challenge which prompts the author of Hebrews into appealing for endurance: 'do not abandon that confidence of yours; it brings a great reward' (10: 35). At least here, the author does not specify what shape this

great reward will take, nor does he distinguish between 'rewards' for his Christian readers and for all those others 'who seek' God. Christians and other 'God-seekers' alike are summoned by faith to put their future in the hands of the just and faithful God (see 10: 23).

(5) 'Seeking' God brings out an attitude that a sincere 'drawing near to God' in worship and prayer presupposes. One approaches God in prayer, because one hopes to receive a favourable response, whatever form it may take. 'Drawing near to the throne of grace' calls for a confidence that one's prayers will be heard. The author of Hebrews leaves matters quite open—as regards the when, the where, and the how of the 'reward' of those who seek God in prayer. What emerges here recalls the open-ended confidence of Jesus' teaching: 'Ask and you will receive. Seek and you will find. Knock and the door will be opened to you' (Matt. 7: 7). Nothing is indicated about when, where, and how persevering prayer will be answered. Everything is concentrated in the assurance that it will be answered.

As I stated above, the five major themes contained in Hebrews 11: 6 let us glimpse something of the shape taken by the faith of outsiders. But to appreciate the richness of this verse, one must read it not only within its immediate context but also within the context of the entire letter. That is rarely, if ever, done. Admittedly, the Letter to the Hebrews addresses Christians and does so in the knowledge that they have been enduring persecution and suffering of various kinds. Yet, as is clear right from its majestic opening verses (1: 1–4), salvation through faith is offered to all people and on the basis of the universal sovereignty of Christ as Son of God and unique high priest. A comment make by Luke Timothy Johnson on 1 Timothy 2: 5 ('God is one') applies equally well to Hebrews and the vision it offers about God and faith: 'If God is to be more than a tribal deity, then God must be one for all humans; and if God is to be righteous (fair), then there must be some principle by which all humans can respond to God: faith.'[9] Here one might take up a NT text originally addressed to Christians (Col. 3: 3) and extend it to God's other peoples: 'through faith your life is hidden with Christ in God's kingdom'.

---

[9] L. T. Johnson, *The First and Second Letters to Timothy* (New York: Doubleday, 2001), 197.

DIVINE INITIATIVE

A casual reading of Hebrews 11: 6 and of the use made of it by some theologians might encourage the conclusion that faith is shown by 'outsiders' through their 'performance' in seeking and approaching God. It could seem that it is a question of their successful initiative in seeking God rather than God's prior initiative in seeking them. They would differ then from Abraham, Sarah, and others listed in Hebrews 11, who by faith obeyed a call that came to them from God. In such cases drawn from the particular story of Judaism, human faith responded to a prior initiative of God. But what of the view of 'outsiders' taken, or at least implied, by Hebrews?

Does Hebrews endorse or at least allow for the notion that we human beings may seek out God in ways that can bring us to the goal of our existence in God? Several hundred years later such an idea lay behind the position taken by Symmachus (d. 402), a rhetorician who defended the ancient Roman religion and petitioned the emperor to reinstate the goddess 'Victory' in the senate. In his memorandum he justified his request by arguing for a plurality of ways to God: 'one cannot approach such a great mystery by only one road (*uno itinere non potest venire ad tam grande secretum*)'. Clearly Symmachus presupposed that it is we human beings who approach and come to God, rather than vice versa. Hebrews, however, begins by highlighting the prior initiative of God, who 'in these last days has spoken to us by a Son' (1: 2). Other NT authors agree with this conviction about the divine initiative being the pre-eminent factor (e.g. John 3: 16–17; Rom. 8: 3–4; Gal. 4: 4–7). Right from the start of its description of faith and examples of faith, Hebrews points to the prior activity of God in rousing faith. By calling faith 'the assurance of things hoped for', our text implies prior promises coming from God and evoking the response of human hope. By naming faith as 'the proof of things not seen', Hebrews suggests the unseen reality of God that gives proof of its existence by its power to call forth faith.

Right from the NT times and the teaching of Hebrews, Paul, and John, Christians have insisted on the prior action of God in summoning forth human faith (in the divine self-revelation) and hope (in the divine promise of salvation). In the second century Irenaeus

wrote: 'no one can know God, unless God teaches [him or her]; that
is to say, without God, God cannot be known (Deum scire nemo
potest, nisi Deo docente; hoc est, sine Deo non cognosci Deum)'
(*Adversus Haereses* 4. 6. 4). Centuries later St Anselm of Canterbury
prayed to God: 'teach me to seek You, and reveal Yourself [to me]
when I seek [You], because I cannot seek You unless you teach [me],
nor find [You] unless You reveal Yourself [to me] (doce me quaerere
Te, et ostende Te quaerenti, quia nec quaerere Te possum nisi Tu
doceas nec invenire nisi Te ostendas)' (*Proslogion* 1).

OBEDIENCE AND SALVATION

The roll call of heroes and heroines of faith in Hebrews 11 introduces
only once obedience, a theme closely allied to that of faith. It does so
in expounding the central example of Abraham: 'by faith Abraham
obeyed when he was called to set out for a place that he was to receive
as an inheritance; and he set out not knowing where he was going'
(Heb. 11: 8). Elsewhere obedience is a key feature in the plot of
Hebrews, not least when it portrays the prayer and obedience of
Jesus himself. By obediently submitting to the divine will and
dying, he 'became the source (cause) of eternal salvation for all
who obey him' (5: 7–9). Thus the faithful obedience of Jesus became
God's way of saving human beings.

But where does that leave all those innumerable outsiders who do
not know Jesus and hence cannot consciously obey him and experience in him the cause/source of their eternal salvation? This question
can be met by observing the qualification that Hebrews 11 introduces
into the drama of human salvation. We presume that the 'great cloud
of witnesses' (12: 1) cited in the previous chapter of Hebrews, either
by name or in general, were eventually blessed with eternal salvation.
Yet they all existed before Christ and could not have consciously
obeyed him. If they had known him, they would have obeyed him.
The same, one can argue, is true of those innumerable outsiders
whose faith enables them to 'please' God. Without knowing Jesus
and hence without the possibility of consciously obeying him, they
mysteriously experience in him (and his Holy Spirit) the cause of

their salvation. In their case faith does not include conscious obedience towards Jesus, but that does not prevent him from being 'the pioneer of their salvation' (2: 10).

We need to say something similar about a verse from John's Gospel that is frequently invoked to establish that access to God is solely through Jesus: 'no one comes to the Father except through me' (John 14: 6). To be sure, no one comes to God explicitly *as* Father except through Jesus.[10] But innumerable people are drawn to God through Jesus, even though they may remain unaware of this role of Jesus. As was said above, Christ and his Holy Spirit do not necessarily and always make their presence consciously felt. This is not to revive, however, any old idea about 'anonymous Christians'. Since they are baptized members of a visible community, by definition Christians cannot be anonymous. What I speak of here is different—the personal presence and power of Jesus and the Spirit, a presence and power that shapes the lives of millions of people who may never in their lifetime become aware of this invisible influence.

The Letter to the Hebrews has dominated this final chapter. But the masterpiece of St Paul deserves the last word. The Apostle argues that 'all have sinned and fallen short of the glory/beauty of God' (Rom. 3: 23) before maintaining that all human beings are to be saved by faith (Rom. 3: 27–31). He returns to these two themes later by saying that 'God has imprisoned all in disobedience so that he may be merciful to all' (Rom. 11: 32). Faith and merciful salvation are available for all. Paul divides his world into Jews and Gentiles, two groups who have been unfaithful to God. But God 'makes use of such infidelity to manifest to all his bountiful mercy'.[11] Paul envisions the divine mercy going out to all through Jesus Christ and his Spirit. This vision of salvation for all human beings arguably forms the crowning point of Paul's greatest letter. It can rightly serve as the closing words of this book: 'God has imprisoned all in disobedience so that he may be merciful to all.'

---

[10] See G. O'Collins, *The Lord's Prayer* (London: Darton, Longman & Todd, 2006), esp. p. 48.

[11] J. A. Fitzmyer, *Romans* (New York: Doubleday, 1993), 628.

Select Bibliography

Baillie, J., *The Sense of the Presence of God* (New York: Scribner, 1962).

Burrell, D., *Faith and Freedom: An Interfaith Perspective* (Oxford: Blackwell, 2004).

Dalferth, I. U., *Becoming Present: An Inquiry into the Christian Sense of the Presence of God* (Leuven: Peeters, 2006).

Davis, S. T., Kendall, D., and O'Collins, G. (eds.), *The Redemption: An Interdisciplinary Symposium on Christ as Redeemer* (Oxford: Oxford University Press, 2004).

D'Costa, G., 'Other Faiths and Christianity', in A. E. McGrath (ed.), *The Blackwell Encyclopedia of Modern Christian Thought* (Oxford: Blackwell, 1993), 411–19.

—— *The Meeting of the Religions and the Trinity* (Maryknoll, NY: Orbis Books, 2000).

Dunn, J. D. G., *The Theology of Paul the Apostle* (Grand Rapids, Mich.: Eerdmans, 1998).

Dupuis, J., *Toward a Christian Theology of Religious Pluralism* (Maryknoll, NY: Orbis Books, 1997).

—— *Christianity and the Religions: From Confrontation to Dialogue* (Maryknoll, NY: Orbis Books, 2002).

Geffré, C., *De Babel à Pentecôte: Essais de Théologie Interreligieuse* (Paris: Cerf, 2006).

Griffiths, P. J. (ed.), *Christianity Through Non-Christian Eyes* (Maryknoll, NY: Orbis Books, 1990).

Hinnells, J. R. (ed.), *The Routledge Companion to the Study of Religion* (London: Routledge, 2005).

Jones, L. (ed.), *Encyclopedia of Religion*, 15 vols. (Detroit: Macmillan, 2005).

Kendall, D. and O'Collins, G. (eds.), *In Many and Diverse Ways: In Honor of Jacques Dupuis* (Maryknoll, NY: Orbis Books, 2003).

King, U. (ed.), *Faith and Praxis in a Postmodern Age* (London: Cassell, 1998).

O'Collins, G., 'Salvation', in *ABD*, v (New York: Doubleday, 1992), 907–14.

—— *Christology: A Biblical, Historical and Systematic Study of Jesus* (Oxford: Oxford University Press, 1995, rev. edn. 2004).

—— 'Christ and Other Religions', *Gregorianum* 84 (2003), 347–62.

—— 'Jacques Dupuis's Contributions to Interreligious Dialogue', *Theological Studies* 64 (2003), 388–97.

O'Collins, G., *Jesus Our Redeemer: A Christian Approach to Salvation* (Oxford: Oxford University Press, 2007).

Preuss, H.-D., *Old Testament Theology*, 2 vols. (Edinburgh: T. & T. Clark, 1996).

Quinn, P. L. and Taliaferro, C. (eds.), *A Companion to Philosophy of Religion* (Cambridge, Mass.: Blackwell, 1997).

Sesboüé, B. *Hors de l'Eglise pas de salut. Histoire d'une formule et problèmes d'interprétation* (Paris: Desclée, 2004).

Smith, M. S., *The Memoirs of God: History, Memory and the Experience of the Divine in Ancient* Israel (Minneapolis: Fortress, 2004).

Sullivan, F. A., *Salvation Outside the Church?* (New York: Paulist Press, 1992).

Wainwright, W. J., *The Oxford Handbook of the Philosophy of Religion* (New York: Oxford University Press, 2005).

Whaling, F., 'Religion, Theories of', in A. E. McGrath (ed.), *The Blackwell Encyclopedia of Modern Christian Thought* (Oxford: Blackwell, 1993), 547–53.

Zenger, E. *et al.*, *Einleitung in das Alte Testament* (Stuttgart: Kohlhammer, 5th edn., 2004).

Note: since it focuses on scriptural data, this book refers to or quotes from numerous biblical commentaries. Information about these commentaries is found in the footnotes, above all in the first twelve chapters.

Index of Names

Biblical Index

II THE NEW TESTAMENT

4: 42 84, 143
4: 46–54 82
5: 1 103
6: 22–58 242
6: 35 99
7: 2–14 84
8: 48 83 n.
9: 1–41 241
9: 5 99, 127, 165
10: 10 211
10: 14 237
11: 25 217
11: 45–53 104 n.
11: 50–2 204
11: 52 99
12: 12 103
12: 15 104
12: 20–2 99
12: 24 99
12: 32–3 99
12: 41 62
14: 6 127, 165, 187, 217
15: 1–10 242
20: 22 246
21: 15–17 199

Acts
1: 3 217
1: 8 144
1: 9–11 145
2: 5–11 144, 226
2: 6–11 145
2: 21 144 n., 147, 164, 167, 196
2: 33 146
2: 36 144, 172
2: 38 167
2: 38–9 148
2: 38–40 147, 164, 196
2: 39 144
2: 41–2 167
4: 1–22 147

4: 8 145
4: 12 143–4, 165, 167
5: 31 143
5: 40 146
6: 8–8: 1 146
6: 13–14 110
7: 55 146
8: 15–17 148
8: 26 148
8: 26–40 148–9
8: 29 145, 148
8: 39 145, 149
9: 10–16 145
9: 10–17 151
10: 1–2 150
10: 1–11: 18 149–52
10: 2 149, 152 n.
10: 3–8 150
10: 9–23 150
10: 19 145
10: 22 149, 151
10: 23 151
10: 23–48 150
10: 28 151
10: 30–2 151
10: 33 152
10: 34–5 197
10: 34–48 167
10: 36 152, 197
10: 42 152
10: 42–3 197
10: 43 152
10: 45–6 148
10: 48 151
11: 3 151
11: 5–17 150
11: 13–14 151
11: 17–18 167
13: 2–4 145
13: 13–52 146
13: 16 152 n.

Biblical Index